AN INTRODUCTION

TO

VULGAR LATIN

AN INTRODUCTION

TO

VULGAR LATIN

BY

C. H. GRANDGENT

PROFESSOR OF ROMANCE LANGUAGES IN HARVARD UNIVERSITY

HAFNER PUBLISHING COMPANY
NEW YORK
1962

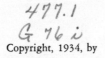
Copyright, 1934, by

C. H. GRANDGENT

REPRINTED BY ARRANGEMENT

Reprinted and Published by
HAFNER PUBLISHING CO., INC.
31 East 10th Street
New York 3, N. Y.

LIBRARY OF CONGRESS CATALOG CARD NUMBER: 61-16902

Printed in the U.S.A.

NOBLE OFFSET PRINTERS, INC.
NEW YORK 3, N. Y.

PREFACE.

WHILE this book is intended primarily for students of
Romance Philology, it will, I hope, be of some interest to
Classical scholars as well. Although it has been long in the
making, I have endeavored to keep it, at every stage, abreast
of current scholarship. I have tried, furthermore, to treat all
portions of the subject, not exhaustively, but with even fulness;
I fear, however, that the Syntax — perhaps unavoidably —
is somewhat scanty as compared with the other parts. It will
be seen that I have continually furnished abundant references
for the guidance of those who wish to look further into special
topics. My principal authorities are listed in the Bibliography; others are cited in the appropriate places in the text.

C. H. GRANDGENT.

TABLE OF CONTENTS.

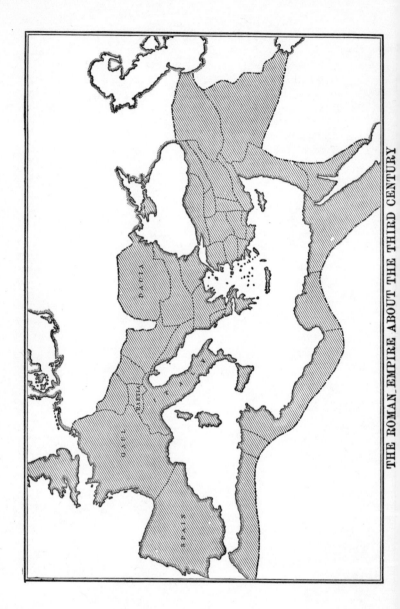

THE ROMAN EMPIRE ABOUT THE THIRD CENTURY

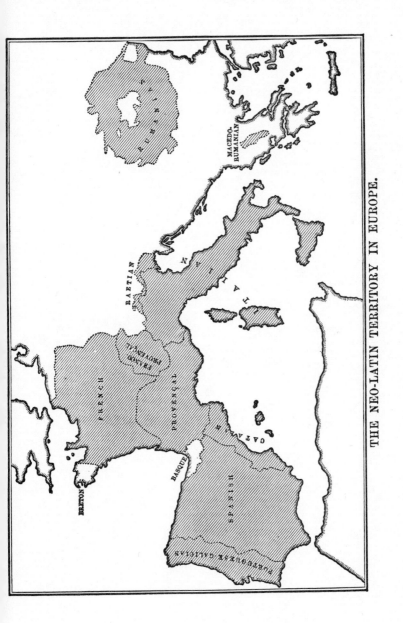

THE NEO-LATIN TERRITORY IN EUROPE.

BIBLIOGRAPHY
WITH ABBREVIATIONS.

App. Pr.: *Die Appendix Probi*, ed. W. Heræus, 1899. A Latin list of correct and incorrect spellings, possibly as early as the third century. Cf. *Mélanges Renier* 301–309; *Mélanges Boissier* 5–9; *Wiener Studien* XIV, 278 ff.; *Romanische Forschungen* VII, 145 ff.

Archiv: *Archiv für lateinische Lexicographie und Grammatik mit Einschluss des älteren Mittellateins.* Quarterly, Leipzig.

Audollent: A. Audollent, *Defixionum Tabellae*, 1904.

Bausteine: *Bausteine zur romanischen Philologie*, 1905. A volume of miscellaneous studies issued in honor of A. Mussafia.

Bayard: L. Bayard, *Le latin de saint Cyprien*, 1902.

Bechtel: E. A. Bechtel, *S. Silviae Peregrinatio, The Text and a Study of the Latinity*, 1902. Cf. **Per.**

Bon.: M. Bonnet, *Le latin de Grégoire de Tours*, 1890.

Buck: C. D. Buck, *A Grammar of Oscan and Umbrian*, 1904.

Carnoy: A. Carnoy, *Le latin d'Espagne d'après les inscriptions*, 2d ed., 1906.

Chronologie: F. G. Mohl, *Introduction à la chronologie du latin vulgaire*, 1899.

C. I. L.: *Corpus Inscriptionum Latinarum*, 1863 —. New ed. (Vol. I, Part 1), 1893 —.

Claussen: T. Claussen, *Die griechischen Wörter im Französischen*, in *Romanische Forschungen* XV, 774.

C. G. L.: G. Goetz, *Corpus Glossariorum Latinorum*, Vol. IV, *Codex Vaticanus 3321*.

Cohn: G. Cohn, *Die Suffixwandlungen im Vulgärlatein und im vorlitterarischen Französisch nach ihren Spuren im Neufranzösischen*, 1891.

Cooper: F. T. Cooper, *Word Formation in the Roman Sermo Plebeius*, 1895.

Corssen: W. Corssen, *Ueber Aussprache, Vocalismus und Betonung der lateinischen Sprache*, 2d ed., 1868–70.

D'Arbois: H. d'Arbois de Jubainville, *La déclinaison en Gaule à l'époque mérovingienne*, 1872.

Densusianu: O. Densusianu, *Histoire de la langue roumaine*, Vol. I, 1901.

Dottin: G. Dottin, *Manuel pour servir à l'étude de l'antiquité celtique*, 1906.

Draeger: A. Draeger, *Historische Syntax der lateinischen Sprache*, 2ᵈ ed., 1878.

Dubois: A. Dubois, *La latinité d'Ennodius*, 1903.

Eckinger: T. Eckinger, *Die Orthographie lateinischer Wörter in griechischen Inschriften*, 1892.

Edon: G. Édon, *Écriture et prononciation du latin savant et du latin populaire*, 1882.

Einf.: W. Meyer-Lübke, *Einführung in das Studium der romanischen Sprachwissenschaft*, 2ᵈ ed., 1909.

Ernoult: A. Ernoult, *Les éléments dialectaux du vocabulaire latin*, 1909.

Facere: G. Rydberg, *Le développement de* facere *dans les langues romanes*, 1893. Reviewed by G. Paris in *Rom.* XXII, 569.

Franz: W. Franz, *Die lateinisch-romanischen Elemente im Althochdeutschen*, 1883.

Franz. ǝ: G. Rydberg, *Zur Geschichte des französischen ǝ*, 1896 —.

Futurum: P. Thielmann, *Habere mit dem Infinitiv und die Entstehung des romanischen Futurums*, in *Archiv* II, 48, 157.

G.: H. Goelzer, *Étude lexicographique et grammaticale de la latinité de saint Jérome*, 1884.

Gl. Cassel: *Kasseler Glossen* in *Altfranzösisches Uebungsbuch*, W. Foerster and E. Koschwitz, 2ᵈ ed., 1902. Made, probably in France, in the eighth or ninth century. Cf. *Zs.* XXVI, 521 ff.

Gl. Reich: *Reichenauer Glossen* in *Altfranzösisches Uebungsbuch*, W. Foerster and E. Koschwitz, 2ᵈ ed., 1902. Made in France in the eighth century. Cf. P. Marchot in *Romanische Forschungen* XII, 641 ff.; K. Hetzer, *Die Reichenauer Glossen* in *Zs.*, Beiheft 7; J. Stalzer, *Die Reichenauer Glossen der Handschrift Karlsruhe 115* in *Sitzungsberichte der philosophisch-historischen Klasse der Kaiserlichen Akademie der Wissenschaften* CLII, Vienna, 1906 (see W. Foerster in *Zs.* XXXI, 513, XXXVI, 47).

Gram.: W. Meyer-Lübke, *Grammaire des langues romanes*, 3 vols., 1890–1900.

Grundriss: G. Gröber, *Grundriss der romanischen Philologie*, 2 vols., 1888–1902; 2ᵈ ed. of Vol. I, 1904 —.

Haag: O. Haag, *Die Latinität Fredegars*, 1898.

Hammer: M. Hammer, *Die locale Verbreitung frühester romanischer Lautwandlungen im alten Italien*, 1894.

Hoppe: H. Hoppe, *Syntax und Stil des Tertullian*, 1903.

Keil: H. Keil, *Grammatici Latini*, 1857–1880.

Kluge: F. Kluge, *Romanen und Germanen in ihren Wechselbeziehungen*, in *Grundriss*, I², 498.

Körting: G. Körting, *Lateinisch-romanisches Wörterbuch*, 3ᵈ ed. 1907.

Koffmane: G. Koffmane, *Entstehung und Entwickelung des Kirchenlateins*, 1879.

Lat. Spr.: W. Meyer-Lübke, *Die lateinische Sprache in den romanischen Ländern*, in *Grundriss*, I², 451.

Lebreton: J. Lebreton, *Études sur la langue et la grammaire de Cicéron*, 1901.

Lexique: F. G. Mohl, *Études sur le lexique du latin vulgaire*, 1900.

Lindsay: W. M. Lindsay, *The Latin Language*, 1894.

Löfstedt: E. Löfstedt, *Beiträge zur Kenntniss der späteren Latinität*, 1907.

Loth: J. Loth, *Les mots latins dans les langues brittoniques*, 1892.

Ltblt.: *Literaturblatt für germanische und romanische Philologie.* Monthly, Leipzig.

Mulomedicina: E. Oder, *Claudii Hermeri Mulomedicina Chironis*, 1901.

Neue: F. Neue, *Formenlehre der lateinischen Sprache*, 3ᵈ ed., 1892–1902.

Neumann: Franz Neumann, *Verzeichniss der auf Aussprache und Rechtschreibung bezüglichen Eigenthümlichkeiten in den Inschriften aus Gallia Narbonensis*, 1897. *Fortsetzung*, 1898.

Olcott: G. N. Olcott, *Studies in the Word Formation of the Latin Inscriptions; Substantives and Adjectives, with special reference to the Latin Sermo Vulgaris*, 1898.

Oliver: A. Oliver, *Observations on the Use of Certain Prepositions in Petronius with special reference to the Roman Sermo Plebeius*, 1899.

Part. Perf.: P. Thielmann, *Habere mit dem Part. Perf. Pass.*, in *Archiv* II, 37², 509.

Per.: *Peregrinatio ad loca sancta*, ed. P. Geyer, in *Itinera hierosolymitana sæculi iiii–viii*, 1898. Written probably in the latter part of the fourth century by an ignorant nun, perhaps from Spain. See **Bechtel.** Cf. J. T. Gamurrini, *S. Hilarii Tractatus de Mysteriis et Hymni et S. Silviæ Aquitanæ Peregrinatio ad loca sancta*, 1887, and *S. Silviæ Aquitanæ Peregrinatio ad loca sancta*, 1888; M. Férotin, *Le véritable auteur de la Peregrinatio Silviæ* in *Revue des questions historiques* LXXIV (N.S.XXX), 367 ff.; J. Anglade, *De latinitate libelli qui inscriptus est Peregrinatio ad loca sancta*, 1905; W. Heræus, *Silviæ vel potius Ætheriæ Peregrinatio ad loca sancta*, 1908; E. Löfstedt, *Philologischer Kommentar zur Peregrinatio Ætheriæ*, 1911. Cf. E. Wölfflin in *Archiv* IV, 259; P. Geyer in *Archiv* XV, 233; D. D. de Bruyne in *Revue Bénédictine*, 1909, 481; K. Meister in *Rheinisches*

Museum für Philologie LXIV, 368; J. Deconinck in *Revue Biblique*, 1910, 432.

Phon. : P. Marchot, *Petite phonétique du français prélittéraire*, 1901.

Pirson : J. Pirson, *La langue des inscriptions de la Gaule*, 1901.

Planta : R. von Planta, *Grammatik der oskisch-umbrischen Dialekte*, 1892–97.

Pogatscher : A. Pogatscher, *Zur Lautlehre der griechischen, lateinischen und romanischen Lehnworte im Altenglischen : II. Teil, Vokalismus der Tonsilben*, 1888.

Pr. Pers. Pl. : F. G. Mohl, *La première personne du pluriel en gallo-roman*, 1900.

Quillacq : J. A. Quillacq, *Quomodo lingua latina usus sit S. Hilarius*, 1903.

R. : H. Rönsch, *Itala und Vulgata*, 1869.

Regnier : A. Regnier, *De la latinité des Sermons de saint Augustin*, 1886.

Richter : Elise Richter, *Zur Entwicklung der romanischen Wortstellung aus der lateinischen*, 1903.

Rom. : *Romania*. Quarterly, Paris.

S. : E. Seelmann, *Die Ausprache des Latein nach physiologisch-historischen Grundsätzen*, 1885.

Sepulcri : A. Sepulcri, *Le alterazioni fonetiche e morfologiche nel latino di Gregorio Magno e del suo tempo*, in *Studi Medievali* I, 171.

Sic. : N. Maccarrone, *Il latino delle iscrizioni di Sicilia*, 1910.

Sittl : K. Sittl, *Die lokalen Verschiedenheiten der lateinischen Sprache*, 1882.

Sommer : F. Sommer, *Lateinische Laut- und Formenlehre*, 1902.

Stolz : F. Stolz, *Historische Grammatik der lateinischen Sprache*, Vol. I, 1894.

Substrate : G. Gröber, *Vulgärlateinische Substrate romanischer Wörter*, in *Archiv* I, 204, 539; II, 100, 276, 424; III, 138, 264, 507; IV, 116, 422; V, 125, 234, 453; VI, 117, 377; VII, 25.

Suchier : H. Suchier, *Die französische und provenzalische Sprache und ihre Mundarten*, in *Grundriss* I², 371.

Thurot : *Notices et Extraits des Manuscrits de la Bibliothèque nationale et autres bibliothèques :* Vol. XII, Paris, 1868, Charles Thurot, *Notices et Extraits de divers manuscrits latins pour servir à l'histoire des doctrines grammaticales au moyen âge.*

Tiktin : H. Tiktin, *Die rumänische Sprache*, in *Grundriss*, I², 564.

Travaglio : C. Travaglio, *La scrittura latina volgare nei papiri dei primi cinque secoli dopo Cristo* in *Atti della R. Accademia delle Scienze di Torino* XLIII, 525.

Urbat : R. Urbat, *Beiträge zu einer Darstellung der romanischen Elemente im Latein der Historia Francorum des Gregor v. Tours,* 1890.

Vok. : H. Schuchardt, *Der Vokalismus des Vulgärlateins,* 3 vols., 1866–68.

Walde : A. Walde, *Lateinisches etymologisches Wörterbuch,* 1906.

Waters : W. E. Waters, *Petronius, Cena Trimalchionis,* 1902.

Wick : F. C. Wick, *La fonetica delle iscrizioni parietarie pompeiane,* 1905.

Windisch : E. Windisch, *Die keltische Sprache,* in *Grundriss* I^2, 371.

Wölfflin : E. Wölfflin, *Lateinische und romanische Comparation,* 1879.

Zauner : A. Zauner, *Romanische Sprachwissenschaft,* 1900.

Zs. : *Zeitschrift für romanische Philologie.* Four to six numbers a year. Halle.

Zs. fr. Spr. : *Zeitschrift für französische Sprache und Litteratur.* Quarterly, Chemnitz and Leipzig.

Works to which only occasional reference is made are cited in full in the text.

PHONETIC ALPHABET

AND OTHER SYMBOLS.

β = bilabial *v*, the sound of Spanish *v* and *b*.

ð = the sound of *th* in English *this*.

ə = the sound of *e* in French *me*.

ŋ = the sound of *ng* in English *long*.

ö = rounded *e*, the sound of German *ö*.

þ = the sound of *th* in English *thin*.

ü = rounded *i*, the sound of German *ü*.

χ = the sound of *ch* in German *ach*.

- · (a dot) under a vowel letter shows that the vowel is close.
- ᴗ (a hook) under a vowel letter shows that the vowel is open.
- ⌒ (a semicircle) under a vowel letter shows that the vowel is not syllabic.
- ╱ (an acute accent) after a consonant letter shows that the consonant is palatal.
- * (an asterisk) before a word shows that the form is conjectural, not attested.
- ﹥ indicates derivation, the *source* standing at the *open* end of the figure, whichever way it be turned.
- SMALL CAPITALS mean that the forms so printed occur in inscriptions (but this indication is used only when for some special reason it seems desirable).

The other marks and abbreviations employed are so generally accepted as to need no explanation.

AN INTRODUCTION TO VULGAR LATIN.

1. The extent of the Roman Empire is shown by the map on p. x. Throughout this territory the official language was Latin, originally the speech of Latium, a little district on the Tiber. The Latin tongue was thus extended to many peoples, representing different races, civilizations, and linguistic habits. In central Italy it was adopted by Etruscans and by various Italic tribes, in northern Italy by Ligurians, Celts, and Illyrians, in southeastern and southwestern Italy respectively by Illyrians and Greeks; beyond the peninsula it spread among Iberians, Ligurians, Celts, Aquitanians, Semites, Germanic tribes, and others still. The Latinization of these peoples was the work of several centuries[1]: by 272 B. C. all Italy was subdued south of the Macra and the Rubicon; Sicily became a province in 241, Sardinia and Corsica in 238; Venetia cast her lot with Rome in 215; Spain was made a province in 197; Illyria was absorbed after 167, Africa after the fall of Carthage in 146, southern Gaul in 120; the Cimbri and Teutones were destroyed in 102–1; northern Gaul was a province in 50, Rætia in 15; Dacia was colonized in 107 A. D., forsaken in the third century, and quite cut off from the rest of the Latin-speaking world in the sixth. The Latin language never gained a foothold in Greece; political changes drove it from Great Britain, the Orient, and Africa; in the rest of the Empire it has remained, for the most part,

---

[1] See Mohl, *Chronologie;* also Meyer-Lübke, *Lat. Spr.*, pp. 451–455.

until the present day, and has been carried thence to America, Africa, and Asia. The map on p. xi marks the parts of Europe where Latin in its modern forms is now spoken.

2. The Latin tongue, like every living language, has always been in an unstable condition. The evidence of inscriptions and of grammarians indicates that from the beginning to the end of Roman history speech was constantly changing, the alteration being most rapid in the earliest and the latest periods. Furthermore, there were at all times, but especially before the Social War, considerable local divergences. The Latin-speaking peoples were not homogeneous, and their speech reflected their varied origin. In Italy the language of Latium was adopted by tribes using, in the main, kindred languages. At first there was sturdy resistance; until the conflict of 90–89 B. C. all southern Italy was under Oscan influence, and Oscan was used in inscriptions until the first century of our era.[1] When Latin conquered, it blended more or less with the native idioms; the resulting geographical discrepancies are manifest in early monuments. The Social War, however, had a levelling effect, and speech in Italy became more uniform; but there doubtless were still noticeable differences in pronunciation and even in vocabulary.[2] In the outlying provinces, and to some degree in the peninsula, Latin was simply substituted for foreign tongues, and there was little or no mixture; nevertheless a few native words were kept, and there must have been a variety of accent. It should be remembered, moreover, that the language carried

---

[1] See *Chronologie* 133 and 116–120. Oscan forms are *ligud* for *lēge*, *pru* for *pro*, *ni* for *nē*, etc.

[2] The S. Italian *nn* for *nd*, *i* for *ē*, and *u* for *ō* may be Oscan. *Pomex*, *ēlex* for *pūmex*, *īlex* are perhaps Umbrian: *Lat. Spr.* 445, 464. The Italian word *zavorra* is possibly Etruscan: *Chronologie* 98–99.

to the several provinces was not identical: it represented
different chronological stages and different local dialects of
Italic Latin; the earlier acquisitions received a more popular,
the later colonies a more official speech.   Administration and
military service tended to obliterate distinctions; under the
Empire the variations probably came to be no greater than
those now to be found in the English of the British Empire.
We may say in general that the Roman territory, excepting
Greece and the East, was completely Latinized by the fourth
century after Christ.

   3. With the beginnings of culture and literature there
came inevitably a divergence between the language of the
upper and that of the lower classes, and also between city
and country speech.   Literary influence is conservative and
refining, while popular usage tends to quick change.   In late
Republican and early Imperial times educated speech became
highly artificial, drawing away from the everyday language;
on the other hand, the common idiom, throughout the Republic and the Empire, was constantly developing away from
the archaic standard of elegant parlance.[1] What we call Vulgar Latin is the speech of the middle classes, as it grew out
of early Classic Latin.   It is not an independent offshoot of
Old Latin: it continues the Classic, not the primitive, vowel
system.[2]   Neither is it the dialect of the slums or of the
fields: grammarians tell us of not a few urban and rustic
vulgarisms that are not perpetuated in the Romance tongues.
It is distinct from the consciously polite utterance of cultivated society, from the brogue of the country, and from the
slang of the lowest quarters of the city, though affected by
all of these.[3]   Vulgar Latin naturally developed differently in

---

[1] Cf. J. Marouzeau, *Notes sur la fixation du latin classique* in *Mémoires de la So-
ciété de Linguistique de Paris*, XVII, 266.
[2] Cf. *Lat. Spr.* 463-464.   [3] Cf. Cooper XV–XXX; W. Konjetzny in *Archiv* XV, 297.

various localities, as far as the levelling influence of school and army permi...d; the universal inclination of language to diverge was reinforced by the original habits of the diverse speakers and by such peculiarities of native accent as had survived.[1] The differentiation progressed, being accelerated when schools decayed and military was replaced by ecclesiastical organization, until the dialects of distant localities became mutually unintelligible. At this point we may say that Vulgar Latin stops and the Romance languages begin. Although any definite date must be arbitrary, we may put it, roughly speaking, in the sixth or seventh century of our era. The Vulgar Latin period lasts, then, from about 200 B. C. to about 600 A. D.; it is most sharply differentiated from Classic Latin in the last few centuries of this epoch.[2]

4. If we compare Classic and Vulgar Latin, we shall see that the latter was always tending to become more flexible and more explicit. We note an enormous development of modifying and determining words, such as articles and prepositions, and an abundant use of prefixes and suffixes. We find also a great simplification of inflections, due partly to phonetic but mainly to syntactic causes. Furthermore, we observe certain changes in pronunciation, some of which can be ascribed to an inclination to discard those parts of words that are not necessary for their identification (as when *viridis*, *vetulus* become *virdis*, *veclus*), some to a tendency to assimilate unlike adjacent sounds (so *ipse* is spoken *isse*, and the diphthong *ai* is reduced to *e*), some to a desire for differentiation (which lowers i̭ to ḙ to make it more remote from i̭), some to unknown reasons. Why, for instance, ai almost

---

[1] Cf. Sittl and Hammer; Pirson and Carnoy; also, for African Latin, B. Kübler in *Archiv* VIII, 161.

[2] For a history of the Latin language, see *Lat. Spr.* 492-497.

universally became ę, while au did not in Latin generally become ǫ, is a problem as yet unsolved.

5. Our sources of information[1] concerning the current spoken Latin are: the statements of grammarians[2]; the non-Classic forms occurring in inscriptions and early manuscripts[3]; the occasional lapses in cultivated authors, early and late; a few texts written by persons of scanty education; some glossaries and lists of incorrect forms; and, most important of all, the subsequent developments of the Romance languages.[4] All of these are to be used with caution. Of especial value are the *Peregrinatio ad loca sancta*, a considerable fragment of a description of travel in the East, by an uneducated woman (probably a Spanish nun) of the latter part of the fourth century[5]; the *Appendix Probi*, a list of good and bad forms, possibly as early as the third century[6]; the veterinary treatise known as *Mulomedicina Chironis*[7]; the so-called *Glossary of Reichenau*, made in France in the eighth century.[8] There is an interesting collection of curses by A. Audollent, — *Defixionum Tabellæ*, 1904.

---

[1] Cf. Meyer-Lübke, *Lat. Spr.* 455-461; G. Gröber, *Sprachquellen und Wortquellen des lateinischen Wörterbuchs* in *Archiv* I, 35.

[2] Utilized by E. Seelmann, *Aussprache des Latein*, 1885. For a brief account of the Latin grammarians, see Stolz, 55-67.

[3] Used by H. Schuchardt, *Vokalismus des Vulgärlateins*, 1866-68. For papyri see Travaglio. For coins see M. Prou in *Mélanges de philologie romane et d'histoire littéraire offerts à M. Maurice Wilmotte*, 1910, 523. This volume contains on p. 485 *Pamphlets bas-latins du VIIe siècle* by J. Pirson.

[4] For the chronology of developments, the distinction of learned and popular words, and the establishment of unattested Vulgar Latin words, see G. Gröber, in *Archiv* I, 204 ff., and VII, 25 ff. Something can be learned from the charters and laws of the barbarians: cf. F. Schramm, *Sprachliches zur Lex Salica*, 1911.

[5] See Bibliography: Bechtel and *Per.*; note E. Wölfflin, *Ueber die Latinität der Peregrinatio ad loca sancta* in *Archiv* IV, 259.

[6] See W. Heræus, *Die Appendix Probi*, 1899, *Zur Appendix Probi* in *Archiv* XI, 61, *Die Appendix Probi* in *Archiv* XI, 301; G. Paris in *Mélanges Renier* 301, *Mélanges Boissier* 5; W. Fœrster in *Wiener Studien* XIV, 278.

[7] See Bibliography; E. Lommatzsch, *Zur Mulomedicina Chironis* in *Archiv* XII, 401, 551, and W. Heræus, *Zur Sprache der Mulomedicina Chironis* in *Archiv* XIV, 119.

[8] See Bibliography.

I. VOCABULARY.[1]

A. WORDS AND THEIR MEANINGS.

6. It is natural that the speech of the literary and fashionable classes should differ from that of the common people; so it is in all civilized communities. Literature inclines to extend the senses of words, popular use tends to restrict them. The polite language, too, has many poetic figures and many abstract terms unknown to the crowd. On the other hand, the vulgar idiom has homely metaphors of its own and numerous specific, technical words not found in literature.

1. WORDS USED ALIKE IN CLASSIC AND VULGAR LATIN.

7. This class includes a great mass of words, forming, so to speak, the nucleus of the language. Examples are: *canis, filius, mater, panis, pater, puteus, vacca; altus, bonus, longus, viridis; amare, audire, dicere, vendere; bene, male; quando, si; in.*

---

[1] See A. Hatzfeld, A. Darmesteter, and A. Thomas, *Dictionnaire général de la langue française*, II, *Traité de la formation de la langue française;* Densusianu, 185–203; W. Heræus, *Die römische Soldatensprache* in *Archiv* XII, 255, *Die Sprache der römischen Kinderstube* in *Archiv* XIII, 149; J. G. Kempf, *Romanorum sermo castrensis quid sit quibusque e fontibus quaque via ac ratione eius reliquiæ hauriantur* in *Jahrbücher für classische Philologie*, Suppl. XXVI, 342. For an approximately complete vocabulary, reconstructed out of Romance words, see G. Körting, *Lateinish-romanisches Wörterbuch*, 1907. For a thorough discussion of reconstructed forms, see G. Gröber, *Vulgärlateinische Substrate romanischer Wörter* in *Archiv:* I, 233 ff. (*abbreviare — buttis*), 539 ff. (*caccubus — curbus*); II, 100 ff. (*damnum — dui*), 276 ff. (*eber — fiticum*), 424 ff. (*flagrare — gutta*); III, 138 ff. (*hædus — ilicem*), 264 ff. (*ille — lamma*), 507 ff. (*lacusta — mille*); IV, 116 ff. (*minaciæ — nutrire*), 422 ff. (*obedire — putidus*); V, 125 ff. (*quadraginta — rasculare*), 234 ff. (*reburrus — runcare*), 453 ff. (*sabanum — suus*); VI, 117 ff. (*tabanus — zirulare*), 377 ff. (supplement.)

6

2. WORDS USED DIFFERENTLY IN CLASSIC AND IN VULGAR LATIN.

8. Very many Classic words are used in Vulgar Latin with a different sense: *comparare* = 'buy', *focus* = 'fire', *paganus* = 'pagan', *viaticum* = 'journey'. *Capit* assumed the meaning of *fieri potest:* R. 351–352, *non capit prophetam perire*, etc.; Hoppe 48, *hæc æstimare non capit, non capit utique videri Deus.*

Most of the examples can be classified under the heads of restriction or extension of meaning.

a. SENSE RESTRICTED.

9. This happens frequently, a word assuming a more definite or concrete signification: *cognatus* = 'brother-in-law'; *collocare* = 'put to bed' (*se collocare* = 'go to bed', Bon. 286); *dominicus* = *divinus; ingenium* = 'trick', Bon. 283; *lectio* = 'text'; *machinari* = 'grind'; *mulier* = 'wife'; *necare* = 'drown', Bon. 286, Dubois 220; *orbus* = 'blind'; *tractatus* = 'treatise'.

Many words kept their literal but lost their metaphorical sense: *captio* = 'act of taking', G. 243, not 'sophism' nor 'deceit'; *robur* = 'oak', not 'strength', 'authority', nor 'best part'.

b. SENSE EXTENDED.[1]

10. The general use of a word in an extended sense is not common, but there are some examples: *fortis* = 'strong' in all senses, Bayard 105; *infans* = 'child', Pirson 257–258; *parentes* = 'relatives', Pirson 260–262; *se plicare* = 'go', *Per.* 46, 11, etc.; *villa* = 'town', G. 272.

Many words, however, assume a new meaning in addition to the old one: *ambulare* = 'march', *Archiv* XII, 269–270, Bechtel 137, etc., and also 'continue', Regnier 24, perhaps

---

[1] Cf. Bayard 63–202, Bon. 235–328, Dubois 185–225, Quillacq 54–79.

'go'; *facere* = 'pass (time)', Regnier 27 (*quadraginta dies fecit*), *Per.* 66, 11 (*fecimus ibi biduum*), etc.; *fascia* means a measure of land, Pirson 255; *habet* is used like the French *il y a* (Old French *a*), G. 422 (*in arca Noe . . . habuit serpentes*), Regnier 29 (*in carne paucas habet virgines sanctimoniales*), Bechtel 127 (*habebat de eo loco forsitan quattuor milia*, etc.), *Per.* 37,13, etc.; *homo* has the sense of French *on*, Regnier 20, Dubois 218; *ille* = 'the' and 'he', Bechtel 144, Bon. 258 ff.; *populus minutus* = 'common people', Waters Ch. 44; *replicare* = 'reply', Dubois, 204; *res* is used of persons, Waters Ch. 58 (*bella res*); *satis* = 'much', Bayard 83, *Per.* 38,25, etc.; *unus* = 'a', Bechtel 144; *virtutes* = 'miracles' (in imitation of the Greek), Bayard 94.

So various prepositions and conjunctions (as *ad, apud, cum, de, per,* and *quasi, quia, quod, quomodo*) assumed new functions. *Unde* came to mean 'and so', Bon. 328.

3. WORDS USED IN CLASSIC BUT NOT IN VULGAR LATIN.

11. Numerous Classic Latin words either were not employed at all in the vulgar speech or went out of use before the earliest monuments of the Romance languages: so *funus, jubere, proles.* Very many adverbs and conjunctions disappeared: *an, at, autem, diu, donec, enim, ergo, etiam, haud, igitur, ita, nam, postquam, quidem, quin, quippe, quoad, quoque, saltem, sed, sive, ut, utrum, vel,* etc.; *tamen* must have been moribund, although it is common in the *Peregrinatio.* Poetic terms and some abstract nouns were not needed: *aurora, frondifer, horrescere, fletus.* Ecclesiastical Latin, to be sure, is very rich in abstract nouns (G. 391–397, Dubois 301–308), but most of them are new formations. When lost terms were needed for literary or other purposes, they were either borrowed from Classic or clerical Latin (as *nobilis*) or replaced by new constructions (as **carrica* for *onus*).

a. SYNONYMS.

12. When Latin had two words nearly syńonymous, one often crowded out the other: *atrium* gave way to *cors; cur* to *quare; equus* to *caballus*, R. 472; *ferre* to *portare*, Dubois 220; *ludus* to *jocus; magnus* to *grandis; os* to *bucca*, R. 472; *parentes* to *genitores*, Olcott XXV; *senex* to *vetulus*.

Sometimes the survivor was far from a synonym in Classic Latin: *discere* was displaced by *apprendere; domus* by *casa*, *mansio*, *hospitale*[1]*; emere* by *comparare; humerus* by *spatula*, R. 324; *ignis* by *focus*, R. 313; *nunc* by *hora; omnes* by *toti*, R. 338, *Zs.* XXXIII, 143 ; *quot, tot* by *quanti, tanti*, R. 336, 337 ; *urbs* by *civitas*, Dubois 209, and by *villa*, G. 272.

b. SUBSTITUTES.

13. Sometimes a term was replaced by a word not found in Classic Latin at all : *anser* was driven out by **auca* (< **avica*, diminutive of *avis*); *noverca* by **matraster; privignus* by **filiaster; vitrĭcus* mostly by *patraster*. Occasionally the substitute was apparently a slang word: *aliquis* yielded in part to *res nata*, R. 345; *caput* to *testa*[2]*; crus* gave way to *gamba; edere* in the main to *manducare*, Bechtel 140; *gena* to *gabata*.

Some words were replaced by diminutives, some nouns by derivative adjectives: *avis* by *aucellus; avus* by **aviolus; sol*

---

[1] According to Olcott XVIII, *casa* occurs only in Italian inscriptions, *mansio* (= 'dwelling') only in Roman. For *mansio*, cf. R. 472, Dubois 212. Among the Romance languages, Rumanian, Rætian, Italian, Spanish, Portuguese prefer *casa*, French and Provençal *mansio* and *hospitale*. Cf. Zauner 41–42.

[2] *Caput* (or rather ** capum*) is preserved by Rumanian, Rætian, Italian, Provençal, French ; *testa* by Italian, Provençal, French ; **capitia* (< *caput*) by Spanish and Portuguese. Cf. Zauner 41–42.

in part by *soliculus; vetus for most part by vetulus; dies largely by diurnus, Gl. Reich.; hiems by hibernum, R. 472; mane extensively by matutinum. Diminutives were extremely common in late Latin: G. 121–130 (cereolus, schedula, etc.), Olcott 250–263 (gemelli, mammula = 'grandmother', naucella, neptilla, etc.), Dubois 147 (novellus). Adjectives used as nouns were frequent also: R. 100–107 (arida, infernus, etc.), G. 108–121 (brevis, credens, infernus, etc.).

Occasionally, too, words were replaced by phrases: diu by longum tempus (Bon. 201, paucum tempus for haud diu); ver by vernum tempus, Bon. 203, and other phrases.

c. PARTICLES.

14. Many prepositions, conjunctions, and adverbs were lost by subsitution.

Ab was made unnecessary by de and per; apud was partially supplanted by ad; cum, in Gaul, yielded to apud; ex gave way to de, R. 395–396; ob to pro and per. Pro, doubtless under the influence of per, became *por, which replaced per and pro in Spain and to a considerable extent in northern Gaul; southern Gaul, Italy, and Dacia preferred per. Cis, erga, præ, propter were displaced by other words.

The functions of an, ne, utrum were assumed by si; the place of cum was taken by quando and other conjunctions; quando, quod, quoniam were often replaced by quomodo, R. 403. Autem, ergo, etiam, etsi, igitur, sed, tamen, ut were ousted by various substitutes. Cf. Densusianu, 184–185.

4. WORDS USED IN VULGAR BUT NOT IN CLASSIC LATIN.

15. Vulgar Latin evidently had many words that do not appear in Classic texts. Some of these were probably old

native terms that do not happen to occur in the works preserved, some were late creations, some were borrowed from
other languages.

a. NATIVE WORDS.

16. Some native words are rarely attested, although they
were doubtless in common use: *amma*, *Archiv* XIII, 154;
atta, *Archiv* XIII, 154; *baro* = 'athlete', Waters Ch. 53, Ch.
63; *battalia*, *Archiv* XII, 270–271; *branca*, Densusianu 196;
circare = 'hunt', *Archiv* VIII, 186; *cloppus*, Densusianu 196;
drappus, *Substrate* II, 106, Körting (found in the 6th century);
ficatum, Densusianu 190; *gavia* (used by Pliny); *mamma*,
Archiv XIII, 151–152; *nonna, nonnus*, *Archiv* XIII, 156–157;
pa(p)pa, *Archiv* XIII, 158, Bayard 179 (applied by St. Cyprian
to the bishop of Carthage); *pappus* = 'grandfather', Pirson
243; *serutinus*, Audollent 199; *tata, tatus*, Pirson 244, *Archiv*
XIII, 151–153; *trepalium*, *Rom.* XVII, 421.

17. A few that must have existed are not attested at all:
*refusare, *Substrate* V, 234; *retina = 'rein', *Substrate* V, 237;
so not improbably the original of the Romance words mean-
ing 'touch', and perhaps those of the words meaning 'find',
'gape', and 'go' (cf. § 405). Likewise words made by ono-
matopœa, as **miaulare;* cf. M. Grammont, *Onomatopées et
mots expressifs* in *Revue des langues romanes* XLIV, 97.

Some of the unattested words were obviously late developments: *finis, adj. (Fr., Pr. *fin;* It. *fine fino*), from the noun
finis in such phrases as *honorum finis, pudoris finis*, etc. (so,
e. g., *finis honoris* > *fins onors*, etc.), E. Herzog in *Bausteine*
484; *gentis, adj. (Fr., Pr. *gent*, It. *gente*), apparently a cross
between *genitus* and *gentilis; prode*, then m. and f. *prodis,
adj., detached from *prodest* (cf. *potis est* = *potest*, Neue II,
176–177), R. 468–469 (*quid enim prode est homini, sed non
fuit prode illis, hoc enim prode fit vobis*, etc.).

18. Late Latin was rich in derivatives, some of popular creation, some made by Christian writers. According to Olcott XIX, African Latin was freest in word formation. This subject will be discussed at length in the following chapter, but a few examples may be given here: post-verbal *dolus* < *dolere*, Regnier VIII; **abbellire;* **ausare; carricare, Gl. Reich.; confessor* = 'martyr'; **coraticum; dulcor,* *dulcior = 'sweetness'; *follía;* **man(u)aria; modernus,* Dubois 144; **nivicare;* **soliculus; vict(u)alia;* **vir(i)dura.*

b. FOREIGN WORDS.

19. A few Celtic terms were adopted, such as *alauda, vertragus.* More Germanic words (cf. *Gram.,* Introduction) found their way into Latin: *bannus,* Bon. 226; *hapja; haribergum, Gl. Reich.* (cf. *alberca,* Pirson 236); *haunjan; watan; wërra.*

We find a large number of Greek words, a few of them apparently borrowed by popular speech: *amygdalum; cata,* a distributive preposition, verging on the sense of 'every', R. 247 (*cata mane mane*), Bechtel 95 (*cata mansiones, cata pascha*), cf. § 71; *colaphus; dactylus,* Bon. 211; *sagma.* More came in through the Christian vocabulary: *angelus; baptizare; blasphemare;* etc. Some were introduced by fashionable society, which affected familiarity with Greek; there are many Greek words in Petronius: *hepatia,* Waters Ch. 66; *schema,* Waters Ch. 44.

Very many Greek terms used by ecclesiastical writers never became popular. Cf. G. 205–226: *anathema, prophetare, zelare;* numerous verbs in *–izare,* as *allegorizare, anathematizare, catechizare, colaphizare, evangelizare, eunuchizare, Judaizare, prophetizare, sabbatizare, scandalizare, thesaurizare;* and not a few new derivatives, as *baptizatio, diaconissa,* G. 225, 224.

B. DERIVATION.

20. Vulgar Latin is very rich in derivatives and compounds; it has many affectionate diminutives, some of them made with new suffixes (as *–icca*, *–itta*).[1] Petronius shows a fondness for long derivatives, such as *gaudimonium* (Waters Ch. 61). Late writings almost all abound in abstract nouns (Cooper 1–2). In strictly Classic texts there seem to be few really living suffixes [2]; but the facility of word formation, which the literary language lost, popular speech preserved and increased.[3] This freedom of formation was abused by African authors, who were especially addicted to prepositional compounds with *con–*, *in–*, *sub–*, etc.[4] We shall consider first postverbal nouns (i. e., substantives taken from the roots of verbs), then prefixes, next suffixes, and finally composite words.

1. POST-VERBAL NOUNS.

21. After the model of *cantus — cantare, saltus — saltare,* etc. (pairs in which the derivative verb seemed to come from the noun, whereas in reality both come from a primitive verb, as *canere, salire*), a fictitious primitive noun was derived from a number of verbs in Vulgar Latin and in the Romance languages: so *dolus* from *dolere, Vok.* I, 35, 98, Bon. 367, Regnier VII (blamed by St. Augustine).

2. PREFIXES.[5]

a. PREFIXES USED WITH NOUNS, ADJECTIVES, AND PRONOUNS.

22. *Bis–* or *bi–* was used with some adjectives and apparently with a few nouns: *bimaritus*, G. 130; *bisacutus*, G. 170; *bisaccium*, Petronius.

---

[1] See *Gram.* II, 430–693; Densusianu 156–173.   [2] Cooper XXXIV.
[3] Cooper XXX ff.   [4] Cooper XXXVI, XLVI, 246–247.   [5] Cooper 246–297.

23. *Ad–*, *con–*, *de–*, *dis–*, *ex–*, *in–*, *re–* and some others were occasionally used to form adjectives: **adaptus; commixtius,* G. 160; *defamatus; *disfactus; exsūcus; inanimatus; *replēnus.* Cf. G. 160 ff.

24. *Ac–*, *atque–*, *ecce–*, *eccu–*, *met–* were used as demonstrative prefixes to pronominal adjectives and to adverbs. *Eccu–* is *eccum*, i.e., *ecce hum;* its origin being forgotten, it was used in late Vulgar Latin as a synonym of *ecce*. *Met*, primarily a suffix, came to be used as a prefix through such combinations as *semet ipsum*, understood as *se metipsum*. In archaic writings such reinforced demonstratives as *eccum, eccam, eccos, eccas, ecca, eccillum, eccillam, eccillud, eccistam* are not uncommon; in Classic texts they are rare. Vulgar Latin examples are: *ac sic; atque ille; ecce hic; * eccu istè; * eccu sic,* Substrate VI, 385; *met ipse.* Cf. A. Köhler, *Die Partikel ecce* in *Archiv* V, 16. See §§ 65, 66.

b. PREFIXES USED WITH VERBS.

25. *Ad–*, *con–*, *de–*, *dis–*, *ex–*, *in–*, *re–* were freely used, *dis–* being mainly a Vulgar Latin prefix: *abbreviare*, G. 179; ** adcap(i)tare; adgenuculari*, R. 181; *adpretiare*, R. 181, G. 180· *adpropiare*, R. 181, G. 180; *adunare*, R. 182; *confortare*, R. 185, G. 181; **cominitiare; complacere*, R. 184; *deaurare*, G. 182; ** disjejunare; exaltare*, G. 183; *excoriare*, G. 182; *impinguare*, G. 183; **infurcare; recapitulare*, G. 185; **requærere*. *Ad–*, *con–*, *de–* lost their special significance; *ad–* was particularly favored in Spain, *con–* in Italy. Cf. *Lat. Spr.* 487. Occasionally there was a change of prefix: *aspectare* was used with the sense of *expectare*, ** convitare* sometimes took the place of *invitare; dis–* was often substituted for *ex–*.

26. *Ab–*, *contra–*, *per–*, *sub–*, *super supra–*, *tra trans–* were used occasionally: *aboculare; *contrafacere; *perdonare; sub-audire, G. 185; *subcludere; subsannare, R. 199, G. 187; superabundare, G. 187; *super–*suprafacere; *trabuccare; *trans-annare; transplantare, G. 188.

27. *Extra–* was sometimes used in Italy and Dacia, *infra–* and *intra–* in Italy: *extrabuccare; *infraponere; *intratenere.

28. *Abs–, e–, ob–, præ–, pre–, pro–, retro–* were apparently not used to form new verbs in the popular spoken language, although some of them are occasionally so employed by late writers: *opprobrare*, G. 184; *prædestinare*, G. 184 (cf. Livy); *prolongare*, G. 184. *Ob–* is sometimes replaced by *ad–*: *ob-dormire* > *addormire*.

29. *Foris* and *minus* came to be used as prefixes in some regions: *forisfacere; *minuscredere. Foris* was confounded in Gaul with the Frankish *fir–* (= *ver–*): *verslahen* = Old Fr. *forbatre*. See G. Baist, *Fränkisches* fir– *im ältesten französi-schen* in *Romanische Forschungen* XII, 650; cf. *Rom.* XXX, 633. For this use of *minus*, compare the phrase *minus est* = *deest*, Regnier 109: *caritas in quantum adest . . . in quantum autem minus est.* Cf. § 245.

30. Some verbs take a double prefix: *adimplere; coexcitare*, R. 207 (cf. Quintilian, *coexercitatus*); *deexacerbare*, R. 207; *deexcitare; *exeligere.

31. Recomposition, i.e., the restoration of the full form of the primitive verb, was a regular process in Vulgar Latin (cf. §139): *aspargo* for *aspergo* is blamed by Velius Longus, Édon 127, and is used by St. Cyprian, Bayard 3; *commando* is, according to Velius Longus, the usual form, rather than *commendo*, S. 60, Édon 131; *consacrati* etc. occur in inscriptions, S. 60; *crededit*, Bon. 490; *reddedit*, Bon. 490; *retenere*, Bon. 489;

tradedit, Bon. 490. Cf. S. 58–64, Bon. 486–493. *Cómpŭto, cóllĭgo, cóllŏco, cónsto, cónsŭo, érĭgo, éxĕo, ínflo, præsto* seem to have been regarded as simple verbs: S. 64.

32. Late writers were in the habit of restoring the full, primitive form of prefixes; but this was doubtless merely a matter of spelling, and did not indicate the common pronunciation. In Tertullian, Cyprian, and some others there is generally no assimilation of the prefix; other writers, such as Gregory of Tours, apparently used both assimilated and unassimilated forms. Bayard 12–15: *adpetere, conpendium, inprobus, obfero, subplanto.* Bon. 178–188: *adtonitus, conmittere, inlatus, obprimere, subcumbere.*

3. SUFFIXES.

a. SUFFIXES FOR VERBS.[1]

33. Verbs *from nouns*[2] generally end in *–are;* occasionally in *–iare* or *–ire;* sometimes in *–icare,* which was eventually supplanted in Italy and in Gaul by *–izare* (for pronunciation see § 339). This last ending came from Greek *–ιζειν* through borrowed words, such as *baptizare.* For a list of Greek verbs in *–ιζειν* adopted by Christian writers, see R. 248–249 (cf. § 19 above); some new formations were used, as *catechizare.* In early Latin this same ending appears as *–issare* (*atticisso, rhetorisso*): see A. Funck, *Die Verba auf issare und izare* in *Archiv* III, 398.

Examples: *oculare; pectinare; plantare; potionare;* * *trepaliare;* — *plagiare;* — *ignire;* — *carricare; follicare;* * *nivicare;* — * *dom'nizare;* * *werrizare.*

---

[1] Cf. Cooper 205–245, Dubois 151–162, Quillacq 41–46, Bonnet 471–474.
[2] Cf. R. 154–162.

34. Verbs *from adjectives and perfect participles* end in *–are,* *–iare, –ire;* also in *–icare* (cf. *albicare*), *–itare* (cf. *debilitare, visitare*), *–ēscere* and *–īscere* (cf. *canescere, mollescere*); possibly in *–izare: angustare;* * *ausare; captivare; confortare; falsare; gravare; levare;* * *oblītare; rŭtare; ūsare;* — *alleviare;* * *altiare;* * *captiare; humiliare;* — * *abbellire; unire;* — *amaricare;* — * *vanitare;* — *fortescere; lætiscere; vilescere;* — **blankizare ?*

Many verbs from perfect participles (frequentatives, etc.) replace the original verbs: *adjuvare* > *adjutare; audere* > *ausare; canere* > *cantare; uti* > *usare.* The endings *–(i)tare, –escere* lost their frequentative or inchoative sense: *adparescere*, Dubois 157; *ostentare*, Dubois 156.

35. Verbs *from other verbs* end in *-icare* (cf. *fodicare* < *fodere*), *–itare* (cf. *clamitare* < *clamare*); also in *–ēscere, –īscere* (cf. *florescere, dormiscere*), which lost its inchoative force: * *bullicare* < *bullire;* — *crocitare;* — *apparescere;* * *finiscere; stupescere.* Vulgar Latin has many old frequentive verbs: G. 178–179, Cooper 205. There are some late diminutives in *–aculare, –iculare, –uculare*, through diminutive nouns or adjectives (cf. *perīculari* < *perīculum*): * *saltīculare.* We find also some miscellaneous imitative formations: * *expaventare* (and some others) apparently after the analogy of *præsentare;* * *misculare* perhaps after *maculare.*

36. *Greek verbs* in *–âν, –ειν*, etc., when taken into Latin, regularly end in *–are: κυβερνᾶν* > *gubernare; βλασφημεῖν* > *blasphemare.* Cf. Claussen 795. But *ψάλλειν* > *psallĕre*, perhaps through the analogy of *fallere:* Claussen 796.

Germanic verbs in *–an* or *–on* regularly passed into the first conjugation in Latin: *wîtan* > It. *guidare; roubôn* > It. *rubare.* Those in *–jan* went into the fourth: *hatjan* > *hatire, Gl. Reich.; warnjan* > It. *guarnire.*

b. SUFFIXES FOR NOUNS.[1]

37. Some 90 endings, apparently, were used in Vulgar Latin. The Christian writers are especially rich in derivatives. Petronius, too, was very fond of diminutives: *adulescentulus*, Waters Ch. 59, Ch. 64; *porcellus*, Ch. 40; *taurellus*, Ch. 39.

The commonest endings are the following: —

–a, used to form feminines: *nepta*, Pirson 123, Bon. 366, Haag 41; *socera*, Bon. 355.

–āgo, –ĭgo, –ūgo were characteristic of rustic speech: Cooper 111.

–al, –āle, used to form adjectives and also nouns, especially names of parts of apparel (as *bracchiale*), was extended: *coxale*, G. 95. Cf. Olcott 238–239.

–alia, a neuter plural, as *victualia* (cf. the collective plural *–ilia*, as *mirabilia, volatilia*, G. 110–111), was used, in a collective sense, as a feminine singular with an augmentative and pejorative signification, in Italy and Gaul: *canalia < *canis*.

–anda, –enda, neuter plural of the gerundive, came to be used as a feminine singular: *facienda and *facenda.

–ans, –ens: see Adjectives.

–antia, –entia, made from present participles + *–ia* (as *benevolentia, essentia, significantia*), were used to form abstract nouns from verbs: **credentia; fragrantia; placentia;* *sperantia. Cf. R. 49–52, G. 79–102, Olcott 73–78.

–ānus: see Adjectives.

–ar, –āre, for nouns and adjectives: *liminare*, G. 95; *pollicare. Cf. Olcott 187–189.

–aría: see *–ia*.

–arium, used to designate a place (as *gallinarium*), was extended: *breviarium;* *calamarium. Cf. R. 31–37, Olcott 176–182.

–arius: see Adjectives.

–aster: see *Modern Language Notes* **XXIV**, 240.

–ata: see *–ta*, etc.   [*cum.*

–atĭcum (as *viaticum*) was extended, to form nouns from nouns: **corati-*

–ātus, as *senatus* (common in Petronius, e. g., *bonatus*, Waters Ch. 74), was extended: *clericatus;* *ducatus. Cf. *–ta*, etc.

---

[1] Cf. Cooper 1–91, Dubois 99–136, Quillacq 15–31, Bon. 453–463.

–cellus, diminutive, was used beside *–culus: avicula, avicella; navicula, navicella.* So **domnicellus*, etc.

–ceus, –cius: see Adjectives.

–culum, –crum (as *miraculum, lavacrum*) were occasionally used: **genuculum.* Cf. G. 91–92, Olcott 131–134.

–ellus, diminutive (as *castellum*), was often used beside *–ŭlus*, which lost its diminutive force: *anulus, anellus; porculus, porcellus; vitulus, vitellus.* So *calamellus*, etc.

–enda: see *–anda.*

–ens: see Adjectives, *–ans.*

–ensis: see Adjectives.

–entia: see *–antia.*

–ĕrium, as *desiderium*, was probably somewhat extended: Old Fr., Pr. *consirier*, etc. Cf. R. 31–37. See A. Thomas, *Les substantifs en* –ier *et le suffixe* –arius, *Rom.* XXXI, 481; and *Nouveaux essais de philologie française* 110.

–eum: see *–ium.*

–eus: see Adjectives.

–ia, unaccented, used to form abstract nouns (as *victoria*), was extended: **fortia* (cf. *fortia* n. pl. = 'mighty deeds of God', Koffmane 76).

–ia, unaccented, used to form feminines (as *avus, avia*): *neptia*, Pirson 123 (cf. *Zs.* XXXII, 640).

–ía, from Greek *–ía* through Christian writers and speakers: *monarchía; philosophía;* etc. It was often attached to words in *–arius;* hence an ending *–aría: *libraría.* Cf. Olcott 173–176.

–ĭca: see *Archiv für das Studium der neueren Sprachen und Literaturen* CXIV, 457.

–īcca (as *Bodicca, Bonica, Karica*) first appears in Africa in feminine proper names; it was then extended to Spain, Sardinia, and Dacia, and came to be used as a diminutive suffix in Spanish, Portuguese, and Rumanian: Sp. *animalico;* Rum. *manică.* It may have arisen in the first place from a childish pronunciation of *–īclus, –īcla*, being used in pet names. Cf. *Einf.* § 173. For *–accus, –iccus, –occus, –uc(c)us*, see A. Horning in *Zs.* XIX, 170, XX, 335; cf. *Gram.* II, 591. Cf. *Zs.* XXXIV, 26.

–īceus, –īcius: see Adjectives, *–ceus.*

–incus or *–inquus* (as *propinquus*), perhaps also **–ingus* and locally *–ancus*, possibly of Ligurian origin (*Rom.* XXXV, 1–21, 283ff., 333ff.), was used for many new words: Pr. *Arbonenca, ramenc;* It. *solingo, Valinca;*

Sp. *Cusanca*. It was probably confounded, in some regions, with the following.

-ing, a German patronymic ending, was used for some nouns and perhaps for adjectives (see *-incus* above): Pr. *lausenga;* It. *camerlingo*.

-īnus (as *caninus, Montaninus*) originally denoted appurtenance, then resemblance, then smallness; it was freely used, especially to form diminutive nouns, but sometimes to form new adjectives: *domnina* = 'young lady', Olcott 134–136; *Florentinus; serpentinus*. Cf. Olcott 200–204.

-io: see *-tio*.

-issa, from the Greek *-ισσα* (as *βασίλισσα*, so *pythonissa*), was used for some new formations: **dukissa; Germanissa*, Pirson 228; *prophetissa*, R. 251. Cf. Cooper 251.

-ĭtas: see *-tas*.

-ĭtia, -ĭties, used to form nouns from adjectives (as *munditia -ies*), were much extended, *-ities* especially in the south; both are rare in Rumanian (Cooper XLV): **altitia; *granditia*. Cf. Olcott 78–80.

-ĭttus first appears during the Empire in inscriptions in Italy and Dacia, sometimes in Spain and Gaul, as a suffix for proper names: feminine *Attitta, Bonitta, Caritta, Julitta, Livitta, Suavitta*, etc.; masculine *Muritta, Nebitta, Sagitta*, etc. Cf. Pirson 226: *Julianeta, Nonnita, Nonnitus*. Its origin is unknown; it may have arisen from a childish pronunciation of *-ĭclus -a:* cf. *-ĭcca*. Meyer-Lübke, *Einf.* § 172, conjectures that it may have come from the Germanic ending that now appears as *z* in such names as *Heinz*. A. Zimmermann, *Zs.* XXVIII, 343, regards *-ăttus, -ĭttus, -ŏttus* as alternative forms of *-ātus, -ītus, -ōtus*, like *lĭttera* beside *lītera*, etc. It came to be very widely used as a diminutive suffix for nouns, and also for adjectives, the *i* being short in Gaul, Rætia, and central and northern Italy, generally long in the Spanish peninsula and in Sardinia: nouns, Fr. *amourette*, It. *fioretto*, Sp. *bacito;* adjectives, Fr. *doucet*, It. *grassetto*, Sp. *bonito*.

-itūdo: see *-tūdo*.

-ium, -eum (as *capitium, calcaneum*)*:* see G. 56–59.

-īvum, -īva: see Olcott 224–226.

-men, -mentum, used to form nouns from verbs (as *certāmen, vestimentum*), were extended, especially *-mentum: *gubernamentum*. Cf. Olcott 123–131, R. 22–25.

-mōnium, -mōnia: see Olcott 81–82.

-o (-ōnem), originally used to indicate a characteristic (as *bĭbo*), was

commonly employed as an augmentative or pejorative, in Gaul often as a diminutive: *gŭlo;* It. *boccone;* Fr. *aiglon.* See *Archiv* V, 56, 223, XIII, 222, 415, 475. Cf. Olcott 83–87, G. 44–45.

–or (–ōrem), used to form abstract nouns (as *candor, sapor*), was employed for many new formations of the same kind, especially in Gaul: *dulcor;* **flator;* **flavor;* **lūcor;* **sentor; viror.* In Gaul these nouns came to be feminine: Bon. 503–504 (*dolor, timor,* etc.).

–or (–ōrem), used to designate the agent: see *–tor.*

–ōrium; see *–tōrium.*

–ŏttus, of unknown origin (cf. *–ĭttus*), was apparently used first of young animals, then as a general moderate diminutive: It. *aquilotto, casotta.*

　–sa: see *–ta,* etc.

　–sio: see *–tio.*

　–sor: see *–tor.*

　–sōrium: see *–tōrium.*

　–sūra: see *–ūra.*

　–sus: see *–ta,* etc.

–ta, –tus, –sa, –sus, later *–āta, –ātus, –uta,* perfect participles used as nouns, started perhaps with such forms as *defensa, remissa,* i. e., feminine perfect participles with a feminine noun understood, and were reinforced by neuter plural forms which became feminine and also by fourth declension nouns in *–tus,* as *collectus, narratus:* cf. C. Collin in *Archiv* XIII, 453; L. H. Alexander, *Participial Substantives of the* -ata *type in the Romance Languages,* 1912. They were considerably used to make abstract nouns from verbs (and *–ata* was sometimes attached to nouns, as *annata); *–tus* and *–sus* were preferred in Dacia (Cooper XLV): *collecta,* G. 111; **debĭta; extensa,* R. 83; **movĭta,* Substrate IV, 122; **perdĭta; recubĭtus;* **reddĭta;* **vendĭta;* It. *andata, fossato, venuta.* Cf. Olcott 33–51, R. 82–83, G. 85–88, Bayard 24–25.

–tas (–tātem), used to make abstract nouns from adjectives, was freely employed: *falsĭtas; nativĭtas; purĭtas; trinĭtas.* So *deĭtas* from *deus.* Cf. Olcott 58–69, G. 102–106, Bayard 19–22 (very common in St. Cyprian).

–tio, –sio (–tiōnem, –siōnem), used to form abstract nouns from verbs (as *lectio, mansio, potio*), are very common in St. Jerome, St. Cyprian, and other late writers: *abbreviatio; aggravatio,* G. 63; **nutritio; ostensio; prensio; revolutio.* Cf. Olcott 2–23, R. 69–82, Bayard 19–22.

–tor, –trix, –sor (–tōrem, –trīcem, –sōrem), used to denote the agent (as *amātor, mensor*), were very freely employed (but show few traces in Rumanian: Cooper XLV): *necātor; ostensor;* Pr. *beveire, trobaire.* Cf. Olcott 88–122, R. 55–63, G. 45–56.

–tōrium, –sōrium, used to form from verbs nouns denoting place, some-

times instrument (as *dormitorium, natatorium, cursorium*), were much extended, often taking the place of *-culum* (*cubiculum* > *accubitorium*): *cæsorium; mensorium; missorium; oratorium; *pressorium; repositorium.* Cf. Olcott 194–196, R. 31–37, G. 96–97.

-tūdo (*-tūdĭnem*), used to make abstract nouns from adjectives (as *fortitudo*), was extended: *certitudo; servitudo.* Cf. Olcott 69–73.

-tūra: see *-ūra.*

-tus: see *-ta,* etc.

-ŭlus, -ŭla, diminutive (as *vitulus*), was used for a few new formations: *alaudula; ossulum,* Bon. 197.

-ūra and *-t-ūra, -s-ūra,* used to form abstract nouns from perfect participles (as *censura, strictura*), later from adjectives also, were extended, in late Latin often replacing *-or* (*fervor* > *fervura*): *frig'dura; messura; nutritura; ornatura; *planura; pressura; tensura; *vir'dura.* See *Einf.* § 171. Cf. Olcott 51–58, R. 40–45, G. 88–90.

-ūta: see *-ta,* etc.

38. When Greek nouns were borrowed by Latin, the endings were adapted as follows: —

-os, -η, -ov regularly became respectively *-us, -a, -um:* Claussen 796. There are a few exceptions for special reasons (Claussen 795): ἔλαιον, influenced by *olere,* gave *oleum;* μηλόφυλλον, by popular etymology, gave *millefolium.*

-as in popular words generally became *-a* (Claussen 798–799): λαμπάς > *lampa.*

-ης, -της became *-a, -ta* or *-us, -tus* (Claussen 798): τρώκτης > *tructa;* βωλίτης > *boletus.*

-ι in popular words either fell or became *-a, -e, -is,* or *-i* (Claussen 799): πέπερι > *piper;* σίναπι > *sinapis, sinape;* κόμμι > *gumma, gummi-s.*

-ις often became *-a,* instead of *-is* (Claussen 798): *pausis* > *pausa.*

-μα in popular words gave a feminine *-ma* (Claussen 796–797): κῦμα > *cima.*

-ρος preceded by a consonant became *-er* (Claussen 797): Ἀλέξανδρος > *Alexander.*

-ων in popular words became *-o* (Claussen 797): λέων > *leo.*

Sometimes the genitive or the accusative was taken as a basis, instead of the nominative (Claussen 800–802): ἐλέφαντος > *elephantus;* μαγίδα > *magĭda.*

The unaccented vowel of the penult was often changed in conformity with Latin habits (Claussen 802–806): διάβολος > *diabolus diabulus; κέρασος > cerăsus *cerĕsus; κιθάρα > cithăra cithĕra; σκόπελος > scopulus; σπατάλη > spatula.

c. SUFFIXES FOR ADJECTIVES.[1]

39. The commonest endings are the following: —

–abĭlis: see *–bĭlis.*

–āceus –ācius, –ĭceus –ĭcius, used to make from nouns adjectives denoting material (as *arenaceus, pelliceus*), were extended (especially in rustic speech: Cooper 111), *–aceus* being employed later as an augmentative and pejorative suffix for adjectives and finally for nouns: *chartaceus; formaceus; mixticius,* G. 143; *setaceus;* It. *tempaccio,* etc. Cf. Olcott 215–220. See E. Wölfflin, *Die Adjectiva auf –icius* in *Archiv* V, 415.

–ālis, –īlis, used to make from nouns adjectives of appurtenance (as *regalis, gentilis*), were extended: *cortilis; *ducalis; episcopalis.* Cf. Olcott 226–238, G. 144.

–āneus –ānius, –ōneus –ōnius (as *extraneus, erroneus*) were slightly extended: *caroneus; spontaneus.*

–ans, –ens (–antem, –entem), present participles (as *amans, potens*), were used freely to make adjectives and nouns from verbs: *credens; *currens; *passans.*

–ānus, denoting appurtenance (as *paganus, Romanus*), was used to form adjectives of place (occasionally time) and nouns of office: *biduanus,* Bechtel 83; *medianus,* Bechtel 83; *Sicilianus; Tuscanus; –*capitanus; decanus.*

–arĭcius, a combination of *–arius* and *–ĭcius* (as *sigillaricius*), became popular in Gaul: see A. Thomas, *Nouveaux essais de philologie française* 62 (*Hacherece,* etc.).

–āris (as *singularis*) was extended: *particularis.* Cf. Olcott 182–187.

–arius, attached to nouns and adjectives, to denote connection, and used also in the masculine to form nouns of occupation (as *aquarius, argentarius, pomarius*), was much extended, especially in the latter function: *imaginarius; *leviarius; — apothecarius; *marinarius; *werrarius.* Cf. Olcott 137–173. The phonetic development of this suffix was apparently peculiar in Gaul and some other regions: the earliest examples are *glan-*

---

[1] Cf. Cooper 92–163 (diminutives, 164–195), Quillacq 32–40, Dubois 136–151, Bon. 464–467.

deria < *glandarius* + *-ia* (6th century) and *sorcerus* < **sortiarius* (8th century); the earliest forms in French and Provençal are *-ers, -er,* then *-iers, -ier.* On the other hand, Spanish *-ero* and Italian *-aio* are perfectly regular, Italian *-aro* is easily explained by the analogy of the plural *-ari,* and Italian *-iere, -iero* are probably borrowed. E. R. Zimmermann, *Die Geschichte des lateinischen Suffixes* -arius *in den romanischen Sprachen,* and E. Staaff, *Le suffixe* -arius *dans les langues romanes,* try to derive all the forms from *-arius.* P. Marchot, *Zs.* XXI, 296 (cf. *Phon.* I, 34–36), postulates *-ar(i)us* and *-er(i)us,* showing that while the French forms may perhaps be derived from *-arius* and *-iarius,* the Provençal cannot. Cf. *Gram.* I, 222, § 227. Zimmermann, *Zs.* XXVI, 591, points out that many words have *c, e,* or *i* before the *a,* that *-iarius* was a real suffix (cf. *anatiarius,* Olcott 142), that *-iarius* and *-carius* may have established *-iers* in French. A. Thomas, *Rom.* XXXI, 481 (cf. *Nouveaux essais de philologie française* 119, and *Bausteine* 641), suggests that the Germans in Gaul associated *-arius* with their proper names in *-areis* or *-ari,* and when *umlaut* affected the *a* of these, pronounced *-arius,* too, as *-erius* or *-erus,* and that this pronunciation spread to the neo-Latin speakers. Cf. *Chairibertus* repeatedly used for *Charibertus* by Fredegarius: Haag 7.

-ātus, a perfect participle ending (as *sceleratus*), was much used to make adjectives in the popular language: *exauguratus;* **fatatus; timoratus.* Cf. Olcott 244–250, G. 159–160.

-bĭlis, or *-ābĭlis, -ĭbĭlis,* an objective suffix used to make adjectives from verbs (as *amabilis, terribilis*), is very common in Christian writers and was much employed in late Latin, especially in learned words; it is rare, however, in Rumanian (Cooper XLV): *acceptabilis; capabilis; *caritabilis; diligibilis; indicibilis,* G. 137. Cf. Olcott 209–213, R. 109–116, G. 135–140.

-ceus -cius : see *-āceus.*

-ens : see *-ans.*

-ensis, used to make from nouns adjectives of appurtenance (as *forensis*), was greatly extended, especially in popular speech, the derivatives being sometimes employed as nouns: * *cortensis;* * *Frankensis; turrensis,* G. 155; *vallensis,* G. 155; —* *markensis;* * *pagensis.*

-eus -ius, denoting material (as *aureus*), was slightly extended (but is rare in Rumanian: Cooper XLV); the derivative was sometimes used as a noun: *panneus; papyrius;* — *fageus; querceus.* Cf. Olcott 339–344.

-ĭbĭlis : see *-bĭlis.*

-īceus -īcius : see *āceus.*

–ĭcus (as *medicus*) was used especially in words from the Greek: *clericus.* Cf. Olcott 220–223.

–ĭdus (as *rapidus*) was slightly extended: *exsūcidus,* G. 155 (Tertullian); **rīpidus; sapidus.*

–īlis: see *–ālis.*

–īnus: see Nouns.

–ĭnus (as *fraxinus*) was used for a few adjectives: *quercinus.*

–ĭscus, probably a fusion of Greek *–ισκος (Syriscus)* and Germanic *–isk (Thiudiscus),* was used for *–ĭcus* in some late words: **Angliscus; *Frankiscus.*

–ĭttus: see Nouns.

–ius: see *–eus.*

–īvus (as *nativus*) occurs in a few new formations: **restivus.* Cf. Olcott 224–226.

–ōneus: see *–āneus.*

–ōrius: see *–tōrius.*

–ōsus, also *–iōsus: Rom.* XXXIX, 217.

–sōrius: see *–tōrius.*

–tōrius, –sōrius, made up of *–t–or, –s–or* $+$ *–ius* (as *noscere notor notorius, censēre censor censorius*), were used for some new formations: *defensorius; mansorius.* In Provençal and Rumanian *–tōrius* was extended, with the sense of *–bĭlis* or of the gerundive: Pr. *punidor;* Rum. *jurătórĭŭ,* Tiktin 597.

–ŭlus, diminutive (as *albulus*), was a favorite with Christian writers; *promptulus,* G. 158. Cf. G. 157–158.

–ŭndus (as *jocundus*) was used in Spanish and Provençal for a few words: Pr. *volon.*

–ūtus (as *canutus*) was somewhat extended: **carnutus.*

d. SUFFIXES FOR ADVERBS.[1]

40. The usual endings are as follows: —

–ce –c (as *ne nec, num nunc, tum tunc*) was apparently used to form *dunc* (*C. I. L.* IX, 4810, etc.) $= dum + ce$ (cf. *Franz.* ∂ I, 10); Pirson 252 cites eight examples of *dunc,* one of them from Gaul. Cf. *dōnique* in *Substrate* II, 103–106. Possibly **anc* is derived from *an* in the same way: cf. *Archiv* I, 241; *Gram.* III, 552.

–e is very common in St. Jerome: G. 193–197 (*angelice,* etc.). It was

---

[1] Cf. Cooper 196–204, Dubois 163–171, Bon. 467–470.

preserved in popular speech in *bene, longe, male, pure, tarde,* and occurs also in *Romanice,* whence such formations as *Brittanice, Normannice,* etc.

–ĭter: see *–ter.*

–o and *–um* generally coincided in pronunciation (*multum = multo,* etc.). They are rare in St. Jerome, but common in other late writers: *clanculo, multum, rato,* etc. Many such adverbs were preserved in common speech, as It. *alto, basso, caldo, chiaro, piano, poco;* hence other adjectives came to be used as adverbs (as It. *forte, soave*), and in Rumanian nearly all adjectives may be so used (as *greŭ, noŭ*).

–ter (as *brevĭter*) was not preserved in common speech, though much used in ecclesiastical Latin (G. 197–201: *infantiliter,* etc.), being especially common in St. Cyprian (Bayard 32–34).

–tim was favored by St. Cyprian (Bayard 34–35) and some other writers, but was not kept alive in popular Latin.

Some adverbial phrases on the model *ad ... –ōnes* (in Italy also without the preposition) came into use: It. *a ginocchioni, bocconi;* Fr. *à reculons.* Cf. *Gram.* II, 689; *Rom.* XXXIII, 230; *Zs.* XXIX, 245, XXX, 337, 339.

Repetition was used, as sometimes in Classic Latin, for emphatic effect. Many examples are to be found in Petronius: *modo modo =* 'only yesterday,' Waters Ch. 37, Ch. 42, Ch. 46.

41. Adverbs of manner came to be made with the ablative *mente.* This noun was first used with an adjective to denote a state of mind, as *forti mente, obstinata mente, jocunda mente, firma mente, sana mente;* Apuleius, *dubia mente,* I, 6, and *saucia mente,* V, 23. Then it was employed in a more general sense: *pari mente,* G. 428; **bona mente;* **ipsa mente;* **mala mente.* Later, perhaps after the Vulgar Latin period, *mente* was used with any adjective that could make an adverb of manner; **longa mente; sola mente, Gl. Reich.* This formation is not common, however, in Rumanian: *Lat. Spr.* 487. In the Romance languages *mente* was sometimes added to adverbs: Fr. *comment;* It. *insiememente.*

e. CHANGE OF SUFFIX.

42. The popular language sometimes substitutes one suffix for another, as *manuplus* for *manipulus*. The principal types are: —

(1) Subsitution of a new or common suffix for an old or rare one: —

-cĭllus > *-cĕllus*: see *-ĭllus*.

-cŭlus > *cĕllus*: see *-ŭlus*.

-ēlus > *-ĕllus* (common in late Latin): *camēlus* > *camĕllus*, Cohn 213–216, R. 460; *loquēla* > *loquĕlla*, Corssen I, 227, R. 460; *querēla* > *querĕlla*, S. 131, R. 321, 460; *suadēla* > *suadĕlla*, R. 460. Cf. Caper (Keil VII, 96): "*querela, loquela* per unum *l.*"

-ēnus > *-īnus*: "*Byzacenus* non *Byzacinus*," *App. Pr.*; *venēnum* > *veninum*. Cf. Cohn 219–226.

-ex(-ēcem) > *-ix(-īcem)*: *vervēcem* > *berbīcem*. Cf. Cohn 41–42.

-ĭllus > *-ĕllus*: *axĭlla* > *ascĕlla*, etc. Cf. Cohn 42–52.

-or(-ōrem) > *-ūra*: *calor* > *calūra*; *pavor* > *pavura*; *rancor* > *rancūra*, etc. Cf. Cohn 172–180.

-ŭlus > *-ĕllus*: *anŭlus* > *anĕllus*; *avicŭla* > *avicĕlla*, etc. Cf. Cohn 17–28.

-ŭus > *-ĭtus*: *vacuus* > *vŏcĭtus* (cf. § 195).

(2) Indiscriminate use of two suffixes: —

-ānus = *-āneus*: *extraneus* *extranus*; *subterraneus* *subterranus*. Cf. Cohn 160–172.

-ātus = *-ĭtus* = *-ūtus*: *barbatus* *barbutus*; *carnatus* *carnutus*; *caudatus cauditus*, Cohn 184; *lanatus lanutus*, Cohn 184. Cf. Cohn 180–205.

-ĭceus -ĭcius = *-ĭceus -ĭcius*: *erĭcius* *erīcius*. Cohn 30–31.

-ĭcŭlus = *-ĭcŭlus*: *capĭtŭlus* *capĭtŭlus*; *cornĭcŭla* *cornĭcŭla*; *lentĭcŭla* *lentĭcŭla*. Cf. Cohn 151–154.

-ĭcŭlus = *-ŭcŭlus*: *ossĭculum ossŭculum*, Waters Ch. 65; *pedīculus pedŭculus*.

-ĭlius = *-ĭlius*: *consĭlium* *consīlium*; *famĭlia* *famīlia*. Cf. Cohn 154–160.

-ĭx(-īcem) = *-ĭx(-ĭcem)*: *sōrĭcem* *sorīcem*. Cf. Cohn 147–151.

(3) Alteration of a suffix: —

-ārius: see Suffixes for Adjectives, *-ārius*. Cf. Cohn 274–291.

–ēnus > *–īnus* through late pronunciation of Greek η as *ī*: σαγήνη >
saginæ (*Vok.* III, 121: 7th century) > Old Fr. *saïne*, etc.

–ĭcŭlus? > *–ŭcŭlus*: *genŭcŭlum; *ranŭcŭla, etc.   Cf. Cohn 226–264.

–ūdo (*–ūdĭnem*) > *–ūmen* (*–ūmĭnem*): *consuetudo* *costumen, *Substrate*
I, 553–554; *incus incūdo* .* *incūmĭnem*, etc.   Cf. Cohn 264–274.

4. COMPOUNDS.

a. NOUNS.

43. *Acer arbor* (> Fr. *érable*); *alba spīna; avis strūthius;
bene placĭtum,* G. 131; *bis cŏctum; in ŏdio; mĕdio die; mĕdio
lŏco.*

b. ADJECTIVES.

44. These compounds generally belonged to the literary
style.   G. 130–134, 160–170: *magnisonans; omnimodus; uni-
cornis; unigenitus;* etc.   But *male habĭtus,* etc., were popular.

c. PRONOUNS.

45. See §§ 24, 65.

d. VERBS.

46. *Calce pistare; crucifĭgĕre,* G. ᴌ.91; *fŏris mĭttĕre; genu-
flectĕre,* G. 191; *ĭnde fŭgĕre* (> Fr. *enfuir*); *ĭntra vidēre; manu
tenēre; mente habēre* (> Pr. *mentaver*); *mĭnus pretiare.* So
antemĭttĕre, etc., in *Gl. Reich.*   In church writers there are
many verbs in *–ficare,* as *mortificare:* G. 190.

e. ADVERBS.

47. There were many compounds made up of a preposition
and an adverb: *ab ante,* R. 234; *ab intus,* R. 231, Bon. 483;
ab olim, Bechtel 101; *a contra,* Bechtel 101; *a foras,* Bechtel
101; *a foris,* R. 231, Bon. 483; *a longe,* G. 203, Bon. 483; *a
modo,* R. 232, Bon. 483; *a semel,* Bechtel 101; — *ad horam* ⚊
'presently', 'just now', G. 426; *ad mane,* Bechtel 101; *ad semel,*
Bon. 194, 484; *ad sero,* Bechtel 101; *ad subito,* Bechtel 101;

ad tunc, Bechtel 101; — *de contra*, Bechtel 101; *de deorsum*, R. 232; *de foris*, R. 232, G. 203; *de intro*, Bechtel 102; *de intus*, R. 232, G. 203; *de magis*, *Lat. Spr.* 487; *de retro*, R. 232; *de semel*, Bechtel 101; *de sursum*, R. 233, G. 203, Bon. 484; — *e contra*, G. 203; *ex tunc*, R. 433; — *in ante*, Bon. 484, *Lat. Spr.* 487; *in contra*, R. 235; *in hodie*, Bechtel 102; *in mane*, Bechtel 102; **in semel*, *Substrate* III, 268.

Petronius (Waters Ch. 38) says: *Ubi semel res inclinata amici de medio.*

The following compounds are of a still different nature: *ac sic*, *Per.* 40,8, etc.; *et sic*, *Per.* 39,17, etc.; *usque hodie*, G. 426, *Per.* 68,13.

f. PREPOSITIONS.

48. Some of these adverbial compounds, and some others similar to them, were used as prepositions: *ab ante*, *Lexique* 40; — *de ante*, Bechtel 102; *de inter*, Bechtel 102, Haag 75; *de intus; de retro; in ante; in contra.* Cf. E. Wölfflin, *Abante*, in *Archiv* I, 437. Slightly different is *intus in*, Bechtel 102.

A compound made up of preposition + noun is found in: *in giro* (followed by the ablative or the accusative), Bechtel 102; *in medio*, Bechtel 102; *per girum* and *per giro = circa*, Bechtel 102.

Some compounds consist of two prepositions: **de ad* (> It. *da*)[1]; *de post*, R. 235; *de sub*, R. 235; *de super*, Bon. 484.

g. CONJUNCTIONS.

49. *At ubi* and *ad ubi*, Bon. 484–486 (cf. *Per.* 74,28, 85,15, etc.); *et at ubi*, *Per.* 72,19, 75,3.

---

[1] Romance *da, dad* may be the result of a fusion rather than a combination of *de* and *ad*. In any case it is probably a late product. Some have thought it came from *de+ab*. Mohl, *Lexique* 38–47, says *da* is found from the 7th century on; he would derive It. and Old Sp. *da*, Sardinian *dave, dae*, Rætian *dad* from the Oscan *da, dat* and from a southern Latin **dabī, *dabe*.

II. SYNTAX.[1]

A. ORDER OF WORDS.[2]

50. The Romance order is simpler and more rational than that of Classic Latin. It does not permit the arbitrary separation of members that belong together, such as the preposition and the word it governs, or the adjective and the noun it modifies, as in Ovid's "In nova fert animus mutatas dicere formas corpora." Neither does it allow the collocation of words of the same part of speech that belong logically in different places, as in the "In multis hoc rebus dicere habemus" of Lucretius. The most irrational features of the Classic Latin construction were surely artifical, and were not characteristic of daily speech. Nevertheless there is really a fundamental difference between the old order and the new: Romance has, so to speak, a *crescendo*, Latin to a certain extent a *diminuendo* movement (*Lat. Spr.* 491); Romance puts the emphasis at the end, Latin very frequently in the middle. The principle, however, is not primarily rhythmic, but psychic, the difference being due to a diverse conception of the structure of language: Romance inclines more to put the modifier after the word modified. The modern order is the more logical, proceeding from the known to the unknown. The old arrangement is exemplified by this sentence: "Fabius

---

[1] See Meyer-Lübke, *Gram.* III, for a comprehensive account of Romance syntax.
[2] See Elise Richter, *Zur Entwicklung der romanischen Wortstellung aus der lateinischen*, 1903, from which work most of the matter of this chapter was taken.

æquatus imperio Hannibalem et virtute et fortuna superiorem vidit." The following examples illustrate the later structure: "Mors perfecit tua ut essent omnia brevia," "Hæc loca sunt montuosa et natura impedita ad rem militarem." The change constitutes a progress in language; all cultivated peoples have made it. It is indigenous in Latin, not imitated from the Greek, which independently effected the same transformation.

51. The modern order was not abruptly substituted for the old. On the contrary, it is to be found in Latin, with generally increasing frequency, in inscriptions and popular writers, from the earliest texts down; it occurs sporadically also in literary authors, especially in Cicero. Petronius has notably short periods and an approach to the new structure. But until the fourth century the majority of Latin sentences have the old arrangement. Classic Latin may be said to represent an intermediate stage, while the revolution was in progress; there was a long struggle, and for centuries the ancient and the modern type were used side by side. By the fourth century the new order prevailed. Here is a characteristic passage from the *Peregrinatio:* "Hæc est autem vallis ingens et planissima, in qua filii Israhel commorati sunt his diebus, quod sanctus Moyses ascendit in montem Domini, et fuit ibi quadraginta diebus et quadraginta noctibus" (*Per.* 37, 21-24). The following is a good sample of the style of the Vulgate: "Cui respondit Dominus: Qui peccaverit mihi, delebo eum de libro meo; tu autem vade, et duc populum istum quo locutus sum tibi; angelus meus præcedet te. Ego autem in die ultionis visitabo et hoc peccatum eorum" (*Exodus* XXXII, 33, 34).

52. There was always a tendency to put a stressed word first, followed by an unaccented one, such as a connective or an atonic pronoun (*Lat. Spr.* 490). According to Meyer-

Lübke, *Zs.* XXI, 313, personal pronouns, when unstressed, were always enclitic in Latin, and were attached preferably to the first word in the sentence ; and so it was in the early stages of the Romance languages : cf. It. *vedolo* but *non lo vedo, aiutatemi* but *or m'aiutate ;* Fr. *voit le* but *qui le voit.* The definite article, however, precedes its noun in all the Romance languages except Rumanian and Albanian (Zauner 40).

53. In dependent clauses, which were naturally of less importance, the old order survived longer than in independent. In a few other respects the old arrangement lingered and under certain conditions is still preserved : negative and intensive adverbs precede their verb ; under some circumstances the object may come before the verb, and sometimes the whole predicate precedes ; in certain constructions the dependent infinitive may stand before the finite verb (as Pr. *morir volgra*).

B. USE OF WORDS.

54. There were great changes in the functions of pronouns, prepositions, conjunctions, and adverbs. Many uses of prepositions are connected with the loss of inflections: these will be discussed under the Use of Inflections. A definite and an indefinite article developed out of *ille* and *unus.*

1. NOUNS AND ADJECTIVES.

55. For the simplification of inflections, see the Use of Inflections.

Repetition for intensive effect is not uncommon in late writers : Commodian, *malum malum*, Wölfflin 4 ; *bene bene, bonis bonis, fortis fortis, malus malus*, etc., R. 280. Cf. § 40.

a. COMPARISON.

56. Little by little the old comparative and superlative lost their precise sense from being employed frequently with merely an intensive force (Wölfflin 83). The comparative came to be used for a superlative, as *omnium levior* (Wölfflin 68–71), and also for a positive, as Ovid's *inertior ætas* (Wölfflin 63–68); and the superlative was often really a positive in meaning, as in St. Augustine's *sancta atque dulcissima* (Wölfflin 57–63), and in *hic est filius meus carissimus*, etc. (R. 415–417). From early times certain periphrases were used to emphasize the comparative idea, as Plautus, *melius sanus* (Wölfflin 16); Anthimus, *plus congruus* and *maxime congruus* (Wölfflin 16; cf. *maxime pessima*, etc., R. 280); Vitruvius, *magis melior*, etc. (Wölfflin 46); Commodian, *plus levior*, etc. (Wölfflin 47). To avoid ambiguity, the *plus* and *magis* constructions were employed more and more to express a distinct comparison : *plus miser* in Tertullian, *plus formosus* in Nemesianus, *plus dulce*, *plus felix*, etc., in Sidonius Apollinaris (Wölfflin 29). Finally, toward the end of the Vulgar Latin period, this formation came to be popularly regarded as the regular one: *magis mirabilem*, Sepulcri 232 ; *plus popularis, magis . . . præclarum*, Bon. 451. Many old comparative forms remained, however, in common use. Cf. Adverbs. In the Romance languages a substitute for the superlative was made by prefixing the definite article to the comparative; it is likely that this device existed in late Vulgar Latin, but no example of it has been found. See *Archiv* VIII, 166–170.

b. NUMERALS.[1]

57. *Unus* was used as an indefinite article, occasionally in Classic Latin, frequently in late and popular writers : *lepida*

---

[1] For the forms of numerals, see Morphology.

... *una* ... *mulier*, Plautus, *Pseud.* 948 ; *unus servus*, Petronius, Waters Ch. 26; *accessit ad eum una sorella*, R. 425; cf. *Per.* 48, 25, etc.

58. Ordinal numerals, except a few of the smallest, were apparently not much used in popular speech after the fifth century.

2. PRONOUNS.

59. Pronouns were much more used than in Classic Latin : G. 408-409.

a. PERSONAL AND POSSESSIVE PRONOUNS.

60. The personal pronouns came into more and more frequent use. *Ego* and *tu* are very common in Petronius. The demonstratives, especially *ille*, were employed as personal pronouns of the third person. The adverb *inde* came to be used occasionally as a genitive neuter pronoun : *nemo inde dubitat*, Regnier 10 ; *exinde* = Fr. *en*, Bon. 580.

Many pronouns developed double forms, according as they were accented or unaccented (as *suus* and *sus*): see Morphology. Cf. § 158.

There was great irregularity in the use of reflexives, especially the possessives, *suus* being generally substituted for *ejus*. See *Lat. Spr.* 489, G. 403-404, Hoppe 102-103, Dubois 333-336.

b. DEMONSTRATIVES.

61. *Idem* went out of popular use, being replaced by *ille* and *ipse*. For the encroachment of *ipse* on *idem*, see Hoppe 104, Bayard 132

62. *Is*, too, was often replaced by *ille* and *ipse* (Bechtel 145), and eventually was preserved in vulgar speech only in the combination *eccum* (= *ecce hum*), where it was not recognized,[1] and in the extremely common phrase *id ipsum* (> It. *desso*), where likewise the *id* lost its significance.   This last compound was used as a neuter pronoun, meaning 'it' or 'that,' as *id ipsum sapite*, R. 424 (cf. R. 424–425, G. 407, Quillacq 126), and also as a demonstrative adjective, generally invariable, as *id ipsum velam*, R. 424, *in id ipsum monastyriu*, *Franz. ə* II, 2, *in id ipsam rem*, *Franz. ə* II, 2.

63. *Hic, ille,* and *iste* came to be used indiscriminately (G. 405–406, Hoppe 104, Bayard 130–132); there are examples of *iste* for *hic* in Cæsar's time (Densusianu 178).   *Hic* and *is*, too, were confused by late writers (Bayard 132).   Toward the end of the Vulgar Latin period *hic* was apparently going out of common use, with the exception of the neuter *hoc*.

64. A combination of two demonstratives was common in Christian writers: *is ipse, iste ipse, ipse ille, ille ipse, iste ille, iste hic, hic ipse.*   The last three have left no trace.

65. *Ecce* and *eccum* (pronounced *eccu*) were used as demonstrative prefixes (cf. §24): we find early *ecce ego, ecce tu, ecce hic, ecce nunc;* also *ecce iste, ecce ille*, such combinations being common in Plautus.   The final stage, probably not reached until the end of the Vulgar Latin period, is the fusion of the two parts into one word.

Atque, too, was perhaps used as a prefix (*Gram.* II, 646): Plautus, *atque ipse illic est* (*Epidicus* 91), *atque is est* (*Stichus* 582).   G. Ascoli, however, *Intorno ai continuatori neolatini del lat.* "*ipsu–*" in *Archivio glottologico italiano* XV, 303 (discussing Sp. *aquese*, Pg. *aquesse*, Catalan *aqueix*, etc.), maintains that *eccu'* was the basis in all the Empire.   At any rate, *eccu'* was influenced in some regions, especially in Spain and southern Gaul, by *atque* or *ac* (as in *ac sic*).

---

[1] Cf. Plautus, *Mil. Glor.* I, 25: "Ubi tu's? — Eccum."

When *iste* and *ille* lost their distinctive force, people said for
'this' *ecc'iste* or *eccu'iste*, for 'that' *ecc'ille* or *eccu'ille*. These
compounds developed into * *ecceste*, * *acceste*, * *ceste*, * *eccueste*,
* *accueste*, * *cueste* and * *eccelle*, * *accelle*, * *celle*, * *eccuelle*,
* *accuelle*, * *cuelle*.

66. The suffix –*met* was used also as an intensive prefix,
ipsemet becoming *metipse* through such combinations as *temet
ipsum* (*Ecclus*. XXX, 22), *semet ipsum* (*Philip*. II, 8). Cf. §24.
Ego met ipse is blamed by Donatus (*Lat. Spr.* 484).

Beside *ipse*, there was an emphatic form *ipsĭmus* (used by
Petronius: Waters Ch. 69, etc.). This, with the prefix *met*–,
became * *metipsĭmus*.

67. *Ille, hic, ipse, is*, especially *ille*, were used as personal
pronouns of the third person. Cf. §60.

68. *Ille, hic, ipse, is* were used also as definite articles. *Ille*
in this function is very common: R. 419–420 (*cito proferte
mihi stolam illam primam*). Examples of the others are by no
means infrequent: *hic*, R. 427 (*virum hunc cujus est zona hæc*);
ipse, R. 423 (*in ipsa multitudine*); *is*, R. 423–425. This use of
is was probably more literary than popular.

c. INTERROGATIVES AND RELATIVES.

69. The forms were greatly confused by late writers. In
Bon. 391–396 we find *qui* used as n. sg. and pl.; *quæ* as m., as
n., as acc. f. sg., as acc. m. pl.; *quod* as m., as f. pl., as n. pl.;
quem as n.; *qua* very often as n. pl. (395–396).

In popular speech *qui* was apparently used regularly for
quis : Audollent 549, Quillacq 126–127, Bon. 391–392; it is
common in inscriptions. Furthermore, the masculine *qui* took
the place of the feminine *quæ ;* it occurs in Christian inscriptions from the fifth century on: cf. R. 276 (*qui, quem* for *quæ*,

quam), Haag 51, Bon. 390–391, 394 (*qui* f. sg. and f. pl., *quem* f.), *Archiv* I, 53 (*qui* for *quæ* in 528 A. D.). *Quid*, moreover, gradually encroached on *quod:* Bon. 393.

70. *Qualis* was kept, and was used as an interrogative and as a relative. The adverb *unde* came to have occasionally the meaning of French *dont* (Bon. 580; *Zs.* Beiheft 7, 178), and eventually * *de unde*, * *d'unde*, was employed as a relative pronoun. Cf. § 84.

d. INDEFINITE PRONOUNS.

71. Some Classic Latin pronouns fell into disuse, and some new compounds were made. The principal indefinite pronouns and adjectives used in late popular speech are as follows: —

aliquanti took the place of *aliqui* and *aliquot: aliquanta oppida cepit*, G. 415.

alĭquis flourished especially in the West: Sp. *alguien*, Pg. *alguem*. The neuter *aliquid* was more extended: Pr. *alques*.

alĭqui ūnus > **aliqu'ūnus* *alicūnus.

alius and *alter* were confused in common speech: G. 415–417; Plautus, *alius filius*, G. 417. This confusion is more frequent in late Latin: St. Jerome, *nemo judicat alterum*, G. 416. There is evidence of the retention of the old neuter *alid* (Lucretius I, 263): *Archiv* I, 237.

cata was probably introduced, along the Mediterranean, by Greek merchants, in such phrases as *cata unum* = καθ' ἕνα, *cata tres* = κατὰ τρεῖς. Hence *cata ūnus, **cat' ūnus*, etc. Cf. § 19.

hŏmo was used sometimes like French *on:* Per. 55, 25.

ĭnde came to mean, in certain constructions, 'some' or 'any.'

magis: see *plus*.

mŭltus.

*nec ente or *ne ente was apparently used as an equivalent for *nihil*. Meyer-Lübke, *Gram.* II, 650, conjectures *ne inde.

* *ne ipse ūnus*, * *ne'ps'ūnus*.

nec unus.

nēmo was kept in Italy, Sardinia, and Dacia: *Lat. Spr.* 485.

nūllus.

omnis: see *tōtus. Omnis* and *omnia* were kept in Italy.

paucus.

persona.

plus and *magis* were confused: G. 427, Regnier 108–109 (*quanto plus tenetur tanto plus timetur*, 109).

qualis.

quantus, tantus replaced *quot, tot.* There are examples as early as Propertius: Densusianu 179. Cf. Dräger 104, § 53, R. 336–337, G. 413–415 (St. Jerome, *quanti justi esuriunt*, 414; Claudian, *tantis lacrimis*, 415).

quī.

quīque.

quĭs.

quĭsque, quĭsquis. *Quisque* was much extended (G. 409–411), being used for *quisquis* and *quicumque* (Bayard 135).

res and *res nata* = 'anyone', 'anything': R. 345.

talis.

tantus : see *quantus.*

tōtus, pronounced also *tottus* (S. 121) and perhaps **tūttus,* was sometimes used for *omnis :* Plautus, *totis horis, Mil. Glor.* 212. This use was common in late Latin: Densusianu 178, Bechtel 143, R. 338, G. 402–403 (*tota tormenta diaboli in me veniant*, 403). Cf. §§ 163, 204, (2).

ūnus.

3. VERBS.

72. Frequent in late Latin is a pleonastic use of *debeo,* Bon. 691–693: *commonens ut . . . custodire debeant,* 692. Cf. § 117. Compare the old Italian use of *dovere.*

There is also a common pleonastic use of *cœpi* with the infinitive, instead of the perfect: see § 124.

Videri, too, is often used pleonastically: Bayard 99–100.

4. ADVERBS.

73. The words referring to the "place in which" and the "place into which" were confused, *ubi* being used for *quo, ibi* for *eo : Lat. Spr.* 488. *Unde* was employed in the sense of 'where' (*Zs.* Beiheft 7, 157); also 'therefore' and 'where-fore': *Dic amice unde tristis es*, Regnier 110; cf. § 84.

74. *Plus* was often substituted for *magis*, and *magis* for *potius:* Bayard 110. *Plus* and *magis* were used more and more for comparison, and the old comparative and superlative forms became rarer: see § 56. Repetition was used for intensive effect: Seneca, *semper semper*, Wölfflin 5. *Bene, multum, satis* were employed as intensives more than in Classic Latin. *Totum* occurs often as an adverb: *Per.* 37, 14, and many other places; Dubois 332.

75. Double negation is frequent: R. 446-447 (*nec facio nihil*, etc.). *Non* for *ne* with the subjunctive is common: G. 435, Regnier 110. The absolute use of *non*, meaning 'no', occurs occasionally: *Dicit unus ex uno angulo: Ecce hic est. Alius ex alio angulo: Non, sed ecce hic est*, Regnier 111.

5. PREPOSITIONS.

76. The functions of prepositions were very much extended (Bayard 137-158): see Use of Inflections, Cases.

77. *Ab*, according to Mohl, *Lexique* 43, is not found in any of the Italic dialects except Latin. It apparently has no successors in the Romance languages, having been replaced by *de*, which also, from the third century on, usurped the place of *ex* (*Lat. Spr.* 487, R. 395-396, Hoppe 38): *de palatio exit*, Bechtel 105; *egredere de ecclesia*, Bechtel 105; *de utero matris nati sunt sic*, R. 395; *egressus de arca*, G. 339; *muri de lapide jaspide*, G. 342; *vivo de decimis*, G. 341; *de adversario . . . aliquid postulare*, Hoppe 38; *nec de cubiculo . . . procedit*, Hoppe 38.

78. *Ad* for *apud* occurs in Plautus, Terence, and others

(Oliver 5–6), and is common in late writers (R. 390–392, Urbat 10): *ad ipsum fontem facta est oratio*, Bechtel 103; *ad nos*, Bechtel 104; cf. *Per.* 42, 27. For the most part *apud* was replaced by *ad*, except in Gaul, where it was kept with the sense of *cum:* Haag 74, Urbat 27 (*tractans apud me metipsum;* also *ab una manu pallas altaris tenerem*, etc., where *ab* seems to be used for *apud*). *Apud* is used for *cum* by Sulpicius Severus, and more frequently by later authors: *Lat. Spr.* 489. According to F. G. Mohl, *La préposition* cum *et ses successeurs en gallo-roman* in *Bausteine* 61, *apud* is repeatedly found for *cum* in the Latin writers of Gaul, and *cum* for *apud* in Gregory of Tours; *cum* probably disappeared from actual use in Gaul by the fourth century; *apud*, being, as he says, a new word, had a great vogue in authors of the second and third centuries, a critical period for Gaul, and so came to supplant *cum* in that country.[1]

79. *Pro* often had the sense of 'for,' and replaced *ob* and *propter: fides pro una muliere perfida*, G. 343; *volo pro legentis facilitate abuti sermone vulgato*, G. 343; *attendimus locum illum pro memoria illius*, Bechtel 106. *Pro* itself was partially replaced by *per* (cf. §14), but was substituted for *per* in other regions (Urbat 34–35).

80. *Circa*, in the Empire, frequently meant 'concerning': *frustrati circa veritatem*, Hoppe 37. *Juxta* often signified 'according to': *juxta consuetudinem*, Bechtel 105; *juxta drachmæ exemplum*, Hoppe 37. *Super* sometimes replaced *de: fallere vos super hanc rem*, Bechtel 106; *super anima commendatus*, Hoppe 41.

---

[1] Mohl would derive the Old It. *appo*, not from *apud*, but from * *ad post* (p. 71); Fr. *avec*, not from *apud* + *hoc*, but from *ad hoc* (pp. 75–76). Pr. *ab* he takes from *apud*, but Pr. *am* from Italic *amb, am*.

81. *Retro, subtus, de foris, foris, foras* were freely used as prepositions (R. 398–400, G. 334): *vade retro me*, R. 399; *subtus terram*, R. 399.

6. CONJUNCTIONS.

82. *Quod, quia, quoniam* (and after *jubere, ut*: R. 427–428) are used very often by late writers instead of the accusative and infinitive construction: R. 402, Regnier 112–113. *Ut* with the infinitive is not infrequent: R. 445–446. *Quod* for *ut* is very common: Audollent 549. *Eo quod* came to be much used in the sense of 'that': *Per.* 48, 27, etc. Eventually *ut* was generally discarded.

Cur, quare sometimes replaced *quod* and *quia:* G. 431–432. *Quia*, which in late Latin was often reduced to *qui* or *qua* (see § 168) frequently took the place of *quod:* Regnier 111–112. *Quomodo* became a great favorite, often supplanting *quando, quod*, and *quoniam:* R. 403. *Quando* displaced *cum* in the temporal sense. *Qua*, 'when', encroaches on *quando* in the *Peregrinatio:* 46, 22, etc.; cf. Bechtel 119–120.

83. *Si* took the place of *an* and *utrum* (R. 403–405, Regnier 111), and was often used for *ne* and *num* (G. 430): *videte si potest dici*, Regnier 111. *Ac si* frequently did service for *quasi:* *Per.* 39, 13, and many other places; Bon. 323.

84. *Aut . . . aut* is sometimes equivalent to *et . . . et: Per.* 49, 24; cf. Bayard 161. *Ac sic* recurs continually in the *Peregrinatio*, meaning 'and so' or 'so': 40, 8, etc. *Tamen* in the same text (37, 2, etc.) seems to be used, in most cases, merely to indicate a subordinate clause. *Magis* is much employed for 'but' by late writers. *Unde* sometimes means 'therefore' and 'wherefore': G. 424 (*unde inquit Dominus*); cf. §§ 70, 73.

C. USE OF INFLECTIONS.

1. CASES.[1]

85. In popular speech prepositions were more used, from the beginning, than in the literary language; prepositional constructions, as time went on, increasingly took the place of pure case distinctions, and the use of cases became more and more restricted.   Hence arises in late writers a great irregularity in the employment of cases[2]: G. 302–326, Quillacq 96–103; for African Latin, *Archiv* VIII, 174–176; for confusion after verbs and adjectives, R. 412–415.

a. LOCATIVE.

86. The locative, rare in Classic Latin, remained eventually only in names of places.   There are, however, several examples in the *Peregrinatio :* Bechtel 110, *et sic fit missa Anastasi, ut fit missa ecclesiæ,* etc.   We find remnants of the locative genitive in *Agrigentī* > *Girgenti, Arimĭnī* > *Rimini, Clusiī* > *Chiusi, Florentiæ* > *Firenze, Palestinæ* (G. 322), etc.; of the locative ablative singular in *Tĭbŭrī* > *Tivoli;* of the locative ablative plural in *Andecāvīs* > *Angers, Aquīs* > *Acqui Aix, Astīs* > *Asti, Fīnĭbus* > *Fimes, Parīsiīs* > *Parigi Paris,* etc.   Cf. B. Bianchi in *Archivio glottologico italiano* IX, 378.   With other words, and very often with place names also, the locative was replaced by *in* with the ablative (Hoppe 32: *in Alexandria*) or by *ad* with the accusative (Urbat 10); the *domi* or *domo* of Cicero becomes *in domo* in Seneca.   When the locative of names of localities was kept, it generally came to be regarded as an in-

---

[1] Cf. Pirson 169–202.

[2] There is confusion even in Petronius, who occasionally uses the accusative for the dative and the ablative.

variable form; we find such locatives used as nominatives from the third century on: *Lat. Spr.* 481.

b. VOCATIVE.

87. The vocative is like the nominative in most words in Classic Latin, and such words as had a separate vocative form tended to discard it: vocatives in *–us*, instead of *–e*, occur in Plautus, Horace, and Livy; *meus* for *mi* is very common (Regnier 34). In Vulgar Latin the vocative form probably disappeared entirely, except perhaps in a few set phrases, such as *mī dŏmĭne*.

c. GENITIVE.

88. The genitive, little by little, was supplanted by other constructions, generally by the ablative with *de* (which occurs as early as Plautus), sometimes by the dative. Examples abound: *expers partis . . . de nostris bonis*, Terence *Heaut.* IV, 1, 39; *partem de istius impudentia*, Cicero, *Verr.* II, 1, 12; *clerici de ipsa ecclesia*, Bechtel 104; *de aceto plenum*, R. 396; *de Deo munus*, R. 396; *curator de sacra via*, R. 426; *de colentibus gentilibusque multitudo magna* (also *quidam ex eis*), Acts XVII, 4; *possessor de propria terra*, Urbat 20; *de sorore nepus*, Pirson 194; *terminus de nostra donatione*, 528 A. D., *Archiv* I, 53; cf. Bon. 610 ff. For the partitive genitive we find: *nil gustabit de meo*, Plautus, cited by Draeger I, 628; *aliquid de lumine*, Hoppe 38; *neminem de præsentibus*, Hoppe 38; *de pomis* = 'some apples,' *Per.* 40, 10; *de spiritu Moysi*, Bechtel 104; *de animalibus, de oleo*, etc., R. 396; *aliquid habet de verecundia discipuli*, R. 342; *numquid Zacchæus de bono habebat*, Regnier 54; *quid de scientia*, Sepulcri 217; *de studentibus*, Pirson 197. Cf. Oliver 14.

89. According to Meyer-Lübke, *Lat. Spr.* 487, the genitive probably ceased to be really popular, save in set combinations, by the beginning of the third century.   In late Latin a wrong form was often used: *a deo honorem* in an inscription in Gaul, *Zs. fr. Spr.* XXV, ii, 135; *matre meœ, alta nocte silentia*, etc., Bon. 341–342; *in fundo illa villa*, etc., D'Arbois 13; *in honore alme Maria*, etc., D'Arbois 91–93.

The genitive was retained, however, in some pronouns, in a good many set phrases, in certain words that belonged especially to clerical Latin, and probably in some proper names: *cūjus, illūjus, illōrum*, etc.; *lūnæ dīes, est ministĕriī, de noctis tempore* > It. *di notte tempore* (later *di notte tempo*), etc.; *angelōrum, paganōrum*, etc.; It. *Paoli, Pieri*, etc.

d. DATIVE.

90. The dative was more stable than the genitive: *Lat. Spr.* 487. We find, however, as early as Plautus, a tendency to replace it by the accusative with *ad: ad carnuficem dabo*, Plautus, *Capt.* 1019; *ad me magna nuntiavit*, Plautus, *Truc.* IV, 1, 4; *si pecunia ad id templum data erit*, inscription of 57 B. C., *C. I. L.* IX, 3513; *apparet ad agricolas*, Varro, *De Re Rustica* I, 40; *ad propinquos restituit*, Livy II, 13 — constructions freely used by Classic authors.   Inasmuch as the dative, in the singular of most nouns and in the plural of all, was identical in form either with the ablative or with the genitive (e. g., *causæ causis, muro muris, mari maribus*), the fear of ambiguity naturally fostered this practice and the substitution became very general in most of the Empire: *ait ad me, Per.* 64, 8; *dicens ad eum*, etc., Bechtel 102–103; *cum hæc ad vestram affectionem darem*, Bechtel 103; *fui ad episcopum* = ' I went to the bishop ', Bechtel 104; *loquitur ad Jeremiam*, G. 329; *ad quem promissio facta*, G. 329; *ad quem dixit*, Sepulcri 218; *Dominus ad Moysen dicit*, Urbat 12; *ad me restituit omne regnum*, Urbat 12; *ad Dei officio paratus*, Pirson 194.   Cf. *Lat. Spr.* 488, Oliver

3–4. Sometimes *super*, not *ad*, was used: *imposuerat manus super eum*, Bechtel 105; *super me misericordiam præstare*, Bechtel 105.

91. The dative remained in Dacia, and lingered rather late in Gaul (*Lat. Spr.* 481); elsewhere it probably disappeared from really popular speech by the end of the Empire, except in pronouns (*cūi, illūi ĭllī*, etc., *mī, tĭbi*, etc.).

Rumanian has kept the dative, in its original function and also as a genitive, in the first declension (as *case*), and so in feminine adjectives (as *romîne*).

e. ABLATIVE.

92. The analytical tendency of speech, reinforced by the analogy of prepositional substitutes for the genitive and dative, favored the use of prepositions with the ablative, to distinguish its various functions.   For *de* = 'than,' see *Zs.* XXX, 641.

Ab is common: *ab omni specie idololatriæ intactum*, Hoppe, 36; *ab sceleribus parce*, G. 335; *a carne superatur*, G. 337; *ab scriptura sancta commemoratos*, Regnier 51; *a præmio minorem esse*, St. Cyprian, cited by Wölfflin 52; *ab Ariulfi astutia deceptus*, Sepulcri 218.

De is the most frequent: *erubescens de infamia sua*, Hoppe 14; *de singularitate famosum*, Hoppe 33; *nobilior de obsoletiore matrice*, Hoppe 33; *digni de cœlo Castores*, Hoppe 34; *gaudet de contumelia sua*, Hoppe 34; *de victus necessitate causatur*, Hoppe 35; *de vestra rideat æmulatione*, Hoppe 36; *de manibus suis*, Bechtel 104; *de oculis*, Bechtel 104 (cf. *de se*, Bechtel 105); *occidam de lancea*, R. 393; *patrem de regno privavit*, R. 426; *de virgine natus est*, Regnier 54; *de te beati sunt*, Regnier 56.   Cf. R. 392–395, G. 339–342, Regnier 54–56.

Ex occurs also: *ex causa humanæ salutis*, Hoppe 33; *ex infirmitate fatigata*, Sepulcri 218.

In is often found: *in illo die*, Hoppe 31 ; *quo in tempore*, Hoppe 31 ; *in maxilla asinæ delevi mille viros*, R. 397 ; *in camo et freno maxillas eorum constringe*, *Ps.* XXXI, 9 ; *in amore Dei ferventes*, G. 347 ; *in bonis operibus abundetis*, Regnier 60. Cf. R. 396–397, G. 344–347, Regnier 58 ff.

93. Sometimes *ad* or *per* with the accusative is substituted for the ablative : *per hoc*, Hoppe 33 ; *ad diem*, Bechtel 103 ; *ad horam sextam aguntur*, etc., Bechtel 103–104 ; *per nomen vocavit*, Sepulcri 218 ; *pugnare ad ursos, ad unum gladii ictum caput desecare*, *Lat. Spr.* 488.

94. The use of prepositions became really neccessary in the late spoken language, because, after the fall of final *m* and the loss of quantitative distinctions in unaccented syllables, the ablative differed little or not at all from the accusative in the singular of most words : *causăm causā, donŭm donō, patrĕm patrĕ, fructŭm fructū, diĕm diē*. It is likely that before the end of the Empire the ablative plural form was generally discarded, the accusative being used in its stead, and that the ablative and accusative singular were pronounced alike, in all words, in most of the Latin territory. The fusion of the two cases was doubtless helped by the fact that certain prepositions might be combined with either accusative or ablative.

95. There is evidence of the confusion of accusative and ablative as early as the first century, but it was probably not very common before the third. *Cum* with the accusative is very frequent: *cum suos discentes, cum sodales*, in inscriptions, *Lat. Spr.* 488; *cum epistolam*, Bechtel 95 ; *cum res nostras*, D'Arbois 27. Cf. E. K. Rand in *Modern Philology* II, 263, footnote 5.

The accusative form is substituted for the ablative after

other prepositions: *a monazontes*, Bechtel 94;—*de eo torrentem*,
Bechtel 96 ; *de actus*, Bechtel 96 ; *de hoc ipsud*, Bechtel 96 ; *de
martyrium*, Bechtel 96; *de carnem*, etc., R. 406–412; *de ipsas
villas*, D'Arbois 27 ; *de rigna nostra*, D'Arbois 70–71 ;— *ex fines
tuos*, etc., R. 406–412;— *videbo te in publicum*, Waters Ch. 58;
in finem Deus fecit cælum et terram, etc., Hoppe 40–41 ; 12 examples of *in* + acc. for abl. in *Per.*, Bechtel 97–98; *erat in
medium maris*, R. 410;—*pro hoc ipsud*, Bechtel 101; *pro nos*,
D'Arbois 152;— *sine fructum*, etc., R. 406–412.

96. Conversely, the ablative form is very often written for
the accusative: *ad ecclesia majore*, Bechtel 94 ;— *ante sole*,
ante cruce, Bechtel 95 ; *ante sole*, etc., R. 406–412 ;— *circa
puteo*, Bechtel 95 ; — *contra ipso loco*, Bechtel 95 ;— *foras
ecclesia*, Bechtel 96 ;— *in carne conversa*, etc., Hoppe 40–41 ;
in the *Per.*, *in* + abl. for acc. is three times as common as the
correct use of *in* + acc., Bechtel 94–101 ; *venit in civitate sua*,
etc., R. 406–412 ;—*intra civitate sua*, Bechtel 99 ; *intro spelunca*, Bechtel 99 ;—*juxta aqua ipsa*, Bechtel 99 ;—*per valle
illa*, and 21 other cases of *per* + abl., Bechtel 100 ;— *post
lectione*, Bechtel 100 ; *post morte*, etc., R. 406–412 ;— *prope
luce*, Bechtel 101 ; — *propter populo*, Bechtel 101 ; — *super
civitate hac*, Bechtel 101.

97. The ablative was kept only in some fixed expressions,
such as *hōrā, ist' annō, quōmŏdo, parī mente*, etc.; perhaps in
such phrases as It. *vendere cento soldi*, etc.; probably in some
proper names with *de*, as *Della Casa*. It is likely, too, that
the ablative absolute survived in a few common expressions,
like It. *ciò fatto;* generally, however, in popular speech, the
nominative absolute took its place: Bechtel 109–110, *et bene-
dicens nos episcopus profecti sumus, visa loca sancta omnia* (*Per.*
45, 8), etc.

f. ACCUSATIVE.

98. After verbs of motion *ad* was often used, sometimes *in*, instead of the simple accusative: *eamus in forum*, Waters Ch. 58; *fui ad ecclesiam*, Bechtel 103; *ad Babyloniam duxit*, G. 327; *consules ad Africam profecti sunt*, G. 328; *ad istam regionem venit*, Regnier 52.   Cf. Regnier 51–52.

99. Duration of time was expressed by *per* with the accusative, also by the ablative: Bechtel 108–9, *per totos octo dies is ornatus est, tota autem nocte vicibus dicuntur psalmi*, etc.

g. FALL OF DECLENSION.

100. By the end of the Vulgar Latin period there probably remained in really popular use (aside from pronouns and a number of set formulas) in Dacia only three cases, in the rest of the Empire only two — a nominative and an accusative-ablative.   Clerics, however, naturally tried to write in accordance with their idea of correct Latin.

2. VERB-FORMS.

101. Many parts of the verb went out of popular use, and were replaced by other locutions; these obsolete parts were employed by writers with more or less inaccuracy.   In the parts that remained many new tendencies manifested themselves.

a. IMPERSONAL PARTS.

102. Only the present active infinitive and the present and perfect participles were left intact.

(1) Supine.

103. The supine disappeared from general use, being replaced, from the first century on, by the infinitive: as *cum*

veneris ad bibere, St. Augustine, *Sermones* 225, Cap. 4. Cf.
Lat. Spr. 490, Dubois 275. In Rumanian, however, the supine
was preserved: Tiktin 596.

(2) Gerund.

104. With the exception of the ablative form, the gerund
came to be replaced by the infinitive, sometimes with a preposition: *dat manducare, Lat. Spr.* 490; *quomodo potest hic
nobis carnem dare ad manducare,* R. 430; *potestatem curare,
necessitas tacere,* etc., G. 363.

The ablative form of the gerund became more and more a
substitute for the present participle: *ita miserrimus fui fugi-
tando,* Terence, *Eun.* V, 2, 8; Draeger II, 847–849, cites Livy,
conciendo ad se multitudinem, and Tacitus, *assurgens et popu-
lando; hanc Marcion captavit sic legendo,* Hoppe 57; *multa vidi
errando,* Densusianu 179; *qui pertransivit benefaciendo et
sanando,* R. 432. Cf. R. 432–433. The ablative gerund was
sometimes used for a conditional clause: *cavendo salvi erimus,*
Hoppe 57.

(3) Gerundive.

105. The gerundive was used as a future passive participle,
with *esse,* from the third century on, in place of the future:
filius hominis tradendus est, R. 433. Cf. R. 433–434, G. 386–
388. Eventually, however, the gerundive was discarded, except in some standing phrases.

(4) Future Active Participle.

106. The future active participle was probably rare in late
Vulgar Latin, except when it was used with *esse* as a substitute
for the future (as *facturus sum*). Sometimes, in a literary
style, it took the place of a relative clause: *faveant mihi pro
ejus nomine pugnaturo,* G. 389. Cf. G. 388–389.

(5) PRESENT PARTICIPLE.

107. The present participle was kept, and was used as an adjective and as a noun: see Derivation, Suffixes for Adjectives, *–ans*. Sometimes it was employed periphrastically with *esse: si ipse est ascendens in cælos*, G. 389. Writers occasionally substituted it for a relative clause: *nemo mentiens plorat*, G. 388. Often, however, it was replaced by the ablative gerund: see Gerund above.

(6) PERFECT PARTICIPLE.

108. The perfect participle was kept, and, as will presently be seen, its use was greatly extended through new methods of forming the passive and the perfect tenses. Verbs that had no perfect participle were obliged to make one.

(7) INFINITIVE.

109. The perfect and passive infinitive forms eventually disappeared: see Voice and Tense below. In late writers, however, the perfect instead of the present infinitive is very common: R. 431–432 (*malunt credidisse*, etc.).

110. The infinitive + accusative construction was more and more avoided from the third century on: G. 371–375. It was replaced sometimes by the passive, but often by a clause introduced by *quia, quod, quoniam, ut*, etc.: *Eva vidisse describitur*, G. 371; *legitur dixisse Deus*, Regnier 63;—Bechtel 112–115, *dicent eo quod filii Israhel eas posuerint, sciens quod libenter haberetis hæc cognoscere, credidit ei quia esset vere filius Dei*, etc.; *perspicue exposuit quod ager mundus sit*, G. 377; *nesciebat quia Jesus erat*, G. 383; *de corpore loquor, ut spiritu valeat non ignoramus*, G. 385. Cf. G. 375–385, Bon. 659–671.

Late writers, wishing to avoid vulgarisms, often misused the infinitive + accusative: G. 371–373.

111. On the other hand, the infinitive assumed many new functions: see Supine and Gerund above. Cf. Hoppe 42–52: *Ninus regnare primus, amant ignorare, aliter exprimere non est, bonus et dicere et facere*, etc.

It was often used as a noun: *totum vivere animæ carnis est*, Hoppe 42; *ipsum vivere accedere est*, Regnier 106; *per malum velle perdidit bonum posse*, Regnier 106.

It replaced the subjunctive with *ut* and similar constructions: *vadent orare*, Bechtel 117; *revertitur omnis populus resumere se*, Bechtel 117: *valeamus assumi*, G. 363; *quæ legi digna sunt*, G. 366; *timuisti...facere*, G. 368; *non venit justos vocare*, G. 370; *venit aliquis audire*, Regnier 73; *male fecisti dare Spiritum sanctum*, Regnier 74; *mihi præcepit hæc loqui*, Bon. 673. Cf. G. 363–370, Regnier 73, Bon. 647, 671–675; P. Thielmann, *Facere mit dem Infinitiv* in *Archiv* III, 177.

It took the place of a relative or indirectly interrogative clause after certain verbs: *nesciendo quæ petere*, Venantius Fortunatus, cited in *Lat. Spr.* 490; *non habent unde reddere tibi*, R. 430.

b. VOICE.

112. Under the influence of *carus est*, etc., *amatus est* came to mean 'he *is* loved', etc. Hence *amatus fuit* signified 'he *was* loved': see Draeger I, 276 ff. Then a whole passive inflection was made up of the perfect participle + *esse* (in northern Italy *fieri*). The old passive forms—except the perfect participle and, to some extent, the gerundive—gradually disappeared from ordinary speech. Although authors kept up the classic practice as far as they were able, some examples of the popular formation may be culled from late writings: *denuo factus filius fui*, Hoppe 60; *mors salva erit cum fuerit devorata*, Hoppe 60; *conjectus in carcerem fuerat*, Hoppe 61; *permissa est accedere*, Regnier 63.

113. As the passive inflection disappeared, deponent verbs became active.   Even in Classic Latin there is often hesitation, as in the case of *frustrare frustrari, irascere irasci*, etc. Many deponent verbs are used as active verbs by Petronius. In late vulgar speech *mori, sequi*, etc., followed the same course.   Cf. Bonnet 402–413.

114. In the intermediate period the passive was frequently replaced by reflexive and active constructions.   When *littera scribitur* seemed archaic, and *littera scripta est* vulgar, people said *littera se scribit* and *litteram scribunt* or *litteram scribit homo:* cf. *facit se hora quinta*, Bechtel 126; *se sanare = sanari* in the 4th century, *Rom.* XXXII, 455 (cf. *Zs.* XXXIII, 135); for the use of *homo* with the force of French *on*, see *Per.* 55, ²⁵.

c. MOOD.
(1) IMPERATIVE.

115. The imperative came to be restricted to the second person singular and plural of the present, the subjunctive being used for the third person, and also for the first.   Dubois 275 notes that the forms in –*o* are very rare in Ennodius, who lived in southern Gaul in the fifth century.

116. In negative commands the imperative was often replaced by the subjunctive, by the indicative (found in Pirminius), and in Italy, Gaul, and Dacia by the infinitive: *Lat. Spr.* 490.

(2) SUBJUNCTIVE.

117. The subjunctive was limited to fewer functions, being replaced by the indicative in many constructions: *cum hi omnes tam excelsi sunt*, Bechtel 115; *si scire vultis quid facitis*, Regnier 69; etc.   At the end of the Vulgar Latin period it was probably used, in popular speech, very much as it is used

in the Romance languages.   Late writers, while trying to
follow the traditional practice, were less logical and evidently
less spontaneous than Classic authors in their employment of
the subjunctive.

Sometimes the subjunctive was replaced by *debeo* with the
infinitive: *debeant accipi = accipiantur*, G. 418.   Cf. § 72.

Sometimes, after *facio*, its place was taken by the infinitive:
Regnier 27–28, *ecce Pater fecit Filium nasci de vergine*, etc.
Cf. § 111.

In conditions not contrary to fact, in indirect discourse and
indirect questions, in dependent clauses that are not adversa-
tive nor dubitative, the indicative was often substituted for
the subjunctive: R. 428–430, G. 355–357, Regnier 68–71.

On the other hand, late writers often put the subjunctive
where Classic authors would have put the indicative: G.
357–362.

118. The imperfect subjunctive gradually gave way to the
pluperfect: this use is common in the *Bellum Africanum* (*Lat.
Spr.* 489); cf. Sittl 133–134.   It apparently began with *debu-
isset, potuisset, voluisset*, used freely for the imperfect by
Gregory the Great (Sepulcri 226) and others, and with perfect infinitives like *tacuisse* for *tacere* (*Lat. Spr.* 489: examples
from the 4th century).

The imperfect subjunctive ultimately went out of use, except in Sardinia.   Writers of the third and fourth centuries
show uncertainty in the use of it; R. 431 cites many examples, as *timui ne inter nos bella fuissent orta*.

In Rumanian the pluperfect subjunctive has assumed the
function of a pluperfect indicative: *cântáse*, etc.

119. The perfect subjunctive was apparently confused with
the future perfect indicative.   It was thus preserved in Spain

and in Italian and Rumanian dialects: cf. C. De Lollis in
Bausteine 1, and V. Crescini in *Zs.* XXIX, 619; Tiktin 596.
Cf. § 124.

d. TENSE.

120. The present and imperfect indicative and the present
subjunctive remained, in general, with their old functions;
see, however, § 117.   For the imperfect and pluperfect subjunctive, see § 118; for the perfect subjunctive, § 119.   In the
perfect, pluperfect, future, and future perfect indicative great
changes took place, which led also to the formation of a new
perfect and pluperfect subjunctive.

(1) THE PERFECT TENSES.

121. In Classic Latin *habeo* with the perfect participle was
used to express a lasting condition: *Hannibal quia fessum
militem prœliis operibusque habebat, Part. perf.* 376.   It was
used in the same way with adjectives: *miserum habere*, etc.,
Part. perf. 372 ff.   Even in Classic Latin, however, the meaning of this locution began to shift to the perfect, or something
akin to it: Cato the elder, *quid Athenis exquisitum habeam,
Part. perf.* 516; Plautus, *illa omnia missa habeo, omnis res re-
lictas habeo, Part. perf.* 535; in legal phraseology, *factum habeo,
Part. perf.* 537–538; Sallust, *compertum ego habeo*, Draeger I,
295.   The construction is very common in Cicero in a sense
that closely approaches the perfect: *satis habeo deliberatum,
Part. perf.* 415; *scriptum habeo, Part. perf.* 422; *rationes cogni-
tas habeo*, Densusianu 181; *pecunias magnas collocatas habent*,
Draeger I, 294; cf. *Part. perf.* 405, 414–415, 423, 518–521,
Draeger I, 294–295.

122. In late Latin this compound often had simply a perfect meaning: *metuo enim ne ibi vos habeam fatigatos*, Regnier
28; *episcopum invitatum habes*, Bon. 690.   Cf. Bon. 689–691.

In popular speech it supplanted more and more the original perfect form, which was increasingly confined to its aorist function: *Lat. Spr.* 489. In the Spanish peninsula, however, and to some extent in Italy, the old perfect meaning was not entirely lost.

123. On the model of this new perfect, a compound pluperfect was constructed: Cicero, *quas in ærario conditas habebant*, Draeger I, 294; *si Dominum iratum haberes*, Regnier 28; *quam semper cognitam habui*, Sepulcri 227. In the same way a future perfect was made: *de Cæsare satis dictum habebo*, *Part. perf.* 537. Eventually an entire perfect inflection was built up with *habere* or, in the case of neuter verbs, with *esse;* its vogue began in Gaul in the fifth century, elsewhere in the sixth: *Part. perf.* 543, 541.

124. The old perfect form remained in popular use, generally with the aorist sense. Some late writers were fond of substituting for it *cœpi* with an infinitive: Waters Ch. 70, etc. Cf. § 72.

The old pluperfect indicative became rarer, but still lingered, sometimes with its original sense, sometimes as a preterit, sometimes as a conditional. The preterit use occurs in *dixerat, ortaret, transalaret* in the *Gl. Reich.;* *auret, furet, pouret*, etc., in the Old French *Sainte Eulalie; boltier'* in the Old Italian *Ritmo Cassinese* (*Zs.* XXIX, 620); etc. The conditional function, which came down from the Classic Latin use in conditional sentences, was preserved in Spanish, in Provençal, in some southern Italian dialects (notably in the *Rosa fresca aulentissima*), and in the Italian *fora < fueram*.

The old future perfect was apparently confused with the perfect subjunctive, and continued to be used, with the force of a future indicative or subjunctive, in the Spanish peninsula.

in some dialects of Italy, and in Dacia: Sp. *cantáre*, Old Sp. *cantáro*.   Cf. § 119.

The old pluperfect subjunctive was used as an imperfect: see § 118.

(2) Future and Conditional.

125. The Latin future was not uniform in the four conjugations; the formation in *–bo*, which was used in three of them and prevailed in two, was native, according to Mohl, *Pr. Pers. Pl.* 141–142, only in Rome and the immediate vicinity.   Furthermore, the future in the first two conjugations was suggestive of the imperfect, and in the other two, in late pronunciation, was liable to confusion with the present subjunctive and indicative.   These causes or others made the future unpopular.   As the tense became rare in speech, mistakes were made in writing: *Vok.* I, 98; Regnier viii.   The old *audibo*, *dormibo* forms were kept late (*Futurum* 161), and we find such errors as *respondeam* for *respondebo* (*Futurum* 158).

126. Classic Latin had some circumlocutions, such as *facturus sum, delenda est, habeo dicere*, which approached the meaning of the future.   During the Empire there was a strong tendency to substitute these or other constructions for the future forms (such periphrases are particularly frequent in African church Latin):—

(1) The present indicative for the future is common in Cicero in conditional sentences: Lebreton 188–190.   The substitution became frequent in all sorts of constructions: *nam si vis ecce modo pedibus duco vos ibi*, Bechtel 112; *cum volueris ire imus tecum et ostendimus tibi*, Bechtel 112; *pervidet*, Bechtel 90–91; *quando corrigis, quando mutaris? cras, inquis*, Regnier 64; *jam crastina non eximus*, Sepulcri 225.   Cf. Draeger I, 286 ff.; Sepulcri 225–226.

(2) The future participle + *esse* was a favorite with late
writers: *sıc et nos futuri sumus resurgere,* Regnier 29. Cf.
Bayard 256. See §§ 105, 106.

(3) *Velle* and *posse* + infinitive were frequent: G. 423.
Velle in this sense was preserved in Dacia; the oldest Rumanian future is *voĭŭ jurá* or *jurá voĭŭ:* Tiktin 599.

(4) *Debere* + infinitive was another substitute. It was
kept in Sardinian.

(5) *Vadere, ire, venire* + infinitive were used also.

127. The form that prevailed, however, was *habeo* with the
infinitive: In Classic Latin *habeo dicere = habeo quod dicam,*
being so used by Cicero and many others; later, as in Suetonius, it means *debeo dicere: Futurum* 48 ff. Cf. Varro, *De Re
Rustica* I, 1, *ut id mihi habeam curàre;* Cicero, *Ad Famil.* I,
5, *tantum habeo tibi polliceri;* Lucretius VI, 711, *in multis hoc
rebus dicere habemus;* Ovid, *Trist.* I, 1, 123, *mandare ... habebam.* In these senses it was very common in late writers:
habes spectare, Hoppe 43; *filius Dei mori habuit,* Hoppe 44;
probare non habent, Hoppe 44; *non habent retribuere,* R. 447;
multa habeo dicere, R. 447; *unde mihi dare habes aquam vivam,*
R. 448; *exire habebat,* R. 449; *nec verba nobis ista dici habent,*
Regnier 28. Cf. R. 447–449.

128. This *habeo* construction finally took the sense of a
simple future: Tertullian, *aliter prædicantur quam evenire habent, cui dare habet Deus corpus,* etc., Hoppe 44–45; — Servius,
velle habet, Futurum 180; — St. Jerome, *qui nasci habent,* G.
370; — St. Augustine, *tollere habet,* Densusianu 181; *et sic nihil
habes invenire in manibus tuis, videre habetis, venire habet,* etc.,
Regnier 28. It had become common in Italy by the sixth
century.

129. In the early stages of the Romance languages, or

possibly in the latest stage of Vulgar Latin, the infinitive came to stand regularly, though not immutably, just before the *habeo*. Finally the two words were fused into one, but this union was not completed until after the beginnings of the Romance literatures, and in Portuguese it is not completed yet: Old Sp. *cantaré* or *he cantar;* separation is common in Old Provençal, and occurs in Old Italian; Pg. *fazel-o-he*. The earliest examples of the Romance future are found in Frede-garius: *Justinianus dicebat 'daras'*, Haag 54; *addarabo*, Haag 55. See Morphology.

130. On the model of this new form, an imperfect of the future, or *conditional*, was constructed. The phrase existed, ready for use, in Classic Latin, where it was employed with an implication of obligation or necessity. So it seems to be used by Tertullian, although sometimes with him the meaning borders on a real conditional: *non traditus autem traduci habebas, ista civitas esterminari haberet, quod esset venturus et pati haberet*, etc., Hoppe 43–45.

In Classic Latin, in place of *amassem* in the conclusion of a conditional sentence, *amaturus eram* or *fui* was often used; and when *amaturus sum* was replaced by *amare habeo*, it was natural that *amaturus eram* should give way to *amare habebam*. Furthermore, to match such a sentence as *dicit quod venire habet*, there was needed a past construction like *dixit quod venire habebat* or *habuit;* and corresponding to *si possum venire habeo*, something like *si potuissem venire habebam* or *habui* was called for.

St. Cyprian and St. Hilary seem to show a simple conditional use of the compound: *quod lex nova dari haberet*, Bayard 256; *manifestari habebat*, Bayard 257;—*Herodes principes sacerdotum ubi nasci habebat Christus interrogat*, Quillacq 116. There are sure examples from the fifth century on: *Lat. Spr.* 489.

The development of this form in the Romance languages was, in general, parallel to that of the future: see Morphology.

The origin of the Rumanian conditional, *cîntareaşĭ*, is not obvious; for a full discussion of the question, see H. Tiktin, *Die Bildung des rumänischen Konditionalis* in *Zs.* XXVIII, 691.

III. PHONOLOGY.

A. SYLLABICATION.

131. The principles of syllabic division are rather difficult to establish. The Latin grammarians seem to have given no heed to actual speech, but to have followed the usage of Greek spelling, supporting it with purely theoretical considerations. Cf. S. 132–151. According to these writers, the syllable always ended in a vowel, or in a liquid or nasal followed by another consonant in the next syllable, or in half of a double consonant: *a-ni-ma, no-ctem, pro-pter, a-mnis; al-ter, in-fans; sic-cus, mit-to.* The division of *s* + consonant they regard as uncertain (*a-s-trum*); doubtless in reality the *s* was nearly syllabic, as in Italian. They add that etymological considerations often disturb the operation of the rule, as in *ob-liviscor*, etc.

132. In point of fact, however, all consonant groups, except a mute + a liquid, made position and attracted the accent: *perféc-tus*, and not *pérfe-ctus*. It is altogether likely, then, that a consonant group, in the spoken language, was usually divided after the first consonant: *noc-tem, prop-ter*. A single consonant between vowels certainly went with the second: *po-si-tus*.

The group mute + liquid makes position in the older dramatists: Nævius accents *intégram*, *Lat. Spr.* 466. In the Classic poets it may or may not make position. Quintilian I, 5 recommends *ténebræ, vólucres, pháretra*, etc. In Vulgar Latin this combination almost invariably attracts the accent: *cathédra*. It is likely that in Old Latin the division came before the

liquid, but subsequently, after the accent had become fixed on
the preceding vowel, both consonants were carried over : *có-
lub-ra, co-lúb-ra, co-lú-bra.*

133. We have reason to believe that in closely connected
speech a final consonant was carried over to the next word, if
that word began with a vowel : *cor exsultat = co r-exsultat.*

B. ACCENT.

134. The Latin accent was probably from the beginning a
stress accent. In the earliest stage of the language it apparently fell regularly on the first syllable : Corssen II, 892–906 ;
S. 30–34; *Franz. ∂* I, 13. The Classic Latin system — according to which the accent falls on the penult if that syllable is
long, otherwise on the antepenult — developed as early as
literature began, and remained, both in the literary and in the
spoken language, through the Classic period ; even after the
distinctions of quantity were lost, the place of the accent was
unchanged : *bonitåtem, cómpŭto, delĕcto.*

The penult vowel before mute + liquid (cf. § 132) normally
has the stress in Vulgar Latin : *cathédra, colúbra, intégram.*
There seem to be a few exceptions to the rule : Old Fr.
palpres < pálpebras, Old Fr. *poltre < *púllitra,* and perhaps
some others.

1. PRIMARY STRESS.

135. We have seen that Vulgar Latin regularly accents
according to the Classic quantitative accentuation. There are,
however, some cases in which the Classic principle fails to
operate or the Classic stress has been shifted : —

a. VOWELS IN HIATUS.

136. Accented *e* and *i,* when immediately followed by the
vowel of the penult, became *y,* the accent falling on the

following vowel: *multĕris* > *muljéris*, S. 51, *Lat. Spr.* 468; *putéŏlis* > *putjólis*, *C. I. L.* X, 1889 (PVTEÓLIS); so *pariĕtes* > *parjétes* > *parētes*,[1] *C. I. L.* VI, 3714 (PARETES). This change seems to be due to a tendency to shift the stress to the more sonorous of two contiguous vowels: cf. O. Jespersen, *Lehrbuch der Phonetik*, p. 192. It was favored also by the analogy of *múlier, púteus, páries*, etc., in which the vowel in hiatus is atonic.

137. Accented *u*, when immediately followed by the vowel of the penult, became *w*, the accent falling on the *preceding* syllable: *bat(t)úĕre* > *báttuere* > *báttere; consúĕre* > *cónsuere* > *cónsere; habúĕrunt* > *hábuerunt; tenúĕram* > *ténueram.* Here the shift was apparently due in each case to analogy, *battuere* being influenced by *báttuo, consuere* by *cónsuo, habuerunt* by *hábuit, tenueram* by *ténui,* etc.

138. Aside from these cases, hiatus seems to have had no effect on the accent in Latin. It is possible, however, that *dúos, súos, túos* were sometimes pronounced *duós, suós, tuós.*

b. COMPOUND VERBS.

139. Verbs compounded with prefixes were generally re-constructed with the accent and the vowel of the simple verb, provided the composite nature of the formation was understood and the parts were recognized (cf. § 31): *défĭcit* > *disfácit, dísplĭcet* > *displácet, ímplĭcat* > *implícat, réddĭdi* > *reddédi, réquĭrit* > *requérit, rétĭnet* > *reténet,* etc. Cf. *Gram.* II, 668–670. So *calefacis,* S. 56; *condedit, perdedit, reddedit, tra-dedit,* S. 54; *addedi, adsteti, conteneo, crededi, inclausus, presteti,* etc., Sepulcri 213–215. On the same plan new verbs were formed: *de-mínat, re-négat,* etc.

---

[1] *Ĭe* regularly became *ē;* but if the preceding consonant was *l,* it was palatalized, hence *parétes,* but *mul'éres.* Cf. § 225.

Récĭpit became * *recípit*, the composite character of the word being felt, although the compound was no longer associated with *capere*.

In *cólligo* and some others not even the composite nature was perceived, the simple verbs having become rare or having taken a different sense: *legere*, for instance, came to be used only in the sense of 'read.'

c. ILLAC, ILLIC.

140. The adverbs *illāc*, *illīc* accented their last syllable through the analogy of *hāc, hīc*. Priscian says "*illîc* pro *illice*": S. 42.

d. FICATUM.

141. There existed in Greek a word συκωτόν (Pirson 40), 'figlike', which was applied by cooks to a liver. It is found in late Latin in the form *sycotum*, which should properly have been pronounced *sȳcōtum;* for some unknown reason, perhaps under the influence of a vulgar * *hēpăte* for *hēpar*, 'liver', it probably became * *sẹcotum.*

Through this word there came into use the culinary terms *fīcătum*, * *fĭcatum*, * *fẹcatum*, * *fẹcotum*, * *fẹcitum*, all meaning 'liver.' *Fīcătum*, a simple translation of συκωτόν, prevailed in Dacia, Rætia, and northern Italy. *Fẹcatum* or *fẹcotum*, a fusion of *fīcătum* and * *sẹcotum*, was preferred in central and southern Italy. *Fĭcatum*, a cross between *fẹcatum* and *fīcătum*, was kept in Sicily and in the Spanish peninsula. Sardinia preserved both *fīcătum* and *fĭcatum*. Gaul had *fĭcatum* and *fẹcatum;* later, by a change of suffix, *fẹcitum*. See G. Paris in *Miscellanea linguistica in onore di Graziadio Ascoli* 41; H. Schuchardt in *Zs.* XXV, 515 and XXVIII, 435; L. Clédat in *Revue de philologie française et de littérature* XV, 235.

e. NUMERALS.

142. The numbers *vīgĭntī, trīgĭnta, quadrāgĭnta, quīnquāgĭnta*, etc., were sometimes accented on the antepenult: Consentius mentions a faulty pronunciation *trígĭnta*, Keil V, 392, lines 4–5; *quarranta* occurs in a late inscription, *Vok.* II, 461, Pirson 97. See M. Ihm in *Archiv* VII, 69–70; G. Rydberg in *Mélanges Wahlund*, 337. The shift was probably due to a natural tendency to differentiate the numerals from one another: compare the floating accent in English *thirteen*, *fourteen*, etc.

d. GREEK WORDS.

143. The accentuation of Greek words was varied. Sometimes the Greek stress was preserved, sometimes the word was made to conform to the Latin principle.

(1) Greek Oxytones.

144. Greek oxytones, when borrowed by Latin, were stressed according to the Latin system: δραχμή > *drách(ŭ)ma*, ἐπιστολή > *epístŭla ˙–ŏla*, λαμπάς > *lámpa(s)*, μηχᾰνή > *mác(h)-ĭna*, παραβολή > *parábŭla*, πειρατής > *pirăta*, σπασμός > *spásmus*, ταπεινός > **tapĭnus*. Cf. S. 42 ff., Claussen 809.

Συκωτόν, however, apparently stressed the first syllable: see § 141.

(2) Greek Paroxytones.

145. Greek paroxytones were mostly accented according to the quantity of the penult: γραφίον > *gráphĭum*, καμάρα > *cámĕra*, μαγιδα > *mágĭda*, παλάμη > *pálma*, πολύπους > *pólўpus*,[1] πορφύρα > *púrpŭra*, φαρέτρα > *phárĕtra* or *pharétra* (cf. § 134).

Πτισάνη (> *ptísăna*) > It. *tisána*, φιάλη (> *phĭăla*) > It. *fiála*, χολέρα (> *chólĕra*) > It. *coléra*, etc., may represent popular terms borrowed by ear from the Greek, with the Greek stress,

---

[1] Occasionally the accent was kept by doubling the consonant, as *polippus*.

but it is more likely that the Italian forms are book-words
with a shifted accent.

Cf. S. 42 ff., Claussen 810–811.

146. The ending –ía was at first generally assimilated to
the Latin –ĭa: βιβλία > bíblia, βλασφημία > blasphémia, ἐκκλησία
> ec(c)lésia, ἱστορία > história, σηπία > sépia, συμφωνία > sym-
phónia. Later a fashionable pronunciation –ía, doubtless
favored by Christian influence, penetrated popular speech
(σοφία > sophía, etc.) and produced a new Latin ending –ía,
which was used to form new words: see Derivation, Suffixes
for Nouns. Cf. Claussen 812. The pronunciations melodĭa,
etc., and sophīa, etc., are attested: S. 55–56.

The endings –εῖα, –εῖον sometimes became –ĕa –ĭa, –ĕum
–ĭum, sometimes –ēa, –ēum: βαλανεῖον > bálnĕum, κωνωπεῖον >
conopēum –ĕum –ĭum, πλατεῖα > platēa platĕa. Cf. Claussen
813–814.

(3) GREEK PROPAROXYTONES.

147. The treatment of proparoxytones is complicated. Cf.
S. 42–49, Claussen 814–821, *Gram.* I, 35, § 17, A. Thomas in
Rom. XXXI, 2–3. Late Latin grammarians mention a pronunciation of Greek words with the Greek accent (S. 42), but
their statements are too vague to be of use.

A few early borrowed words perhaps show the Old Latin
accentuation: κυπάρισσος > *cúparissos > cupressus. Cf. Claussen 809.

148. When the penult was short, the accent remained unchanged: γένεσις > génĕsis, κάλαμος > cálămus, κόλαφος > cólă-
phus, πρεσβύτερον > presbýtĕrum (with a new nominative
présbyter).

149. When the penult vowel was in position, it took the
accent: ἄβυσσος > abýssus, βάπτισμα > baptísma, τάλαντον >
taléntum.

Ἔγκαυστον, however, became both *encáustum* and *éncaustum*.
Occasionally the consonant group was simplified and the
accent remained: καρνόφυλλον > *garófŭlum.*

150. When the penult vowel was long and not in position,
it apparently took the accent in book-words but not in words
learned by ear (S. 48–49): κάμηλος > *camēlus –ĕllus,* κάμινος >
camínus, κροκόδειλος > *crocodílus,* φάλλαινα > *ballǽna;* ἄγκῡρα >
áncŏra, βλάσφημος > *blásphĕmus* (Prudentius), βουτῡρον >
bútўrum (Æmilius Macer), Ἰάκωβος > *Jácobus,* σέλῑνον > * sé-
linum.*

Some words have both pronunciations: εἴδωλον > *īdŏlum*
(both in Prudentius: *Lat. Spr.* 466), ἔρημος > *erēmus erĕmus*
(Prudentius), σίνᾱπι > *sínapi sināpi.*

e. OTHER FOREIGN WORDS.

151. Some words borrowed from other languages kept their
original accent, contrary to Latin rules (S. 49): Umbrian
Pisaurum > It. *Pésaro,* etc.; Celtic *Baiócasses* > Fr. *Bayeux,*
Durócasses > Fr. *Dreux, Trícasses* > Fr. *Troyes,* etc., Dottin 103.

152. Germanic words were apparently made to conform to
Latin types: *Hûgo Hûgun > Húgo Hugónem >* Fr. *Húes Huón;*
Kluge 500.

2. SECONDARY STRESS.

153. As far as we can determine the rhythm of Vulgaɩ
Latin, judging from phonetic changes and from semi-popular
late Latin verse, it consisted in a tolerably regular alternation
of accented and unaccented syllables.   Thus Sedulius, at the
beginning of the fifth century, writes:

> Beátus áuctor sæculí
>   Servíle córpus induít,
> Ut cárne cárnem líberáns
>   Ne pérderét quos cóndidít.

The secondary stress, then, fell on the second syllable from the tonic: *cupĭdĭtôsus, felĭcĭtâtem; dŏlōrósa, lăcrĭmósa; Cĕsărĕm, Gállĭăs.* In some derivatives, however, the root syllable may have received an irregular stress through the analogy of the primitive: *árboricéllus.*

In late formations *e* or *i* in hiatus did not count as a syllable: *comĭnitĭáre.*

154. When the secondary stress *preceded* the tonic, it was strong, and the vowel bearing it was apparently treated as an accented vowel: *amĭcĭtâtem* > Pr. *amistát;* so, in Italian, *Buólogníno* beside *Bológna, Fiórentíno* beside *Firénze, véttováglia* beside *vittória.*

When it *followed* the tonic, it was weak, but probably the vowel bearing it had more force than a wholly unaccented final vowel: *sócĕrí* > Pr. *sózer, plácĭtúm* > Pr. *plach;* but *clérĭcúm* > Pr. *clérgue* while *clér'cum* > Pr. *clerc, cólăphúm* > Pr. *cólbe* while *cól'pum* > Pr. *colp.*

155. In many cases the intervening vowel fell out or lost its syllabic value. Then the primary and the secondary accent were brought together, and the secondary was shifted or lost: *parábuláre* > *paráuláre* > *párauláre, cálidús* > *cáldus, fíliús* > *fílius.*

UNSTRESSED WORDS.

156. Short, unemphatic words, in Latin as in other languages, had no accent, and were attached as additional syllables to the beginning or end of other words (S. 38–39): *non-ámat, áma-me, te-vídet, dó-tibi, cave-fácias, circum-lítora* (Quintilian I, 5). Many words, especially prepositions and conjunctions, as well as some adverbs and pronouns, were used only as enclitics or proclitics.

157. If such particles had more than one syllable, they tended to become monosyllabic: unstressed *magis*, perhaps influenced by *plus*, became *mais and *mas. A dissyllabic proclitic beginning with a vowel seems to have regularly lost that vowel: *illum vídet* > *'lu' vídet; ecce híc* > *'c'ic* (but *écce híc* > *ecc'íc*); *eccum ístum* > *'cu' ístu'* (but *éccum ístum* > *eccu'ístu'*). For elision, see *Franz.* ₂ II, 73–79, 379–390.

158. Words sometimes stressed and sometimes unstressed tended to develop double forms: *illās* > *illas* and *las, *sŭa* > *súa* and *sa*. Cf. S. 56–57.

C. QUANTITY.

159. We must distinguish between the quantity of vowels and the quantity of syllables. Every Latin *vowel* was by nature either long or short; how great the difference was we do not know, but we may surmise that in common speech it was more marked in stressed than in unstressed vowels. A *syllable* was long if it contained (1) a long vowel or a diphthong or (2) any vowel + a following consonant. If, however, the consonant was final and the next word began with a vowel, the consonant, in connected speech, was doubtless carried over to the next syllable and did not make position: see § 133. For the syllabication of mute + liquid, see §§ 132, 134.

1. POSITION.

160. In some of the Romance languages position checked the development of the preceding vowel, and it is probable that the beginnings of this differentiation go back to Vulgar Latin times: *pa-rem* > Old Fr. *per*, *par-tem* > Fr. *part*. Mute + liquid did not prevent the development: *pa-trem* > Fr. *pere*. Neither, apparently, did a final consonant (cf. § 133): *sa-l* > Fr. *sel*.

Compare Italian *fiero* < *fĕ-rus, ferro* < *fĕr-rum ; petto* < *pĕc-tus, pietra* < *pĕ-tra, fiel(e)* < *fĕ-l; — fuore* < *fŏ-ris, collo* < *cŏl-lum ; corpo* < *cŏr-pus, cuopre* < ** cŏ-p'rit, cuor(e)* < *cŏ-r.*

161. Early in the Empire *ss* after diphthongs and long vowels was apparently reduced to *s* (S. 112–120): *cāssus* > *cāsus, caussa* > *causa, formōssus* > *formōsus, glōssa* > *glōsa, mīssit* (S. 118: MISSIT) > *mīsit.* This did not occur, however, in the contracted endings *–āsse –āssem* etc., *–ēsse –ēssem* etc., *–īsse –īssem* etc.

Similarly one *l* was lost in *māllo, mīllia* (but not in *mĭlle :* Pompeius, S. 127), *nōllo, paullum.*

162. In Latin texts there is much confusion of single and double consonants, especially before the accent: *bal(l)æna, buc(c)ĭna, cot(t)idie,*[1] *ec(c)lesia,*[2] *glut(t)īre, mut(t)īre, tap(p)ēte, ves(s)īca,* etc. Cf. S. 111–132, Stolz 223–224. In some words this may result merely from bad spelling; but often it must represent an actual difference in pronunciation, as seems to be the case with the doublet *cĭto* > Sp. *cedo, cĭtto (C. I. L.* VIII, 11594) > It. *cetto.* Cf. § 163.

163. Many words certainly had two forms, doubtless belonging to different Latin dialects, — one with a long vowel + a single consonant, the other with a short vowel + a double consonant: *brāchium brăcchium; būca bŭcca; camēlus camĕllus,* where we have perhaps only a change of suffix, cf. § 42; *cīpus cĭppus; cūpa, cŭppa,* giving Sp. *cuba,* Fr. *cuve,* It. *cupola* and Sp. *copa,* Fr. *coupe,* It. *coppa; glūto glŭtto; hōc erat hŏcc erat,* S. 125–126 (Velius Longus and Pompeius); *Jūpiter Jŭppiter;* perhaps *lītera lĭttera; mūcus mŭccus; pūpa pŭppa; stūpa stŭppa; sūcus sŭccus.* Cf. Stolz 222–225.

---

[1] The antiquity of double *t* is attested by an old inscription : *Lexique* 101.

[2] The single *c,* which prevailed in Romance, is common in Greek and Latin manuscripts: S. 129.

To these may perhaps be added: *bāca bacca; bāsium
bǎssium (> It. *bascio*); *brāca bracca;* *būtis (< βοῦτις) *bŭttis
(> It. *botte*); *cāseus* *cǎsseus (> It. *cascio*); *chāne*(< χάνη)
channe; conservāmus conservammus, Vok. I, 261; *jubēmus
jubemmus, Vok.* I, 261 (*iubimmus iobemmus*); *lītus littus:
mīsi* * *mǐssi* (> It. *messi*).

Beside the two forms indicated, there was occasionally a
third, seemingly a cross between the other two, having both
the long vowel and the double consonant: *anguīla* (> Sp.
anguila) + *anguĭlla* = *anguīlla (> It. *anguilla*); *stēla (> Old
Fr. *esteile:* cf. *Lexique* 95–98) + *stĕlla* (> It. dialect *stẹlla*) =
*stēlla (> It. *stẹlla;* cf. *Vok.* I, 339, *stilla*); *strēna* (> Old Fr.
estreine) + *strĕnna* = *strēnna (> It. *strẹnna*, Sic. *strinna*); *tōta*
(> Sp. *toda*) + *tŏtta* (Keil V, 392[1]) = *tōtta (> Pr. *tota*, Fr.
toute).[2]   So perhaps Diomedes' *līttera: Archiv* XIV, 403.

164. In late Latin inscriptions and manuscripts a consonant
was sometimes doubled before *r* or *u̯: acqua, bellua, frattrĕ,
lattrones, mattrona, strennuor, suppra, suppremis, tennuis.* Cf.
S. 122, Stolz 223.   This doubling indicates in most cases a
local pronunciation, prevalent in Africa or in Italy.   According
to F. G. Mohl, *Zs.* XXVI, 612, a consonant was doubled
before *i̯* and *u̯* in the old Italic dialects: compare the Italian
doubling in *fabbro, tenne, volle,* etc.   In *aqua* the double consonant, attested by inscriptions and by Christian poets, was
very widespread and prevailed in Italy, Rætia, and a large
part of Gaul.   See Clara Hürlimann, *Die Entwicklung des
lateinischen* aqua *in den romanischen Sprachen,* reviewed by
Meyer-Lübke in *Ltblt.* XXIV, 334.

---

[1] Consentius: "per adjectionem litteræ *tottum* pro *toto.*"   Cf. *Gram.* I, 488, § 547;
Lexique 98–104.   According to *Lat. Spr.* 485, *tottus* was used by Pirminius.
[2] For * *tŭttus* see § 204 (2).

2. VOWEL QUANTITY.

165. Originally, perhaps, long and short vowels were distinguished only by duration, the vowels having, for instance, the same sound in *lātus* and *lătus*, in *dēbet* and *rĕdit*, in *vīnum* and *mĭnus*, in *nōmen* and *nŏvus*, in *ūllus* and *mŭltus*. However this may have been, long and short *e, i, o,* and *u* were eventually differentiated, the short vowels being open while the long were close: *vendo sęntio, pinus pįper, solus sǫlet, mųlus gųla.* That is, for the vowels of brief duration the tongue was not lifted quite so high as for those held longer. Later, in most of the Empire, *į* and *ų* were allowed to drop still lower, and became *ę* and *ǫ*: see §§ 201, 208. In the case of *a*, which is made with the tongue lying flat in the bottom of the mouth, there was no such differentiation.

According to Meyer-Lübke, *Lat. Spr.* 467, the distinction was clear by the first century of our era. In *Vok.* I, 461, II, 146, III, 151, 212, is given the testimony of grammarians, all of later date; in *Vok.* II, 1 ff., the evidence of inscriptions. Marius Victorinus, about 350 A. D., distinguishes two *e*-sounds (S. 174, 182); Pompeius, about 480, cites Tertullian for an *ę* similar to *i*, and several fifth century grammarians plainly distinguish *ę* from *ę* (S. 176, 182); from the second century on *æ* was often used for *ę* in inscriptions (S. 183–184). Terentianus Maurus, by 250, distinguishes *ǫ* from *ǫ* (S. 175, 211), and so do other grammarians (S. 211). Writers do not clearly distinguish *i* and *į*, until Consentius, in the fifth century (S. 193); *e*, however, is often used for *į* in inscriptions, as *menus*, etc., and *i* for *ę*, as *minses*, etc. (S. 195, 200–201). None of the grammarians apparently distinguished *u* and *ų*, but *o* is used for *ų* in inscriptions, as *ocsor, secondus*, etc. (S. 216–217).

166. In open syllables, if the word is used in verse, the quantity of the vowel is in general easily ascertained. In

closed syllables and in words not used by poets the quantity
is in many cases doubtful; but it is sometimes given by grammarians, sometimes marked in inscriptions, sometimes con-
jectured from the etymology, and often shown by subsequent
developments in the Romance languages. Occasionally the
testimony conflicts: some inscriptions have CARISSIMO, etc.,
others KARESSIMO, etc. (S. 98, 99); Aulus Gellius prescribes
dĭctum, but an inscription has DICTATORI (S. 105); Classic
Latin offers frĭgĭdus (cf. FRÍGIDA, S. 105), but the Romance
languages, except Spanish, require a short i; some Romance
forms support Classic nūtrīre, others demand ŭ; ūndĕcim,
lūrĭdus, ūltra were apparently pronounced also with short u
(S. 81–82); Fr. loir calls for *glĭrem beside glīrem.

a. VOWELS IN HIATUS.

167. Vowels in hiatus with the last syllable offer difficulties.
The Classic rule that a vowel before another vowel is short is
not absolute even for verse, and the practice of poets was not
always in accordance with spoken usage. Dīes, pīus kept
their originally long vowel, attested by inscriptions (DIES
PIIVS PIIVS, S. 93; cf. Substrate II, 101–102); so cūi, proved
by old inscriptions; and, at least in part, fūi, found in inscriptions, in Plautus, and in Ennius (S. 93): these preserved their
close vowel in the Romance languages.

Naturally long vowels, then, probably kept their original
quantity in hiatus. Naturally short vowels doubtless had
their regular development also: dĕus = dẹus, although we do
find the spellings dius and mius (S. 187); dŭo > dŭi = dụi;
vĭa = vịa. At a later stage, after ụ had become ọ (see §§ 165,
208), any ọ before u was apparently differentiated into ọ;
ōvum > ọum (cf. § 324) > ọum (and also ọvum, with a restoration of the v through the plural ova); sŭus > sọus > sọus (S.

216, Pirson 16). There may have been other special variations in different countries. Cf. § 217.

For a different theory, see *Gram.* I, 246–248. For another
still, see A. Horning in *Zs.* XXV, 341.

168. *Quĭa*, used for *quod* in late Latin, had a peculiar
development from the sixth century on: before a vowel it was
pronounced *quĭ'* and was confused with *quĭd*, which had begun
to assume the functions of *quod* (see §§ 69, 82; cf. *Franz. ∂* II,
352–355); before a consonant, under the influence of *qua* and
qua(m), it became *qua*. Cf. *Franz. ∂* II, 357–390; J. Jean-
jaquet, *Recherches sur l'origine de la conjonction 'que' et des
formes romanes équivalentes*, 1894.

169. *Plŭere* was supplanted in popular usage by *plŏvere*
(*Lat. Spr.* 468). *Plŭvia*, on the other hand, gave way to
*plŏja. Cf. § 208,(4).

b. LENGTHENING BEFORE CONSONANTS.

170. According to some grammarians, vowels were lengthened before *j*, as in *ējus*, *mājor*. The Romance languages,
however, point to open vowels in *pejor*, *Troja*. The apparent
contradiction disappears if we accept the statement of Terentianus Maurus, 250 A. D., who says (S. 104) that the vowels
in these words were short, but the *j* was doubled — that is,
there was a glide from the vowel to the *j*, which prolonged the
first syllable: not *pējor*, *Trōja*, but *pĕijor*, *Trŏija*. We find in
inscriptions such spellings as *Aiiax*, *coiiux*, *cuiius*, *eiius*,
maiiorem, etc.: S. 236, Pirson 74. Quintilian states that
Cicero preferred *aiio*, *Maiiam*, with double *i* (S. 236). Velius
Longus adds that as Cicero approved of *Aiiacem*, *Maiiam*, we
should write *Troiia* also (S. 236). Priscian analyzes *pejus*,
etc., into *pei-ius*, *ei-ius*, *mai-ius* (Édon 207).

171. When *n* was followed by a fricative (*f*, *j*, *s*, or *v*), it regularly fell early in Latin, and the preceding vowel was lengthened by compensation: *cēsor*, *cōjugi*, *cōventio*, *īferi*. But inasmuch as *n* occurs before *f*, *j*, and *v* only at the end of prefixes, it was usually restored by the analogy of the full forms *con–*, *in–*: so *infantem* through *indignus*, etc.; *conjungere* through *conducere*, etc.; *convenire* through *continere*, etc. Before *s*, however, *n* occurred in the middle of many words, and the fall was permanent, the *n* being restored only in compounds before initial *s*: *cōsul*, *īsula*, *mēsis*, *spōsus*; but *insignare*. Cf. § 311.

It is altogether likely that the *n* fell through nasalization of the vowel: *consul cōnsul cõsul cõsul*. If so, all trace of the nasality disappeared, but the length and the close quality of the vowel remained. Cf. *Archiv* XIV, 400.

Romance and late Vulgar Latin words with *ns* (except in compounds as above) are either learned terms or new formations: so *pensare*, beside the old popular **pēsare*.

See S. 77–78; for the usage of Cicero and others, S. 86; for inscriptions, S. 89.

172. (1) Vowels were apparently lengthened before *ŋk*: *quīnque*, *sānctus*, etc. Cf. S. 78; for inscriptions, S. 90.

(2) Before *gn* vowels were lengthened according to Priscian (S. 91), and inscriptions mark length in *dīgnus*, *rēgnum*, *sīgnum* (cf. *sĭgillum*), S. 91. The Romance languages, however, call for *dĭgnus*, *lĭgnum*, *pĭgnus*, *pŭgnus*, *sĭgnum*. Priscian, who wrote in the sixth century, is a very late authority, and some philologists regard the passage in question as an interpolation of still later date; still the evidence of the inscriptions remains. According to Meyer-Lübke (*Gram.* I, 54, *Lat. Spr.* 467), the vowel was lengthened, but only after *ĭ*, *ŭ* had become *i̯*, *u̯*, so that the result was *ị*, *ụ̄*, not *ī*, *ū*; cf. BENEGNVS

in *C. I. L.* XII, 2153, which is doubtless equivalent to the benIgnus of *C. I. L.* XII, 722. This seems a very plausible explanation. C. D. Buck, however, in the *Classical Review* XV, 311, prefers to regard such forms as *dĭgnus*, in so far as they existed at all, as due to a vulgar or local pronunciation.

c. DISAPPEARANCE OF THE OLD QUANTITY.

173. The difference in quantity was probably greater and more constant in accented than in unaccented vowels. The distinctions in quality, resulting from the original quantity, remained, in stressed syllables, through the Latin period and developed further in the Romance languages; in unaccented syllables the distinctions were doubtless weaker, and were often obliterated.

174. The old quantity itself was lost, for the most part during the Empire. It seems to have disappeared from *unstressed syllables* by the third or fourth century; but confusion set in as early as the second. The nominative singular *–ĭs* and the plural *–ēs* were confounded by 150 A. D. (S. 75), and *æ* was often used for *ĕ* in inscriptions (S. 183–184: *benæ*, etc.). Terentianus Maurus, about 250, tells us that *au* is short in unaccented syllables, as in *aut* (S. 66). Other grammarians warn against quantitative mistakes. Servius says, in the fourth century, "*miseræ* dativus est non adverbium," etc. (S. 226). The poetry of Commodian, in the third or fourth century, seems to observe quantity in stressed and to neglect it in unstressed syllables, and we find numerous metrical errors in other late poets: cf. J. Cornu, *Versbau des Commodian* in *Bausteine* 576.

On the other hand, Latin words borrowed by the Britons, mostly in the third and fourth centuries, show, through a shift of accent, the preservation of quantity in post-tonic

syllables: Loth 72, 65. Moreover, Latin words borrowed by
Old High German indicate a retention of long *i* and *u* before
the accent: Franz.

It is possible that the quantity of unstressed vowels was
better kept in the provinces than in Italy.

175. In *accented syllables* there are sporadic examples of
confusion by the second century, as *æques* for *ĕques* in 197
(S. 225); but probably the disappearance of the old distinction was not general before the fourth and fifth centuries, and
not complete before the end of the sixth. Servius, in the
fourth century, criticizes *Rŏma* (S. 106). St. Augustine declares that "Afræ aures de correptione vocalium vel produc-
tione non judicant" (*Lat. Spr.* 467). Pompeius and other
grammarians blame the confusion of *æquus* and *ĕquus* (S. 107,
178). Much late poetry disregards quantity altogether.

On the other hand, Latin words borrowed by the Britons
from the second to the fifth century, but mostly in the third
and fourth, show the preservation of the quantity of stressed
vowels: Loth 64. Latin words in Anglo-Saxon, taken over in
the fifth and sixth centuries, retain the quantity of vowels that
bear the accent: Pogatscher. The Latin words in Old High
German, too, distinguish by quantity *ī* and *ĭ*, *ē* and *ĕ*, *ō* and *ŏ*,
ū and *ŭ; ĕ, ŏ* are distinguished by quality also, for *ē* > *î* while
ĕ > *e* or *i*, *ō* > *û* or *ô* while *ŏ* > *o:* Franz.

d. DEVELOPMENT OF A NEW QUANTITY.

176. At the end of the Latin period a new system of quantity grew up, entirely diverse from the old, and based on the
situation of the vowel. In most of the Empire accented
vowels not in position were pronounced long, all other vowels
short: *sănctŏ vālĕs, vĕndŏ vĕnĭs, dĭxĭ plĭcăs, fŏrmăs fŏrĭ, frŭctŭs*

gū̆lĕ; că-thẹ̄-dră tĕ-nẹ̄-brăs; cọ̄-r mẹ-l nọ̄-s rẹ̄-m trẹ̄-s.   In Spain
and in some parts of Gaul, *all* stressed vowels were apparently long: *tẹ̄mpŭs, pọ̄rta.*

This new pronunciation doubtless sprang up with the disappearance of the old, which it displaced.   Meyer-Lübke in
Gram. I, 561–562, says that the development was different
and independent in the several Romance languages; in *Einf.*
103–104, he describes it as common to all, but as posterior to
the fifth century; in *Lat. Spr.* 467, he puts it in the fourth
and fifth centuries.

177. It is likely that these new long vowels were pronounced in most regions with a circumflex intonation, which
in the transition from Latin to the Romance languages resulted in diphthongization in a large part of the Empire, particularly in northern Gaul: *vẹ̄nis* > It. *vieni, gū̆la* > Old Fr.
goule, cǫr > It. *cuor, nǭs* > Fr. *nous, trẹ̄s* > Old Fr. *treis.*   Portugal, southern Gaul, Lombardy, and Sicily apparently did
not participate in this early breaking; and the conditions of
diphthongization were very diverse in different localities.
The vowels most affected were *ẹ* and *ǫ.*

An isolated example, perhaps only a blunder, occurs in an
inscription made a little before 120 A. D.: NIÉPOS, beside
NEPOTIS (A. Zimmermann in *Zs.* XXV, 735).   In 419 A. D.
we find VOBIT for *obiit* (S. 213).

D. VOWELS.

178. Latin had the vowels *ă, ĕ, ĭ, ŏ, ŭ,* and in unaccented
syllables before a labial (as in *prox*u*mus*) a short *ü;* furthermore, the groups *æ, au, eu, œ,* also *ui.*   We have seen (§ 165)
that *ē, ī, ō, ū* were pronounced close, and *ĕ, ĭ, ŏ, ŭ* open, while
ă was not affected by quantity.   We shall see presently

(§§ 209, 210) that *æ* > *ę* and *ce* > *ę*, while *au*, *eu* generally remained *áu̯*, *éu̯* (*cáutus*, *céu̯*), and *ui* (as in *cui*) was *úi*.

179. The foreign vowels of borrowed words were assimilated in some fashion to the Latin system. In the few Celtic words that were taken over there are no important peculiarities. In the Germanic vocabulary there is not much to be noted: *ai* in words adopted early apparently became *a*, as **waiðanjan* > **wadaniare*; *eu* (or *iu*) appears in *treuwa* (or *triuwa*), which became **treu̯a*; *iu* is found in *skiuhan* > **skiu̯are*.

The history of Greek vowels is very complicated:—

GREEK VOWELS.

180. According to Quintilian (Édon 64–65), the Greek letters were sounded as in Greek. This pronunciation was doubtless the ideal of people of fashion, but popular speech substituted for unfamiliar vowels the sounds of the vernacular. The inconsistencies in this substitution arise partly from the different dates at which words were borrowed, partly from the channel (written or oral) through which they came, and partly from the various pronunciations of the vowels in the several Greek dialects.

181. *A*, long or short, was pronounced *ă*: Φᾶσις > *Phāsis*, φάλαγξ > *phălanx*.

182. *H* was in Greek originally a long *ę*, but early in our era it became *ī*. In book-words it was assimilated to Latin *ē*: ἀποθήκη > *apothēca* > It. *bottęga;* so in some late words, as βλασφημία > *blasphēmia* > It. *bestemmia*. In words of more popular origin it often had the Greek open sound: ἐκκλησία > *eclęsia;* σηπία > *sæpia*, but also *sēpia* > It. *sęppia;* σκηνή > *scæna scēna*. Late words often show *i*: ἀσκητής > *ascitis, Per*.

40, ı, etc.; ἐκκλησίαι > *eclisiæ*, Neumann 9; μοναστήριον > mo-
nastirium, μυστήριον > mistirium, etc., Claussen 854–855; ταπή-
τιον > Fr. *tapis*, Pr. *tapit*.

183. *E* was close in some Greek dialects, open in others.
In book-words it was assimilated to Latin *ĕ:* γένεσις > *gĕnĕsis*.
In popular words it was sometimes close, sometimes open:
ἔρημος > *er'mus er'mus* > It. *ermo*, Sp. *yermo;* κέδρος > *cedrus* >
It. *cedro;* πέπερι > *pĭper;* Στέφανος > *Stephanus Stephanus.* Cf.
Claussen 853–854.

184. *I*, at least in the principal dialects, seems to have had
a very open sound, even when long. In book-words it was
assimilated to Latin *ĭ:* φῖμός > *phīmus;* φίλος > *phĭlus.* In
popular words *ī* apparently became *į*, later *e* or *ę; ĭ* apparently
became *ĕ*, later often *ę:* ἀρθρῖτικός > *arthrīticus* > It. *artętico;*
ἀρτεμισία > *artemīsia* > Old Fr. *armeise;* βωλίτης > *boletus;*
ὀρίγανος > It. *regamo;* χρῖσμα > *chrīsma* > It. *cresima*, Old Fr.
cresme; Χριστός > *Chrīstus Chrestus*, cf. *Christianus Chres-
tianus;* etc.;—ἀντίφονος > **antefona* > Old Fr. *antiefne;* βλίτον
> *blĭtum* > It. *bieta;* μίνθη > *menta* > It. *menta*, Sp. *mienta;*
σίναπι > *sĭnapi* > It. *senape;* etc. Cf. Claussen 855–857.

185. Ω was probably *ǭ*, but perhaps dialectically *ọ̄* (cf. ὥρα
> *hǭra*). In book-words it was assimilated to Latin *ō:* φώκη
> *phōca.* In popular words it apparently became *ǫ*, occasion-
ally *u:* γλῶσσα > It. *chiǫsa;* πτωχός > It. *pitǫcco;* τρώκτης >
trŭcta. Cf. Claussen 869–870.

186. *O* in most dialects was *ǫ̆*. In book-words it was
assimilated to Latin *ŏ:* κόφινος > *cŏphĭnus;* ὀρφανός > *ŏrphănus.*
In popular words it was generally close, but sometimes open,
and occasionally the same word had both pronunciations:
ἀμόργη > *amŭrca;* δοχή > *dǫ̆ga* > It. *doga*, etc.; κόμμι > *gŭmmi;*
ὀσμή > ? It. *orma;* πορφύρα > *pŭrpŭra;* τόρνος > *tǫ̆rnus* > It.

torno, etc.;— κόγχη > *cǫncha;* στρόφος > *strǫppus; χορδή >*
chǫrda;—κόλαφος > *cǫlaphus cǫlaphus.* Cf. Claussen 857–860.

187. *Y* was originally pronounced *u;* later in Attic and
Ionic it became *ü*, which subsequently, in the 9th or 10th
century, was unrounded into *i.*

In the older borrowed words, perhaps taken mostly from
Doric (Claussen 865), υ regularly was assimilated to Latin *u*
(S. 219–221): βύρσα > *bŭrsa;* κρύπτη > *crŭpta;* κύμβη > *cŭmba;*
μύλλος > *mŭllus;* μύρτος > *mŭrta, App. Pr.;* πύξος > *bŭxus.* It.
busta seems to represent a peculiar local development: cf.
buxida (=*pyxis*) in Theodorus Priscianus and in glosses,
Lat. Spr. 468. Cf. *Zefurus*, Audollent 536; "*tymum* non *tu-*
mum," *App. Pr.; Olumpus*, etc., Pirson 39. In τρῡτάνη >
trŭtīna the υ was shortened. In ἄγκῡρα > *ancŏra*, στύραξ >
stŏrax, and a few other words the υ for some reason became *ŏ;*
these probably have nothing to do with καλύπτρα > It. *calǫtta*,
κρύπτη > It. *grǫtta*, μῦδος > It. *mǫtto*, in which the *ǫ* is a later
local development. For some words we find an occasional spelling *œ*, which may represent a Greek dialect pronunciation between *u* and *ü:* γῦρος > *gyrus gœrus;* Μυσία > *Mysia Mœsia;* etc.

Towards the end of the Republic, cultivated people adopted
for Greek words the Ionic-Attic pronunciation, which is generally represented, in the case of υ, by the spelling *y.* Cicero
says: "*Burrum* semper Ennius, nunquam *Pyrrhum*" (S. 221).
According to Cassiodorus, *u* is the spelling in some words, *y*
in others (S. 221). In the *App. Pr.* we find: "*Marsyas* non
Marsuas," "*myrta* non *murta*," "*porphyreticum marmor* non
purpureticum marmor," "*tymum* non *tumum*." Among the
common people the unfamiliar *ü* was assimilated to *i.* The
spelling *i* occurs sometimes before Augustus: ἀγκύλια > *ancilia;*
Ὀδυσσεία > *Odissia*, Livius Andronicus; Ὀλυσσεύς > *Ulixes.*
In inscriptions we find *misteriis*, etc., S. 221. The *App. Pr.*

has "*gyrus* non *girus.*" Cf. *giro, misterii,* etc., Bechtel 76–77;
giret, Audollent 535; *Frigia,* etc., Pirson 39. This *i,* if long,
was usually pronounced *i;* if short, *į,* which became *ę:* γῦρος
> It. *giro;* κῦμα > It. *cima;* σύριγγα > It. *scilinga;*—κύκνος >
It. *cęcino;* etc. For σῦκωτόν, see § 141; γύψος > It. *gęsso* is
probably a local development. Κυ frequently became *qui:*
κολοκύντη > *coloquinta,* etc.; cf. §.223.

The modern Greek pronunciation is represented by some
Romance words: ἄμυλον > It. *amido;* βυζαντίς > It. *bisante;*
τύμπανον > Fr. *timbre;* etc.

Cf. Claussen 860–869.

188. *AI* originally became *ai,* as in Αἴας > *Aiax,* Μαῖα >
Maia; later *æ* (as in αἰγίς > *ægis*), which came to be pronounced *ę,* as in Αἰθιοπία > *Æthiopia Ethiopia.* Cf. Claussen
871–872.

189. *AY* > *au:* θησαυρός > *thesaurus.* Cf. Claussen 872–873.

190. *EI* was doubtless originally pronounced *ei* in Greek,
then, from the sixth to the fourth century B. C., *ē;* finally,
about the third century, *ī,* except before vowels. In Latin, ει
became *ī* before consonants, *ē* or *ī* before vowels; εἴδωλον >
īdolum; παράδεισος > *paradīsus;* πειρατής > *pīrāta;* — Κλειώ >
Clīo; Μήδεια > *Medēa.* In -ειος -εια -ειον, the penult was often
shortened: πλατεῖα > *platĕa.* Cf. Claussen 873–875.

191. *EY* generally became *eu:* Εὖρος > *Eurus.* Such forms
as *"ermĕneumata* non *erminomata"* (*App. Pr.*), *toreomatum*
from τόρευμα, may be merely misspellings: cf. *Clepatra* for
Cleopatra. Some Romance forms show *u:* κέλευσμα >? It.
ciurma. Cf. Claussen 875–877.

192. *OI* originally became *oi,* as in ποινή > *poina;* later *œ*
(as in *pœna*), which came to be pronounced *ę,* as in Φοῖβος >
Phœbus Phebus (S. 277). Sometimes, however, it became *o,*

as in ποιητής > *poēta*. *Cimiterium cymiterium*, for *cœmeterium*
< κοιμητήριον, perhaps indicates an ignorant confusion of *ü*
and *ö*. Cf. Claussen 877–878.

Like οι, ῳ became *œ:* κωμῳδία > *comœdia*.

193. *O Y* was doubtless originally pronounced *ou* in Greek,
then *ọ̄*, then *ū*. In Latin it usually became *ū:* βροῦχος >
brūchus; οὐρανός > *Ūrănus*. Cf. Claussen 878–879.

1. ACCENTED VOWELS.

a. SINGLE VOWELS.

N.B.— For vowels in hiatus, see § 167.   For nasal vowels, see § 171.

a

194. *A* regularly remained unchanged in the greater part
of the Empire: *caput, dare, factum, latus, manus, patrem, tantus.*
But in Gaul, especially in the north, it probably had a forward
pronunciation tending somewhat toward *ẹ:* cf. *crepere* (probably
for *crepare*) in *Gl. Reich.;* and *agnetus* (for *agnātus?*) in Fredegarius, Haag 6.

195. Some words had a peculiar development:—

(1) Beside *alǎcrem* the Romance languages seem to postulate *alẹcrem*
and *alẹcrem*. It is possible that *álǎcer* (whence *alǎcrem*) > *álǒcer* (whence
alẹcrem), then *alǐcer* (whence *alǐcrem alẹcrem*).

(2) For the suffix *–arius,* see § 39, *–arius.*

(3) Beside *cĕrǎsus* (< κέρασος) there must have been a Latin *cĕrěsus.*
So beside *cĕrǎsěus,* which was used in southern Italy, Rome, and Sar-
dinia, there was a *cĕrěsěus,* which was used elsewhere: *Lat. Spr.* 468; cf.
Substrate I, 544.

(4) Beside *grǎvis* there was a *grěvis,* under the influence of *lěvis:*
GREVE, *Lat. Spr.* 46 , cf. *Substrate* II, 441.

(5) Beside *mǎlum* (< Doric μᾶλον) there was a *mēlum* (< μῆλον), used
by Petronius and others: *Lat. Spr.* 468.

(6) Beside *vacuus* there was a *vŏcuus: vocuam, C. I. L.* VI, 1527 d 33;
cf. *vocatio, C. I. L.* I, 198, etc.   Cf. S. 171, Olcott 33.   The *o* was probably

original; old *vocáre, vocívus* regularly became *vacáre, vacívus* (> *vacuus*), whence by analogy *vácat* for *vócat: Lat. Spr.* 466. By a change of suffix *vŏcuus* became **vŏcĭtus.*

ē

196. Long *e*, which was pronounced *ẹ* (§ 165), probably remained unchanged in Vulgar Latin, at least in most regions: *debēre, dēbet, habētis, mercēdem, vēndere, vērus.*

In Sicily, Calabria, and southern Apulia *ẹ* has become *i.* In old Oscan, which was spoken in nearly the same region, *ē* became *i* in late Republican times, as in *cinsum, dibeto,* etc. (*Lexique* 106). There is, however, no proof of historical connection between the phenomena: cf. *Lat. Spr.* 468.

197. *I* is very often used for *ē* in inscriptions and late writings: Gregory the Great has *crudilitas, dulcido, ficit, filix, minsam, vindo,* etc., *–ido* for *–edo, –isco* for *–esco, –isimus* for *–esimus;* and conversely *ver* for *vir,* etc.: Sepulcri 193–194. Cf. S. 189–190; Carnoy 15 ff. (*ficet* in the 3d century, etc.). Also *Vok.:* for the confusion of *–ēre* and *–īre,* I, 260 ff., II, 69 ff.; for *–ēsco* and *–īsco,* I, 359–364; for *–ēlis* and *–īlis, –ēlius* and *–īlius,* I, 287–289; for *vindimia* instead of *vindēmia,* I, 328, III, 127 (*Lexique* 115). These spellings are due in the main to the identity of *ē* and *ĭ* in late pronunciation: see § 165.

A. Sepulcri, in *Studi Medievali* I, 614–615, conjectures that *s* + consonant may have tended to raise *ẹ* to *i, ọ* to *u.* This would account for *bistia* (= *bēstia*) found in late Latin, *Studi Medievali* I, 613; for *crisco* and other verbs in *–isco* for *–ēsco;* for *adimplisti,* etc.; for *fistus,* etc.;— also for *colustra;* for *cognusco* and other verbs in *–usco* for *–ōsco.* Some of the *–ēsco* > *–īsco* cases are surely due to a shift of conjugation: see §§ 414–415.

198. In Gaul this substitution of *i* for *ē* was so very common that it must signify something. It probably indicates an

extremely close pronunciation of the *ę* (cf. *ǫ*); later, in north-
ern Gaul, this very high *ę* > *ei* (*vērum* > Old Fr. *veir*): *Lat.
Spr.* 468. It is interesting to note that Celtic *ē* also became *i:*
Dottin 99.

Lexique 104–105: *criscit, riges, tris, vexit,* etc.   Pirson 2–5:
ficerent, ficit, requiiscit, rictu, rigna, etc.   Neumann 10–11:
adoliscens, minses, quiiscit, rigna.   Bon. 106–113: *minse, quin-
quaginsima,* etc.   Haag 8–9: *adoliscens, criscens, ingraviscente,
seniscit, tepiscit; delitus, fedilis, habitur, minsis, sidibus, stilla,*
etc.   Cf. *Vok.* I, 311 ff.

ĕ

199. Short *e*, which was pronounced *ę* (see § 165), remained
unchanged: *bĕne, ĕxit, fĕrrum, fĕrus, fĕsta, tĕneo, vĕnit.*

For the development of diphthongs, see § 177.

(1) According to *Lat. Spr.* 466, *voster,* which supplanted *vester,* is to be
regarded as a new formation on the model of *noster* rather than as the
old form.

ī

200. Long *i*, pronounced *i* (§ 165), remained unchanged:
audīre, dīco, mīlle, quīnque (*Substrate* I, 546), *vīlla, vīnum.*

(1) *Frīgĭdus,* except in Spain, must have become *frīgĭdus (> *frīgdus*),
perhaps through association with *rĭgĭdus.* Cf. § 166.

(2) Beside *īlex* there was an *ēlex,* found in Gregory of Tours: *Archiv
für das Studium der neueren Sprachen* CXV, 397. Cf. *Lexique* 114.

(3) Beside *sīcula* there was a *sēcula* (*Lexique* 119) > It. *segolo.* Varro
(*Lexique* 119) mentions a rustic *speca* for *spīca.* It. *stegola,* Sp. and Port.
esteva postulate *stēva for *stīva;* cf. *C. G. L.* IV, 177, l. 1.

(4) For *sī,* see § 229, (4).

ĭ

201. Short *i*, pronounced *į* (§ 165), became, doubtless by
the third century and sporadically earlier, *ę* in nearly all the
Empire: *bĭbo, cĭrculus, ĭlle, mĭnus, pĭscem, sĭtis, vĭtium.* The
spelling *e* for *ĭ* is common from the third century on: *frecare,*

legare, menus, etc., S. 200–201; *elud* (= *illud*), Audollent 535; *minester*, etc., Pirson 8–10; *karessemo*, etc., Carnoy 15 ff.; *minester, sebe, semul, sene, vea*, Neumann 23–25; *corregia*, etc., R. 463; *accepere, trea*, etc., Bon. 117–123; *æteneris, trebus*, etc., Haag 11.　　Conversely *i* is often used for *ē* (cf. §§ 197, 198): *minses*, etc., S. 195; *benivolus*, etc., R. 463.　Quintilian and Varro mention (S. 166) a rustic *e* for *ĭ*, attested also by inscriptions (S. 202).

In Sardinia and a part of Corsica this change did not take place, and both *ī* and *ĭ* > *i*.　These two islands were taken from Rome by the Vandals in 458 and added to the African kingdom; after that they were perhaps isolated: *Einf.* 106.

In southern Italy *ẹ* from *ĭ*, like *ẹ* from *ē*, became *i:* cf. § 196.

(1) Beside *camĭsia* there was a *camīsia*: *Substrate* I, 541.

(2) Beside *sĭmul* there was a *sĕmul, perhaps through the analogy of *sĕmel*: *Lat. Spr.* 468.

(3) *Sinĭster* was replaced by *sinĕxter*, under the influence of *dĕxter*: *Lat. Spr.* 469.

ō

202.　Long *o*, pronounced *ọ* (§ 165), remained unchanged in Vulgar Latin, at least in most regions: *colōrem, fōrma, hōra, nōmen, sōlus, spōnsus*.　In Sicily, Calabria, and southern Apulia *ọ* has become *u*, as it did in old Oscan: cf. the change of *ẹ* to *i*, § 196.

For *agnusco, cognusco*, etc., used by Gregory the Great and others, see the end of § 197.　The popular *ūstium* for *ōstium* (*Lat. Spr.* 468; *Studi Medievali* I, 613) is perhaps to be explained in this way.

For *ọu* > *ọu*, see § 167.

203.　The spelling *u* for *ō* is very common in Gaul (*Lat. Spr.* 468): *furma*, etc., S. 214; *amure*, etc., Pirson 13; *victurias*, etc., Bon. 126–130; *cognusco, gluria, nun, puni,* etc., Haag 13. It probably represents a very close sound, which later, in northern Gaul, became *ou* or *u: cōrtem* > Old Fr. *court.* Cf. § 198.

204. There are a few peculiar cases:—

(1) Fr. and Sp. *meuble, mueble* postulate ǫ in *mōbilis,* presumably through the analogy of *mǒveo.* Cf. § 217.

(2) Beside *tōtus* and *tottus* (§ 163), some of the Romance forms point to **tūttus* or **tūctus,* or at least to a nom. pl. **tūtti* or **tūcti:* It. sg. *tutto,* pl. *tutti;* Neapolitan sg. *totto,* pl. *tuttɔ;* old Fr., Pr. sg. *tot,* pl. *tuit.* The Italian *tutto* may have come through the plural. Such a form seems to be attested by the *Gl. Cassel:* "aiatutti. uuela alle," where *tutti* is defined as *alle.* No satisfactory explanation has been proposed; the most plausible, perhaps, is that of Mohl, *Lexique* 102–104, namely, the influence of *cūncti* on *tōti.* Cf. *Zs.* XXXIII, 143.

ǒ

205. Short *o,* pronounced ǫ (§ 165), remained unchanged: *bǒnus, fǒlia, fǒris, fǒrum, lǒcus, mǒrtem, sǒlet, sǒrtem.* The rustic Latin *funtes, frundes* (for *fǒntes, frǒndes*) are perhaps connected with Italian *fǫnte* and other words containing ǫ for ǫ before *n* + dental.

U is occasionally used for ǒ in inscriptions: *lucus,* etc., S. 211–212. Cf. *App. Pr.,* "*formica* non *furmica.*"

For the development of diphthongs, see § 177.

ū

206. Long *u,* pronounced ṵ (§ 165), remained unchanged in most of the Empire: *cūra, dūrus, nūllus, ūna.* Grammarians mention the protrusion of the lips: S. 216.

But in Gaul, a large part of northern Italy, and western Rætia it was probably formed a little forward of its normal position. It was certainly not *ü,* cf. K. Nyrop, *Grammaire historique de langue française* I, § 187; but it doubtless slightly approached it. This pronunciation may have been due to the linguistic habits of the Celts: cf. Windisch 396–397. Celtic $\bar{u} > \bar{\imath}$ in Great Britain by the second century; in Latin words borrowed by the Celts $\bar{u}$ is generally treated like Celtic $\bar{\rho}$ (*mūrus* > *mur*), but in a few, presumably taken very early, $\bar{u} > \bar{\imath}$ (*cūpa* > *cib*, *crūdus* > *criz*): Loth 67–68.

207. The following special cases are to be noted:—

(1) Beside *lūrĭdus* there probably was a **lūrdus: Substrate* III, 517.

(2) *Nūptiæ*, through the analogy of *nŏvius ("bridegroom," from *nŏvus*) and *nŏra*, became *nŏptiæ: Lat. Spr.* 469. Cf. *Substrate* IV, 134.

(3) Beside *pūmex* there was a *pōmex: Bon.* 136, *pomice.* Cf. F. G. Mohl in *Zs.* XXVI, 617–618.

ŭ

208. Short *u*, pronounced *ų* (§ 165), became, probably by the fourth century or earlier, *ǫ* in most of the Empire: *bŭcca, cŭlpa, gŭla, rŭptus, ŭnda.* The spelling *o* is common in late documents: "*columna* non *colomna*," "*turma* non *torma*" (cf. "*coluber* non *colober*," "*formosus* non *formunsus*," "*puella* non *poella*"), *App. Pr.; tomolus*, etc., Pirson 15–17; *tonica*, etc., Bon. 132–135; *corso, covetum* (= *cŭbĭtum*), *toneca*, Haag 14. The old spelling *o* for *u* after *v* (*voltus, servos*, etc.), which lasted down into the Empire, is perhaps only orthographic: *Lat. Spr.* 464.

In Sardinia, a part of Corsica, Albania, and Dacia this change did not take place, and both $\bar{u}$ and $\breve{u} > u$: *Lat. Spr.* 467.

For *ǫu* > *ou*, see § 167.

(1) Beside *angŭstia* there must have been *angǫstia.

(2) Fr. *couleuvre, fleuve, jeune* call for local *ǫ* in *colŭbra, flŭvium, jŭvĕnis.* There are other local irregularities. Cf. § 217.

(3) In place of *nŭrus* we find *nŏrus* (R. 465) and *nŏra* (S. 216), due to the analogy of *sŏror* and *nŏvia ("bride," from *nŏvus*).

(4) Instead of *plŭere* and *plŭvia* people said *plŏvere* (used by Petronius and others) and **plŏja: Lat. Spr.* 468. Cf. §§ 169, 217.

b. DIPHTHONGS.

æ

209. *Æ* was originally written and pronounced *ai*, but through the mutual attraction of its two parts it became *æ*, later *ẹ: cæcus, cælum, quæro.*

In certain words a vulgar and dialect pronunciation *ẹ̄*, common to Volscian and Faliscan (Hammer 7, 8), came into general use: *fēnum, prēda, sēpes, sēptum, sēta.* Cf. S. 166–168, 188; Carnoy 79–80. For *fēnum fænum, prēda præda, sēpes sæpes* both forms were preserved. Hence, by analogy, such spellings as *fæcit*, etc., S. 190. Cf. Neumann 13 (and *Fortsetzung* 21–23): *fæmina, quiæti*, etc.

210. The regular change of *æ* to *ẹ* took place largely in Republican times in unaccented syllables; in stressed syllables in the first century of our era and later. *E* for *æ* in dative endings occurs early: Corssen I, 687 ff. About the middle of the first century B. C., when Varro cited *edus* for *hædus* as a rural form, stressed *æ* was probably still a diphthong in the city but had become *ẹ* in rustic Latium; some hundred years later *ẹ* came into the city and pervaded the provinces: *Lat. Spr.* 465. Terentius Scaurus, in the first century, says that *æ* represents the sound better than *ai:* S. 224. *E* is found early in Campania, especially in Pompeii (*presta*, etc.): S. 225. In Spanish inscriptions *e* occurs from the first century on (Carnoy 78): *questus* (2d century), etc., Carnoy 69–84. It was probably general everywhere by the second century: *Einf.* § 78. Pompeius blames the confusion of *æquus* and *ĕquus:* S. 178. The spelling *e* for *æ* was usual in unaccented syllables (as *sancte*) before the third century, in stressed syllables (as *questor*) from the fourth century on; it may be called regular by the fifth century: S. 178, 225. Cf. Bechtel

75–76: *cedat, grece*, etc.   Conversely *æ* was often erroneously used for *ĕ* (S. 183–184) and for Greek *η* (as *scænam, Lexique* 104).

au

211.   *Au*, pronounced *áu̯*, generally remained in Vulgar Latin: *aura, gaudium, taurus*.   In Rumanian and Provençal it was preserved as *au*, in Portuguese as *ou;* its existence in the earliest stage of French is proved by the treatment of *c* in *causa* > *chose;* in Italian and Spanish it did not become *ǫ* until original *ǫ* had broken into *uo* or *ue*.

(1) The spellings *Cladius, Glacus, Scarus*, etc., with *a* for *au* when there is an *u* in the next syllable, are pretty common in various countries: S. 223; Carnoy 86–95.   Perhaps they represent a provincial pronunciation, or possibly they are only orthographic.

(2) *Clūdo* for *claudo* is common, coming through derivatives, such as *occlūdo: Vok.* II, 304; Carnoy 100 (*cludo* in two Sp. inscriptions of the 1st and 2d centuries); Bayard 6.   Cf. Carnoy 85–86 (*clusa*, etc.).

212.   Umbrian and Faliscan had *o* in place of Latin *au:* Hammer 4–5, 8.   So, in general, the dialects of northern and central Italy: *Chronologie* 158–164.   There are some examples in Pompeii, in Oscan territory, where *au* was normally preserved; this pronunciation was used also in the country around Rome, and in the first and second centuries B.C. crept into the city, where it was used by the lower classes: *Lat. Spr.* 465–466.   In Umbrian inscriptions we find *toru*, etc.: Hammer 4.   In Latin, *Clodius* and *Plotus* are common in first century inscriptions: Carnoy 85, Pirson 27.   *Closa*, etc., occur in the second century: Carnoy 85.

The grammarians — Probus, Diomedes, Festus, and others — speak of a rustic or archaic *o* for *au:* Corssen I, 655–663; *Vok.* II, 301 ff.; S. 162–164; Hammer 15–19.   Festus cites *orum;* Priscian, *cotes, ostrum, plostrum : *Carnoy 95.   Cf. *App. Pr.*, "*auris* non *oricla*"; R. 464, *coda, orata, orum*.

Conversely, *au* was occasionally used for *ō* (*Chronologie* 160): Festus, *ausculum;* Marius Victorinus, "*sorex* vel *saurex*." Cf. *aucīdere for *occīdere*, postulated by some Romance forms.

213. This rustic and vulgar *ō*, — which was pronounced *ǫ*, while the Romance *o* from *au* was *ǫ*, — was generally adopted in Vulgar Latin in a few words: *cōda; fōces;* *ōt (cf. Umbrian *ote,* Hammer 4)= *aut; plōdere.* Cf. Classic *fauces, suffōco; plaudo, explōdo; si audes, sōdes.* Cicero used *loreola, oricla, plodo, pollulum*: Carnoy 95. *Ōla, cōdex, cōles* = *caulis, lōtus, plōtus* occur also.

eu

214. *Eu,* pronounced *éu̯* (as in *ceu, eu, Europa, eurus, eheu, heu, neu, neuter, seu*), was not preserved in any popular words. Cf. S. 228.

œ

215. *Œ* was originally written and pronounced *oi*, but through the mutual attraction of its two parts it became presumably *ö*, later *ę: cœpi, pœna, pœnitet.* It may be that the intermediate stage is reflected by the spelling PHYEBÆ for *Phœbe*, S. 227.

E is attested by inscriptions in the first century of our era: *ceperint,* Carnoy 84; *Phebus, C. I. L.* IV, 1890; etc. Cf. S. 227, *Lat. Spr.* 464. In the *Per.* we find *amenus, cepi,* etc., Bechtel 76. The confusion of *œ* and *e* is mentioned by late grammarians: S. 227. In late Latin a bad spelling, *œ* for *æ* and *e*, became popular: *cœcus, cœlum, cœmenta, fœmina, fœnum, mœrore, mœstus, pœnates.* Cf. S. 228; *Vok.* II, 293ff.

ui

216. *Ui,* pronounced *úi̯*, was preserved: *cūi, hūic, illūi.* For the development of *fui,* see § 431.

c. INFLUENCE OF LABIALS.

217. According to some philologists, a following labial tends to open a vowel: *colŭbra* > **colǫbra, flŭvium* > **flǫvium, jŭvĕnis* > **jǫvenis, mōbĭlis* > **mǫbĭlis, ōvum* > **ǫvum, plŭĕre* > *plǫvĕre,* etc.   A general influence of this kind can hardly be regarded as proved for any combination except *ǫu*, which became *ǫu :* see § 167.

S. Pieri, *La vocal tonica alterata dal contatto d'una consonante labiale* in *Archivio glottologico italiano* XV, 457, maintains that *i, ẹ, ǫ, u* were lowered one stage—to *ẹ, ę, ǫ, ǫ*—by a preceding or following labial, even if it was separated from the vowel by a liquid.   Although many examples are cited, the evidence is not convincing.   For a criticism of the theory, see G. Ascoli, *Osservazioni al precedente lavoro,* ibid., p. 476. The discussion is continued by Pieri, *La vocal tonica alterata da una consonante labiale* in *Zs.* XXVII, 579.

d. CLERICAL LATIN.

218. In clerical Latin the vowels were probably pronounced for the most part as in vulgar speech, until the reforms of Charlemagne.   After that, in general, *ă = a, ĕ = ę, ĭ = i, ŏ = ǫ, ŭ = u* (or *ü*), *æ* and *œ = ę, au = ǫ* or *au.*

2. UNACCENTED VOWELS.

N. B.—For secondary stress, see §§ 153-155.

219. Among unstressed vowels, those of the first syllable had most resistance, possibly through a lingering influence of the Old Latin accent: cf. § 134.

The vowels of the final syllable lost much of their distinctness, but did not fall, except sporadically, until long after the Vulgar Latin period, and then only in a part of the Empire.

Grammarians testify to the confusion of *o* and *u:* S. 212. *Quase,* *sibe* are found in place of *quasi, sibi:* S. 199–200. According to Quintilian I, iv, 7, "in *here* neque *e* plane nequi *i* auditur."

Weakest were medial vowels immediately following the secondary or the primary stress. In early Latin there was an inclination to syncope: *ar(i)dōrem, av(i)dēre, bál(i)nĕum, cal(e)fácĕre, júr(i)go,* etc. This tendency continued, in moderation, in Classic and Vulgar Latin: *cal(i)dus, ŏc(u)lus, frig(i)daria, vĭr(i)dis,* etc. In inscriptions we find such forms as *infri, vetranus:* S. 251.

For the confusion of unaccented *e* and *i,* see Pirson, 30–36, 47–48; for *o* and *u,* see Pirson 41–47. Fredegarius is very uncertain in his use of unstressed vowels: Haag 15–24.

220. *Ü* was employed only before labials, in unaccented syllables: cf. S. 196–198, 203–208; Lindsay 25–26, 35; *Franz.* I, 21–24. During the Classic period it generally became *ĭ: decumus > decimus, maxumus > maximus, pontufex > pontifex, quodlubet > quodlibet,* etc.; cf. *Lat. Spr.* 466. In Spanish inscriptions we find *maximus,* etc., spelled both with *u* and with *i:* Carnoy 65–69.

Sümus, being sometimes accented, developed two forms, *sŭmus* and *sĭmus.* The former was the one generally adopted in Classic Latin, but *sĭmus* was favored by Augustus and by some purists of his time (Lindsay 29). According to Marius Victorinus (Keil VI, 9), "Messala, Brutus, Agrippa pro *sumus simus* scripserunt." In the vulgar speech *sĭmus* seems to have prevailed in Italy and southern Gaul. Cf. § 419, (1).

221. In general Latin quantity did not sensibly affect the quality of unstressed vowels, except in initial syllables, and even there the difference must have been small. In final syllables, however, *ī* was certainly distinct from *ĭ: sentīs,*

sentĭt > It. *senti, sente; fēcī, fēcĭt* > Pr. *fis, fes*.   In *sĭbi, tĭbi*
the final vowel was sometimes long, sometimes short.

a. UNACCENTED VOWELS IN HIATUS.

222. *I* and *u* followed by a vowel and beginning a syllable
were apparently pronounced as consonants from the earliest
times.   Quintilian says that *u* and *i* in *uos* and *iam* are
not vowels: S. 232.   Quintilian and Velius Longus cite the
spellings *Aiiax, aiio, Maiiam* as approved by Cicero: S. 236.
Bonnet notes that *a*, not *ab*, is used before *Joseph, Judæis*,
etc.   These, then, will be treated as consonants, and will be
left out of consideration in the present chapter.

223. After gutturals, *u* followed by a vowel was originally
a vowel itself, but lost its syllabic value in early Classic times:
acua > *aqua, distinguere* > *distinguere*.   So it was in *qualis,
quæro, quem, qui*.   In Greek transliterations κυ for *qui* (as in
ἀκύλας) is very common: Eckinger 123–125; cf. § 187.

In perfects, however, such as *nocuit, placuit*, the *u* was apparently not reduced to a semivowel until the end of the
Classic period.

In some other words the syllabic value of *u* was kept, at
least in theory, rather late: Velius Longus distinguishes *aquam*
from *acuam*, S. 234; *App. Pr.*, "*vacua* non *vaqua*," "*vacui* non
vaqui."

224. Otherwise, *e, i*, and *u* in hiatus with following vowels
lost their syllabic value probably by the first century of our
era, and sporadically earlier.   Occasional examples (such as
dormio, facias, fluviorum) are found in Ennius, Plautus, Lu-
cilius, Lucretius, Horace, Virgil, Ovid, Juvenal, and Seneca:
e.g., *deorsum* in Lucretius; *vindemiator* in Horace; *abiete, abieti-
bus* in Virgil.   *Italia* counts as three syllables in poets of the

early Empire. Cf. S. 232. Valerius Probus has *parietibus:* Édon 208. Consentius declares that trisyllabic *soluit* and four-syllable *induruit* are barbarisms; Cæsellius is undecided whether *tenuis* has three syllables or two: S. 234. *Suavis*, however, was used as a trisyllable by Sedulius in the fifth century; it was probably a semi-learned word, as it became *soef* in French, *soave* in Italian.

The pronunciation *ę̣, į̣, ų̣* was probably regular in popular speech by the first century or before; by the third century, with a narrowing of the mouth-passage, the semivowels presumably developed into the fricative consonants *y* and *w:* S. 231–232. So *alea* > *alęa* > *alja, fīlius* > *fīlį̣us* > *filjus, sapui* > *sapuį̣* > *sapwi.* In the same way *filíolus* > *filjólus* (§ 136), *tenúeram* > *tênweram* (§ 137); likewise *eccu'hīc* > **eccwįc, eccu'ísta* > **ecwįsta* (§ 65), etc. We have, then, in late Latin, a new *y* and a new *w*.

Hence arises, in late Latin spelling, a great confusion of *e* and *i* in hiatus: CAPRIOLVS (cf. § 136), S. 187; Caper, "non *iamus* sed *eamus*," "*sobrius* per *i* non per *e* scribendum," Keil VII, 106, 103; *aleum, calcius, cavia, coclia, fasiolus, lancia, lintium, noxeus, solia, vinia, App. Pr.;* *abias, abiat, exiat, Lauriatus, valiat*, Audollent 535; *palleum*, etc., R. 463; *calciare, liniamenta*, Bayard 4; *eacit* (=*jacet*), *eam* (=*jam*), *Vok.* II, 43; cf. Carnoy 33–35.

225. But the combinations *ęé, įé, ǫó, ųó* developed differently, *eé* and *ié* apparently being contracted into *ē, oó* and *uó* into *ō*, at an early date: *arĭĕtem* (§ 136) > *arētem* (Varro, "*ares* veteres pro *aries* dixisse*": Carnoy 43); **dē-ĕxcĭto* > **dēxcĭto* > It. *desto; faciēbam* > **facēbam; mulĭĕrem* (§ 136) > *mul'ērem*, the *į* remaining long enough to palatalize the *l* (the Romance *ę* was doubtless a later analogical development); *parĭĕtes* (§ 136) > *parētes, C. I. L.* VI, 3714 (Rome); *prĕhĕndĕre* >

prĕndĕre, then *prĕndĕre through the analogy of *rĕddĕre* and perhaps also of *ascĕndĕre*, *defĕndĕre*, *pĕndĕre*, *tĕndĕre*; *quĭētus* > *quētus*, common in late inscriptions, Pirson 57 (cf. *requebit*, Carnoy 43); — *cŏhŏrtem* > *cōrtem*; *cŏŏpĕrīre* > *cōpĕrīre*, then *cŏpĕrīre **cŏp'rīre* through the analogy of *cŏ*– and perhaps also of *ŏpĕra*, *ŏpus*; *dŭōdĕcim* > *dōdĕcim* (Pirson 58: *dodece*).

226. Furthermore, *u* after all consonants fell before unaccented *u* probably by the middle of the first century, before unaccented *o* by the second century: *antīquus* > *antīcus*; *carduus* > *cardus*; *cŏquus* > *cŏcus* (*App. Pr.*, "*coqui* non *coci*," "*coqus* non *cocus*"; cf. S. 351); *distĭnguunt* > *distĭngunt* (according to Velius Longus, some writers use no *u* in *distinguere*, Édon 130); *ĕquus* > *ĕcus* (*App. Pr.*, "*equs* non *ecus*"; cf. Velius Longus, S. 217); *innŏcuus* > *innŏcus*, Koffmane 111; *mŏrtuus* > *mŏrtus*; *suus* > *sus*, *tuum* > *tum*, Carnoy 117; — *battuo* > *batto* (cf. *abattas*, *Gl. Reich.*); *cŏquo* > *cŏco* (*App. Pr.*, "*coquens* non *cocens*"; hence *cocīna); *quat*(*t*)*uor* > *quattoȝ* (S. 218) *quator* (Pirson 58) *quatro* (7th century, Carnoy 221); *quot*(*t*)*īdie* > *cottīdie*, S. 352; *stĭnguo* > *stĭngo*; *tĭnguo* > *tĭngo* (Caper, "*tinguere* ... non *tingere*," Keil VII, 106); *tŏrqueo* > *torquo > *tŏrco; *ŭnguo* > *ŭngo* (*ungo*, *unguntur*, *ungi*, Bayard 7; Caper, "*ungue* non *unge*," Keil VII, 105; *uncis* = *unguis*, Audollent 536). So apparently *aruum* > *arum, *ĕruum* > *ĕrum* (*Lat. Spr.* 472: *ero*). *Vĭduus*, however, doubtless under the influence of the commoner *vĭdua*, kept its *u*: Old Fr. *vef*.

After gutturals, *u* fell before stressed *u* and *o*: *quum* > *cum*; *quōmŏdo* > *cōmŏdo*, Audollent 536. See § 354.

U often fell irregularly in *contin*(*u*)*ari*, *Febr*(*u*)*arius*, *Jan*(*u*)*arius*: *Vok.* II, 468–469; S. 217–218.

227. Similarly, *i* after a consonant fell before unaccented *i*: *audīi* > *audi*, *consĭlīi* > *consĭli*, *ministĕrīi* > *ministĕrī*. Velius

Longus found it necessary to say that *Claudii, Cornelii, Julii,* etc., should be spelled with double *i:* Keil VII, 57.

Some late words, however, kept *-ĭī* and *-ĭīs: Dionysii* > It. *Dionigi, Parisiis* > It. *Parigi.*

b. INITIAL SYLLABLE.

228. As far as one can judge from spellings and subsequent developments, *ă* was pronounced *a; æ, ĕ, ĭ, œ* all came to be sounded *ẹ; ī* remained *i; ō* and *ŭ* were finally all pronounced *ọ* or *ụ; ŏ* remained *ọ; au* became *a* if there was an accented *u* in the next syllable, but otherwise remained unchanged (cf. *Lat. Spr.* 470): *rādīcem, vălēre; ætātem, dēbēre, tĕnēre, vĭdēre, fœdāre; rīdēmus, cīvĭtātem, hībernus; plōrāre, frūmentum, sŭbĭnde; cŏlōrem, dŏlēre, mŏvētis; A(u)gŭstus, A(u)runci, a(u)scŭlto, audēre, gaudēre, naufragium.* For the confusion of *e* and *i,* see Audollent 535, Carnoy 17–33, Bon. 135–138. Cf. *œcclesia,* Bechtel 76; "*senatus* non *sinatus,*" *App. Pr.; golosus gylosus* (for *gulōsus*), Koffmane 110; *moniti* (for *mūnīti*), Bon. 136. *Agustus* is frequent from the second century on, S. 223 (cf. *agustas,* Pirson 26); *Arunci* occurs in manuscripts of Virgil; Caper says "*ausculta* non *asculta,*" S. 223; **agŭrium* must have existed also.

229. In a few words the vowel of the initial syllable was lost before an *r: *corrŏtŭlare* > **c'rŏt'lare; dīrēctus* generally > *d'rēctus* (*Vok.* II, 422: *drictus*); *quĭrītare* > **c'rītare. Jejūnus* after prefixes lost its first syllable: **dis-junare.*

Some minor peculiarities are to be noted: —

(1) *A* after *j* apparently tended to become *e:* Old Latin *jajŭnus* > Classic *jejŭnus* (the original *a* seems to be preserved in some Italian dialect forms); Classic *Januarius* > *Jenuarius* (common in inscriptions, S. 171–172, *Lat. Spr.* 470); Classic *janua* > **jenua* > Sardinian *genna.*

(2) *E,* long or short, is very often replaced by *i* in Gallic inscriptions (*Lat. Spr.* 470): *divota, mimoriæ,* etc.; *dilevit,* Bon. 109; cf. *Vok.* I,

422–424. This perhaps indicates a close pronunciation: cf. § 198. *Di–* for
de–, possibly through confusion with *dis–*, is common in Gregory the
Great: *dirivare*, etc. According to Mohl, *Lexique* 105–108, *e* became *i* in
southern Italy from the fourth to the sixth century: RIVOCAVERIT, etc.
A form *ni* for *ne* is found from early times: Pirson 3.

(3) *Ĭ* was occasionally assimilated to a following accented *a: gĭgántem*
> **jagante* > Old Fr. *jaiant*, Pr. *jaian*, Old Genoese *zagante; sĭlváticus* >
salvaticus (*Gl. Reich.*, cf. *Lat. Spr.* 470) > Old Fr. *salvage*, It. *salvatico*,
Rum. *sălbatec.* Cf. *Einf.* § 111.

(4) *Ī* tended to become *e*, by dissimilation, if there was an accented *ī* in
the next syllable:[1] *dīvīdĕre* > **devīdĕre; dīvīnus* > *devīnus*, in fourth
century inscriptions, *Lexique* 122; *fīnīre* > *fenīre*, in manuscripts and
inscriptions, *Lexique* 123; *vīcīnus* > *vecīnus*, attested by Servius, *Lexique*
104 ff. *Sī*, in late Latin, sometimes became *se*, attested from the sixth
century on (*Vok.* II, 87; *Lexique* 120; *Franz. ∂* II, 224 ff.; Bon. 126;
Haag 11; cf. *nise*, *C. I. L.* I, 205); in very late texts there is frequent confusion of *si* and *sed* (*Franz. ∂* II, 225, 234–235); the *e* is perhaps due to the
analogy of **que* < *quĭd* = *quod* (cf. §§ 69, 82), cf. Italian *sed* on the model
of *ched: si* is preserved in French, Provençal, and Spanish, *se* in Portuguese, Old French, Italian, and Old Rumanian. In *mīrabĭlia* the *ī* apparently became *e* and *a*.

(5) *Ū* was kept by analogy in many words: *dūrare, mūrare, mūtare,
nūtrire* (beside **nŏtrire*). *Jūnĭpĕrus* > *jeniperus* (*Lat. Spr.* 470) and *jini-
perus* (*App. Pr.*).

(6) *O* appears as *u* in *furmica* (*App. Pr.*, cf. *Rom.* XXXV, 164), *putator*
(*Bon.* 127), *turrente* (Bon. 131). *O* is changed to *e* in *retundus* (*Vok.* II,
213; cf. Vitruvius, *retundatio, Lat. Spr.* 470), through the influence of the
prefix *re–;* also sometimes in *serore* (*Lat. Spr.* 470; cf. *serori, seroribus*,
Carnoy 107).

(7) *Au* in vulgar speech was often replaced by *o* (cf. §§ 212, 213):
oricla, App. Pr., Pirson 27; so **ot* (for *aut:* cf. Umbrian *ote*, Lindsay 40),
which prevailed in Vulgar Latin.

230. *S* before a consonant was doubtless long and sharp,
as in modern Italian, so that at the beginning of a word it had
a syllabic effect — *s-chola*. This led to the prefixing of a
front vowel (until the seventh century nearly always an *i*, later

---

[1] Mohl's view, *Lexique* 122–126, is that original Latin *ei*, if *i* followed, became *e*
instead of *ī*.

often *e*) to the *s* when no vowel preceded — *in i-schola*. This *i* or *e* came to be regarded as a regular part of the word. The prosthetic vowel occurs first in Greek inscriptions. The earliest Latin example is probably *iscolasticus*, written in Barcelona in the second century; it is found repeatedly, though not frequently, in the third century (Carnoy 114–116); in the fourth and fifth it is very common: *espiritum, ischola, iscripta, isperabi, ispose, istatuam, istudio,* S. 317; *ismaragdus,* Pirson 60; *estatio, Estephanus, iscola, istare,* R. 467. Grammarians took no note of it until St. Isidore, in the seventh century. But in late Latin texts *ab* rather than *a* was used before words beginning with *sc, sp, st: ab scandalo,* Dubois 171; *ab sceleribus,* Bon. 445; cf. Dubois 171–172, Bon. 445–446.

The *es-, is-* thus produced was confounded with *ex-, exs-* (pronounced *es-*) and *ins-, his-* (pronounced *is-*): *explendido, splorator, instruo* for *struo, Spania,* etc., S. 317; *hispatii* for *spatii,* Bechtel 78; *spiratio* for *inspiratio,* Koffmane 109; *scalciare* for *excalceare, scoriare* for *excoriare, spandere* for *expandere, Spania, Spanus, stantia* for *instantia, strumentum,* etc., R. 469–470; *spectante* for *expectante,* etc., Bon. 148.   Cf. *Vok.* II, 365 ff.; S. 316–319; Pirson 59–60.

c. INTERTONIC SYLLABLE.

N. B.— By this term is meant the syllable following the secondary and preceding the primary stress.

231. Vowels so situated probably became more and more indistinct towards the end of the Empire, and occasionally disappeared.   In some regions they began to fall regularly before the close of the Vulgar Latin period, but *a* was generally kept: *bón(i)tátem, cáp(i)tális, cárr(i)cáre, cérebéllum, cív(i)tátem, cóll(o)cáre, cómparáre cómperáre, dél(i)cátus, dúb(i)táre, éleméntum éliméntum, frígidária frigdária, mírabília,*

sácraméntum, séparáre séperáre, vérecúndia. Frigdaria occurs
in the second century B. C.: *Franz. ∂* I, 12. Cf. *dedcavit,* Pirson 52; *vetranus,* Pirson 51; *cornare* for *coronare,* Koffmane
111; *stablarius,* R. 467. The fall of the vowel of course dis-
turbed the Vulgar Latin rhythm: see § 153. Cf. F. Neumann
in *Zs.* XIV, 559.

Mĭnĭstĕrium apparently became *mĭnstĕrium* early enough for
the *n* to fall before the *s:* see § 171. Cf. *Substrate* IV, 116.

d. PENULT.

232. The Vulgar Latin rhythmic principle tended to obliterate one of the two post-tonic syllables of proparoxytones.
The penult, being next to the accent, was weaker and more
exposed to syncope. We find in late Latin much confusion
of *e* and *i: anemis, meretis,* etc., Neumann 22; *dixemus,* etc.,
Bon. 118. Likewise *o* and *u: ambolare,* etc., R. 464; *insola,*
etc., Bon. 131–135; cf. Sepulcri 201–202.

The treatment of this vowel, however, was apparently very
inconsistent in Vulgar Latin, and the conditions differed
widely in different regions. There was probably a conflict
between cultivated and popular pronunciation, both types
often being preserved in the Romance languages: thus while
the literary and official world said (*h*)*ŏmĭnes* (> It. *uomini*),
the uneducated pronounced *'ŏm'nes* (> Pr. *omne*); similarly
beside *sŏcĕrum* there was *sŏcrum.*

As far as the general phenomena can be classified, we may
say that in popular words in common speech the vowel of the
penult tended to fall under the following conditions:—

(1) Between any Consonant and a Liquid.

233. A vowel preceded by a consonant and followed by a
liquid weakened and fell in the earlier part of the Vulgar

Latin period: *altra; anglus; aspra; dedro* for *déderunt, Lex-ique* 63; *fecrunt fecru, Lexique* 64; *íns(u)la; juglus; maníplus; socro*, Pirson 51. In some words we find *a* weakened to *e: cítera, App. Pr.; hilerus,* Carnoy 12; *Cæseris, compera, seperat* (about 500 A. D.), *Vok.* I, 195–196; *Eseram* for *Isaram*, Bon. 96. For a vowel between a *labial* and a liquid, see (2) below.

But if the first consonant was a palatal, the vowel seems to have been kept, at any rate in some regions: *bájulus, frágilis, grácilis, vírginem.* In *vígilat* > *vǐglat* the vowel fell before the *g* began to be palatalized (so apparently in *dígitum* > *dic-tum, Franz. ?* I, 15–16; *frígidus* > *frigdus, App. Pr.*). Cf. § 259.

234. Latin originally had the two diminutive endings –*clus* (< –*tlo*), as in *sæclum,* and –*cǔlus* (< –*co-lo*), as in *aurǐcǔla.* These were kept distinct by Plautus. Later they were con-fused, both becoming –*cǔlus* in Classic Latin, both –*clus* in vulgar speech: *artíc(u)lus, bác(u)lus, másc(u)lus, óc(u)lus, spéc(u)lum, vernác(u)lus, víc(u)lus. Oclus* and some others occur in Petronius: see W. Heræus, *Die Sprache des Petronius und die Glossen,* 1899; cf. *peduclum,* Waters Ch. 57. Many ex-amples are found in inscriptions: *oclos, scaplas,* Audollent 538; *aunclus, felicla, masclus,* Pirson 49–50. Cf. *Franz. ?* I, 16–18.

To –*clus* was assimilated in popular Latin the ending –*tǔlus: capítulus* > *capiclus; fístula* > *fiscla; vétulus* > *veclus, App. Pr.* (cf. *vitlus,* Pirson 51). But a few words, which must have been slow in entering the common vocabulary, escaped this absorption: *crústulum* > *crustlum* (found in 18 A. D.); *spatula* > *spatla.* Cf. § 284.

(2) BETWEEN A LABIAL AND ANY CONSONANT.

235. A vowel preceded by a labial and followed by a con-sonant was inclined to fall early: *bublus; cóm(i)tem; comp'tus;*

déb(i)tum; dóm(i)nus; fíb(u)la; póp(u)lus; sablum; tríb(u)la; vápulo baplo. In *dóm(i)nus* the *mn* form may be the older: *domni*, Pirson 50; *domnus* in St. Augustine, Koffmane 109; *domnicus*, R. 467; *domnulus*, Koffmane 111. *Lamna* occurs in Horace and Vitruvius, *Franz. ɔ* I, 13. Petronius has *bublum*, Waters Ch. 44, *offla*, Waters Ch. 56. Cf. *fibla, poplus, sablum*, etc., in R. 467.

In some words, however, the vowel was kept, either everywhere or in a large region: *árb(o)rem; hámula; hóm(i)nes; júv(e)nis; nébula; trémulat.*

236. When *ab* or *av* was brought next to a consonant by the fall of a following vowel, it generally became *au*, but often there were double forms; the process began very early: **ávica > auca*, found in glosses; *ávidus > audus*, Plautus (cf. *avunculus > aunculus*, Plautus); **clávido > claudo* (cf. **navifragus > naufragus*); *fábula > *faula *fabla; gábata > *gauta *gabta; *návitat > *nautat; parábula > *paraula *parabla; tábula > *taula *tabla.* Cf. *Franz. ɔ* I, 12.

(3) BETWEEN A LIQUID AND ANY CONSONANT.

237. A vowel preceded by a liquid and followed by a consonant was subject to syncope at all periods: *ardus*, Plautus; *caldus*, Plautus, Cato, Varro, Petronius; *cól(a)phus* (cf. *percolopabat*, Waters Ch. 44; *colpus, Gl. Reich.*); *fúlica fulca, Franz. ɔ* I, 13; *lardum*, Ovid, Martial, Juvenal, Pliny; *merto*, Pirson 51, *Franz. ɔ* I, 15; *soldus*, Cæsar, Horace, Varro; *valde; virdis, App. Pr.* (cf. *virdiaria*, Vegetius, 4th century). Cf. *Franz. ɔ* I, 12 ff.

(4) MISCELLANEOUS.

238. In some words the vowel fell under different conditions: *dígitum > dictum, Franz. ɔ* I, 15–16 (cf. § 233); *frígidus*

> *frigdus* (cf. § 233), *App. Pr.* (*fricda*), Pompeii (FRIDAM); *máxima* > *masma*, 2d century, Suchier 732; *nítidus* > **nittus*, *pútidus* > **puttus*, probably late; *postus*, Lucretius, Pirson 50, *Franz.* 2 I, 13–14 (cf. *posturus*, Cato).

239. In the transition from Vulgar Latin to the Romance languages the vowels in classes (1), (2), (3), — in so far as they had not fallen already, — were syncopated with some regularity; and a number of vowels otherwise placed fell under different conditions in various regions: *pónere* > **ponre*, *tóllere* > ** tolre; fémina* > **femna, hábitus* > ** abtus, rápidus* > **rapdus; cárrico* > **carco, cléricus* > **clercus, cóllocat* > **colcat; déc(i)mus, fráx(i)nus, pérs(i)ca, séd(e)cim.* Cf. *Gl. Reich.*: *carcatus, culicet culcet = collŏcat.*

In a part of Gaul *ámita* > ** anta, débita* > **depta, domínica* > ** dominca, mánica* > ** manca, sémita* > **senta.* Some of these shortened forms were used in other regions.

A vowel preceded by *d* or *t* and followed by *c* seems to have remained longer than most other vowels that fell at all: *júdico, médicus, viáticum, víndico,* etc.

e. FINAL SYLLABLE.

240. The vowels regularly remained through the Vulgar Latin period. Later, about the eighth century, they generally fell, except *a* and *ī*, in Celtic, Aquitanian, and Ligurian territory.

241. In the *App. Pr.* we find "*avus* non *aus*," "*flavus* non *flaus*," "*rivus* non *rius*." *Aus* and *flaus* have left no representatives, but *rius* is evidently the ancestor of Italian and Spanish *rio*. All three forms are probably examples of a phonetic reduction that affected certain regions.

Through a large part of the Empire *–āvit* > *–aut: triumphaut* is found in Pompeii. See Morphology.

242. Final vowels, as in modern Italian, must have been often elided or syncopated in the interior of a phrase, especially *e* after liquids: Caper, "*bibere* non *biber*"; *haber* in an inscription; *conder*, *præber*, *prædiscer*, *tanger* in manuscripts. See *Franz.* ₂ I, 41. So, perhaps, *autumnal(e)*, *tribunal(e)*, etc.

The *App. Pr.* has "*barbarus* non *barbar*," "*figulus* non *figel*," "*masculus* non *mascel*." These curious forms are probably not the result of a phonetic development, but are rather due to a local change of inflection, which left no trace in the Romance languages. Cf. Old Latin *facul = facilis, famul = famulus*.

243. *A*, long or short, was naturally pronounced *a; æ, ĕ, ĭ,* according to the testimony of numerous inscriptions (*Lat. Spr.* 469), were all probably sounded *e*, which in Sicily became eventually *i; ī* remained *i; ŏ* was *o*, which became *u* in Sicily; *ŭ* was *u*. In some localities this *o* and this *u* were kept distinct, but generally they were confounded (*Lat. Spr.* 469). Examples: *ămās, ămăt; sanctæ, trīstēs, trīstĕm, trīstĭs; fēcī, bŏnī, sĕntīs; bŏnōs, mŏriŏr; cŏrpŭs, frūctū.* About the eighth century *a* probably became *ə* in northern Gaul.

244. The changes in pronunciation led to great confusion in spelling. It is likely that final vowels were especially obscure in Gaul in the sixth and seventh centuries.

Neumann 7–8 cites ten cases of *e* for *a: Italice*, etc.

E and *æ*, in late Latin, were not usually distinguished (cf. § 210): *apte = aptæ, cotidiæ*, etc., Bechtel 75–76.

E and *i* came to be used almost indiscriminately. Quintilian I, vii, says that Livy wrote *sibe* and *quase;* in I, iv and I, vii, he describes the final vowel of *here* as neither quite *e* nor quite *i*. Cf. *mihe, tibe*, etc., *Lexique* 118. *E* for *i* is frequent in the dative and ablative, Carnoy 45: *luce*, dative; *uxore*, ablative.

Es and *is* are continually interchanged: *Vok.* I, 244 ff., III, 116; *mares = maris*, etc., Audollent 535; *Joannis*, etc., Neumann 11–13; *jacis, omnes = omnis* (3d century), etc., Carnoy 13–15; *regis = reges*, etc. Bon. 111; *omnes =omnis*, etc., Bon. 121.   So *et* and *it:* Bechtel 88–89, very common in *Per.; tenit*, etc., Neumann 11–13; *posuet*, etc., Carnoy 13; *movit*, etc., Bon. 115; Sepulcri 229–230.

With *o* and *u* it was the same.   In *Vok.* II, 91 ff., there are 61 examples of *u* for ablative *o* between 126 and 563 A. D., as well as frequent instances of ablative in *um*, of *om* for *um*, *os* for *us*, and *us* for *os*.   The confusion of *o* and *um* is very common in *Per.;* also in Gregory the Great, Sepulcri 203–204; cf. Carnoy 48, *monumento = monumentum*.   Bon. 131 has *spoliatur* for *spoliator*.   *Os* and *us* were interchanged from the third century on: *anus = annos*, Carnoy 48; *bonus = bonos*, etc., Sepulcri 201.   The accusative plural in *us* was particularly common in Gaul: *filius = filios*, etc., Bon. 128; cf. Haag 42.

245. In words often used as proclitics final *–er, –or* became *–re, –ro: ĭnter > *intre; quat(u)or > quatro*, Carnoy 221; *sĕmper > * sempre; sŭper > * supre*.   Cf. *Lat. Spr.* 474.

Mĭnus, used as a prefix (cf. § 29) as in *minus-pretiare*, became in Gaul *mis–*, perhaps at the end of the Vulgar Latin period, under the influence of *dis–*.   Cf. *Phon.* 43–44.

E. CONSONANTS.

246. The Latin consonant letters were B, C, D, F, G, H, I, K, L, M, N, P, Q, R, S, T, V, X, Z.   *I* and *V* were used both for the vowels *i* and *u* and for the consonants *j* and *v*.   *K*, an old letter equivalent to *C*, was kept in some formulas; it need not be separately considered. Q was generally used only in the combination $QV = kw$ (cf. § 223). X stands for ks. Z in Old Latin apparently meant s or ss (S. 319–320); later it represented a different Latin version of Greek ζ, which will be treated below (§§ 338–339).

In addition to the above, Vulgar Latin had a new w and y coming from originally syllabic u, e, or i in hiatus: see § 224. In words borrowed from Greek and German there were several foreign consonants, which will be discussed after the native ones.

247. Double consonants regularly kept their long pronunciation: *annus, nullus, passus, terra, vacca.*   For $ss > s$ and $ll > l$ after long vowels, see § 161.   For double forms like *cīpus cippus,* see §§ 162, 163.

In late spelling there is some confusion of single and double consonants: *anos,* Pirson 88; *fillio,* Pirson 85; *serra,* Bon. 158; cf. Pirson 83–91.   For Fredegarius see Haag 39–40.   Double consonants are often written single in early inscriptions.

248. The principal developments that affected Latin consonants may be summed up as follows: b between vowels was opened into the bilabial fricative β, and thus became identical with v, which also changed to β; c and g before front vowels were palatalized and were then subject to further alterations; h was silent; m and n became silent at the end of a word, and n ceased to be sounded before s.   The voicing of intervocalic surds began during the Vulgar Latin period.

The consonants will now be considered in detail, first the native Latin, next the Greek, lastly the Germanic; the Celtic need not be separately studied.   The Latin consonants will be taken up in the following order: aspirate, gutturals, palatals, dentals, liquids, sibilants, nasals, labials.

1. LATIN CONSONANTS.

a. ASPIRATE.

249. *H* was weak and uncertain at all times in Latin, being doubtless little or nothing more than a breathed on-glide: S. 255–256. Grammarians say that *h* is not a letter but a mark of aspiration: S. 262–263. There is no trace of Latin *h* in the Romance languages. Cf. G. Paris in *Rom.* XI, 399.

250. It probably disappeared first when medial: S. 266. Quintilian commends the spelling *deprendere:* S. 266. Gellius says *ahenum, vehemens, incohare* are archaic; Terentius Scaurus calls *reprehensus* and *vehemens* incorrect, and both he and Velius Longus declare there is no *h* in *prendo:* S. 266. Probus states that *traho* is pronounced *trao:* Lindsay 57. Cf. *App. Pr.*, "*adhuc* non *aduc.*" In inscriptions we find such forms as *aduc, comprendit, cortis, mi, nil, vemens:* S. 267–268.

251. Initial *h* was surely very feeble and often silent during the Republic. In Cicero's time and in the early Empire there was an attempt to revive it in polite society, which led to frequent misuse by the ignorant, very much as happens in Cockney English to-day: for the would-be elegant *chommoda, hinsidias*, etc., of "Arrius," see S. 264.

Quintilian says the ancients used *h* but little, and cites "*œdos ircos*que": S. 263. Gellius quotes P. Nigidius Figulus to the effect that "rusticus fit sermo si aspires perperam"; but speaks of bygone generations—i.e., Cicero's contemporaries—as using *h* very much, in such words as *sepulchrum, honera:* S. 263–264. Pompeius notes that *h* sometimes makes position, as in *terga fatigamus hasta*, sometimes does not, as in *quisquis honos tumuli:* Keil V, 117. Grammarians felt obliged to discuss in detail the spelling of words with or without *h:* S. 264–265.

H is dropped in a few inscriptions towards the end of the Republic: *arrespex* (for *haruspex*), etc., S. 264.   In Rome are found: E[REDES], *C. I. L.* I, 1034; ORATIA, *C. I. L.* I, 924; OSTIA, *C. I. L.* I, 819.   In Pompeii *h* is freely omitted; and after the third century it is everywhere more or less indiscriminately used: *abeo, abitat, anc, eres, ic, oc, omo, ora,* etc., *haram, hegit, hossa,* etc., S. 265–266.   Cf. *ospitium, ymnus,* etc., *heremum, hiens, hostium,* etc., Bechtel 77–78; *ortus,* etc., *hodio,* etc., R. 462–463.

252. After *h* had become sīlent, there grew up a school pronunciation of medial *h* as *k*, which has persisted in the Italian pronunciation of Latin and has affected some words in other languages: *michi, nichil,* Bechtel 78, R. 455.   Cf. E. S. Sheldon in *Harvard Studies and Notes in Philology and Literature* I (1892), 82–87.

b. GUTTURALS.

253. *C* and *K* did not differ in value except that *C* sometimes did service for *G: App. Pr., "digitus* non *dicitus"; dicitos = digitos,* Audollent 536; cf. S. 341–344.   There was some confusion, too, of *Q* and *C:* S. 345.

254. *Q V* was pronounced *kw:* S. 340–341, 345–346, 350–351.   Before *u* and *o,* however, the *kw* was reduced to *k* by the first or second century, probably earlier in local or vulgar dialects: Quintilian VI, iii, records a pun of Cicero on *coque* and *quoque; condam, cot, cottidie,* S. 351–352; *in quo ante = inchoante, quooperta = coperta, secuntur,* Bechtel 78–79.   Cf. § 226.

Before other vowels the *kw* was regularly kept in most of the Empire, unless analogy led to a substitution of *k,* as in *coci* for *coqui* through *cocus:* see § 226.   But in Dacia, southeastern Italy, and Sicily subsequent developments point to a Vulgar Latin reduction of *que* to *ke, qui* to *ki: Lat. Spr.* 473.

In *quinque* the first *w* was lost by dissimilation: CINQVE, Carnoy 221, found in Spain (so CINQV, *Lexique* 93); CINCTIVS, CINQVAGINTA, S. 351. *Laqueus* seems, for some reason, to have become **laceus: Substrate* III, 274.

255. *X* stood for *ks:* S. 341, 346, 352. After a consonant *ks* early tended to become *s:* Plautus uses *mers* for *merx;* Caper, "*cals* dicendum, ubi materia est, per *s*," Keil VII, 98.

By the second or third century *ks* before a consonant was reduced to *s: sestus* is common in inscriptions, cf. Carnoy 170, Eckinger 126 (Σέστος); *destera*, Carnoy 171; *dester,* S. 353; *mextum* for *mæstum*, Audollent 537. So *ex->es-* in *excutere*, *exponere*, etc.: cf. *extimare* for *æstimare*, Bechtel 139. Hence sometimes, by analogy, *es-* for *ex-* before vowels, as in **essagium*, but not in *exire.*

At about the same time final *ks* became *s*, except in monosyllables: *cojus, conjus, milex, pregnax = prægnans, subornatris*, etc., in inscriptions, S. 353 (cf. *xanto*, etc.); *felis*, fifth century, Carnoy 159; *App. Pr.*, "*aries* non *ariex*," "*locuples* non *lucuplex*," "*miles* non *milex*," "*poples* non *poplex*."

In parts of Italy *ks* between vowels was assimilated into *ss* by the first century, but this was only local: ALESAN[DER], S. 353; BISSIT BISIT VISIT = *vixit*, S. 353. For *ks > χs*, see § 266.

There are some examples, in late Latin, of a metathesis of *ks* into *sk: axilla > ascella*, Lindsay 102; *buxus > *buscus; vixit >* VIXCIT (i. e., *viscit*), Carnoy 157. Cf. *Vok.* I, 145. On the other hand, *Priscilla >* PRIXSILLA, Carnoy 158. In northern Gaul apparently *sk* regularly became *ks*, as in *cresco, nasco*, etc.: see *Mélanges Wahlund* 145.

256. The voicing of intervocalic surds doubtless began as early as the fifth century; it is shown by Anglo-Saxon borrowings and by such Latin forms as *frigare, migat* in inscriptions and manuscripts; there are many examples from the sixth century: *Lat. Spr.* 474. A. Zimmermann, *Zs.* XXV, 731, finds in inscriptions some slight evidence of a change of *t* to *d* during the Empire, in some places perhaps as early as the first century. According to Loth 21–26, intervocalic *c, p, t* were voiced in Gaul in the second half of the sixth century. Rydberg, *Franz.* ɔ I, 32, maintains, on the evidence of inscriptions and manuscripts, that *t* > *d* in the fifth century and the beginning of the sixth, while *c* > *g* at least two centuries earlier. Cf. *Vok.* I, 125 ff.; *immudavit,* 2d century, Carnoy 121; *eglesia, lebra, pontivicatus,* 7th century, Carnoy 123; *negat, pagandum,* etc., *sigricius* = *secretius,* etc., Haag 27; *cubidus, occubavit,* etc., *stubri,* etc., Haag 27–28; *cataveris* = *cadaveris,* etc., Haag 28–29. Some of the above examples show that consonants followed by *r* shared in the voicing, at least as early as the seventh century.

Voicing was not general, however, in central and southern Italy, Dalmatia, and Dacia.

257. Initial *c* and *cr,* in a few words, became *g* and *gr:* *gaveola; *gratis; crassus + grossus > grassus,* found in the 4th century. Cf. Densusianu 111–112.

(1) *C* AND *G* BEFORE FRONT VOWELS.

258. Before the front vowels *e* and *i* the velar stops *k* and *g* were drawn forward, early in the Empire or before, into a mediopalatal position—*k', g'.* *G* seems to have been attracted sooner than *k:* in Sardinian we find *k* before *e* or *i* preserved as a stop while *g* is not—*kelu, kena, kera, kima, kircare, deghe* < *decem, noghe* < *nucem,* but *reina,* etc.

In Central Sardinia, Dalmatia, and Illyria *k'* went no further, and in Sicily, southern Italy, and Dacia the *k'* stage was apparently kept longer than in most regions: *Lat. Spr.* 472.

259. *G'* by the fourth century had become præpalatal and had opened into *y*, both in popular and in clerical Latin: *Gerapolis* for *Hierapolis*, *Per.* 61, 3; "*calcostegis* non *calcosteis*," *App. Pr.*; CON.GI.GI = *conjugi*, S. 349; *geiuna* = *jejuna*, Stolz 275, Neumann 5, *Lat. Spr.* 473; GENVARIVS, S. 239; GENARIVS, Pirson 75; *agebat* = *aiebat*, *Ienubam* = *Genavam*, *ingens* = *iniens*, Bon. 173; *agebat* = *aiebat*, *agere* = *aiere*, Sepulcri 205; *Gepte*, *Tragani*, *Troge*, Haag 33; *iesta*, D'Arbois 10. Before this happened, *frīgĭdus* in most of the Empire had become *frĭgdus* (*App. Pr.*, "*frigida* non *fricda*"), *vĭgĭlat* had become *vĭglat, and *dĭgĭtus* in some places had become *dĭctus* (*Franz. ə* I, 15–16): cf. § 233.

This *y*, when it was intervocalic, fused, in nearly all the Empire, with the following *e* or *i* if this vowel was stressed: *magĭster* > *mayister > *maẹster;* so *pa(*g*)*é*(*n*)*sis*, *re*(*g*)*ína*, *vi-* (*g*)*ínti*, etc.; similarly perhaps the proclitic *ma*(*g*)*is.* Cf. *Agrientum*, βειεντι = *viginti*, μαειστρο, etc., *Vok.* II, 461 (cf. *maestati*, *Vok.* II, 460); *trienta*, S. 349, Pirson 97; *quarranta* = *quadraginta*, Pirson 97; *æliens*, *colliens*, *diriens*, *negliencia*, Haag 34; *recolliendo*, etc., F. Diez, *Grammaire des langues romanes* I, 250. After the accent, and after a consonant, the *y* regularly remained, except when analogy forced its disappearance (as in *colliens* through *colliente, etc.): *légit*, *léges*, *plángit*, *argéntum.* But sometimes it fused with a following *i* in proparoxytones: *roitus* (= *rógitus* = *rogátus*), *Vok.* II, 461.

Spain, a part of southwestern Gaul, and portions of Sardinia, Sicily, and southwestern Italy remained at the *y* stage; elsewhere the *y* developed further in the Romance languages. Cf. *Lat. Spr.* 473.[1]

---

[1] Some light is thrown on the later *clerical* pronunciation by a statement in a fragment of a tenth century treatise on Latin pronunciation, Thurot 77, to the effect ·*g* has "its own sound" (i. e., that of English *g* in *gem*) before *e* and *i*, but is "weak" before other vowels.

260. *K'* as early as the third century must have had nearly everywhere a front, or præpalatal, articulation: *k'entu, duk'ere.* The next step was the development of an audible glide, a short *y*, between the *k'* and the following vowel: *k'yentu, duk'yere.* By the fifth century the *k'* had passed a little further forward and the *k'y* had become *t'y: t'yentu, dut'yere.* Through a modification of this glide the group then, in the sixth or seventh century, developed into *t's'* or *ts: t's'entu* or *tsentu.*

Speakers were apparently unaware of the phenomenon until the assibilation was complete. There is no mention of it by the earlier grammarians: S. 340. In the first half of the third century some writers distinguish *ce, ka,* and *qu,* apparently as præpalatal, mediopalatal, and postpalatal; in the fifth century we find BINTCENTE, INTCITAMENTO: P. E. Guarnerio in *Supplementi all' Archivio glottologico italiano* IV (1897), 21–51 (cf. *Rom.* XXX, 617). S. 348 cites FES[IT], PAZE (6th or 7th century). Cf. *Vok.* I, 163. Frankish *tins* (German *zins*) is from *census,* borrowed probably in the fifth century: F. G. Mohl, *Zs.* XXVI, 595.[1]

Sc was palatalized also: *crēscĕre, co(g)nōscĕre, fascem, nascĕre, pĭscem,* etc. Cf. CONSIENSIA, SEPTRVM, S. 348.

261. For a discussion of the subject, see H. Schuchardt, *Vok.* I, 151, and *Ltblt.* XIV, 360; G. Paris in *Journal des savants,* 1900, 359, in the *Annuaire de l'École pratique des Hautes-Études,* 1893, 7, in the *Comptes rendus des séances de l'Académie des Inscriptions,* 1893, 81, and in *Rom.* XXXIII, 322; P. Marchot, *Petite phonétique du français prélittéraire,* 1901, 51–53; W. Meyer-Lübke in *Einf.* 123–126, in *Lat.*

---

[1] In the school pronunciation of the seventh and eighth centuries *c* before *e* and *i* was probably *ts.* In the treatise cited in the preceding note, Thurot 77, it is stated that *c* has "its own sound" before *e* and *i,* and is almost like *q* before other vowels.

Spr. 472, in *Bausteine zur romanischen Philologie* 313 ff.; Carnoy 155–160 (who puts the assibilation in the sixth century and earlier). For a possible indication, through alliteration, of a local assibilation of *c* as early as the second century, see *Archiv* XV, 146.

262. For *ce*, *ci*, see Palatals below.

(2) *C* AND *G* BEFORE BACK VOWELS.

263. *K* and *g* before vowels not formed in the front of the mouth usually remained unchanged: *canis, gustus, pacare, negare.* See, however, § 256. Inasmuch as *a* had in Gaul a front pronunciation (§ 194), *ka, ga* in most of that country became *k'a, g'a*, probably by the end of the seventh century, and then developed further: *carum* > Fr. *cher, gamba* > Fr. *jambe.*

Intervocalic *g* before the accent fell in many words in all or a part of the Empire, and apparently remained — perhaps under learned or under analogical influence — in others: AVSTVS from the second century on, Carnoy 127 (cf. AVSTE, S. 349); FRVALITAS, S. 349; so **leālis, *liāmen, *reālis* (for *realis* in *Gl. Reich.*, see *Zs.* XXX, 50); so, too, the proclitic *eo* for *ego*, found about the sixth century, *Vok.* I, 129 (other examples in manuscripts, *Franz. ?* II, 242–243). But *lĭgāre, nĕgāre, pagānus.*

(3) *C* AND *G* FINAL AND BEFORE CONSONANTS.

264. At the end of a word the guttural seems to have been regularly preserved in Vulgar Latin: *dīc, dūc, ecce hīc, eccu'hāc, fac, hŏc, sīc;* cf. Italian *dimmi* (< *dīc mī*), *fammi* (< *fac mī*), *siffatto* (< *sīc factum*).

Occasionally, however, the *c* must have been lost, — mainly,

no doubt, through assimilation to a following initial consonant: FA for *fac*, *Zs.* XXV, 735. In late texts *nec* is often
written *ne* before a consonant, and there is a confusion of *si*
and *sic: Franz.* ǝ II, 215–224, 236–240.

265. Before another consonant *k* and *g* were for the most
part kept through the Vulgar Latin period: *actus, oclus; frigdus,* *viglat (§ 233).

For *kw = qu*, see § 254. For *ks = x*, see § 255.

266. *Kt* in some parts of Italy was assimilated into *tt* by
the beginning of the fourth century, in the south even in the
first century: FATA, OTOGENTOS, in Pompeii, *Lat. Spr.* 476;
AVTOR, LATTVCÆ (301 A. D.), OTOBRIS (380 A. D.), PRÆFETTO,
etc., S. 348; *App. Pr.*, "*auctor* non *autor*"; Festus, "*dumecta*
antiqui quasi *dumecita* appellabant quæ nos *dumeta*," S. 348.

The Celts perhaps pronounced the Latin *ct* as χ*t* from the
beginning, inasmuch as their own *ct* had become χ*t* (e. g., Old
Irish *ocht-n* corresponding to Latin *octo*, Windisch 394, 398–
399); and likewise substituted χ*s* for *ks:* **fa*χ*tum* > Fr. *fait*,
**e*χ*sīre* > Pr. *eissir.* Cf. *Einf.* § 186, *Gram.* I, § 650. The
resultant phenomena can, however, be explained otherwise:
Suchier 735.

267. *Nkt* became ŋ*t*, which seems to have been assimilated
into *nt* in parts of the Empire, probably by the first century·
defuntus, regnancte, sante, Lat. Spr. 472; *santo,* S. 278; *cuntis,
santus,* Carnoy 172.

There is reason to believe, however, that the ŋ was retained
very generally in Gaul and perhaps some other regions, and
subsequently drawn forward to the præpalatal position—*n′:
sanctum* > Fr., Pr. *saint, sanh,* etc.

268. *Gm* became *um: fraumenta, fleuma, Lat. Spr.* 472;
App. Pr. "*pegma* non *peuma*" (i.e., πῆγμα); St. Isidore, "*sagma*

quæ corrupte vulgo *sauma* [or *salma*] dicitur" (i.e., σάγμα),
S. 327. Cf. Italian *soma;* and also *salma*, which comes from
sauma as *calma* from καῦμα. *Soma* occurs in *Gl. Reich.*

269. *Gn* was variously treated in different regions, being
preserved in some, assimilated into *n'* or *n* in others, and sub-
jected to still further modifications: *rænante, renum,* Haag 34.
Cf. *Lat. Spr.* 476.

In *cognōsco* the *g* generally disappeared, the word being
decomposed — after the fall of initial *g* in *gnosco* — into *co-* and
nōsco; similarly the *g* was sometimes lost in *cognatus: Vok.* I,
115–116, *connato, cunnuscit,* etc.

270. *Gr,* between vowels, in popular words apparently
became *r* in parts of the Empire: *fra(g)rare, intĕ(g)rum,
nĭ(g)rum, pere(g)rīnum, pi(g)rĭtia.*

c. PALATALS.

271. Latin *j* was pronounced *y,* being identical in sound
with the consonant that developed out of *ę* and *ị* (§ 224):
jam, conjux, cūjus; ęāmus, habęam, tĕnęat, fīlịa, vĕnịo. Instead
of *i* (=*j*) the spelling *ii* was often used: *coiiugi, eiius,* Neumann, *Fortsetzung* 7.

When *y* followed a consonant, that consonant was often
more or less assimilated, sometimes entirely absorbed by the
y. Palatalization was commonest in Gaul, rarest in Dacia.

272. *Dy* and *gy,* in the latter part of the Empire, probably
were reduced to *y* in vulgar speech: *deōrsum, diŭrnus; adjutare, audịam, gaudịum, hŏdie, ŏdịum, pŏdịum, vĭdęam; exagium,
fageus.* Compare oze = *hodie* (S. 323) and Ζουλεία = *Julia*
(Eckinger 80); zaconvs = *diaconus,* etc. (S. 324) and zesv
= *Jesu,* zvnior = *junior* (S. 239). Cf. *ajutit* = *adjutet,* Pirson
76; *madias* = *maias,* 364 A.D., Stolz 275, Pirson 75, Carnoy

162; *madio = maio*, Haag 34; *magias = maias*, Carnoy 162,
S. 349; *juria = jurgia*, Σεριος *= Sergius*, Carnoy 161; *aios =*
ἅγιος, *Vok.* II, 461; *Congianus = Condianus*, Carnoy 162; *cor-*
ridiæ = corrigiæ, *Remidium = Remigium*, Haag 34; *anoget =*
*inodiat, *Gl. Reich.*

De̦, di̦, however, towards the end of the Empire, had
another—doubtless more elegant—pronunciation, which was
probably *dz: pŏdium >* It. *po̦ggio*, but *mĕdium >* It. *me̦zzo*.
Servius *in Virg. Georg.* II, 216, says, "*Media, di* sine sibilo
proferenda est, græcum enim nomen est," S. 320.   St. Isidore
writes, "solent Itali dicere *ozie* pro *hodie*," S. 321.   The letter
Z is often used in inscriptions, but we generally cannot tell
whether it means *dy, y*, or *dz* (cf. § 339): ZES *= dies*, S. 323;
ζιε *= die*, Audollent 537; ZOGENES, S. 324; cf. *sacritus =* διάκριτος,
Waters Ch. 63.

In most words the vulgar *y* prevailed, in others—especially
in Italy—the cultivated *dz;* from *radius* Italian has both *raggio*
and *razzo*.   The *dz* pronunciation was especially favored after
a consonant: *hŏrdeum >* It. *o̦rzo, prandium >* It. *pranzo*.

273. It appears that the labials were not regularly assimilated in Vulgar Latin: *sapiam >* It. *sappia*, Pr. *sapcha*, etc.
But through the analogy of *audio >* **auyo, vĭdeo >* *veyo, etc.,
and perhaps through slurring due to constant and careless use,
habeo, dēbeo often became *ayo, **deyo:* cf. It. *aggio, deggio*,
beside *abbio, debbio*.   The reduced forms generally prevailed,
but not everywhere.   For *plŭvia* a form *plŏja was substituted
in most of the Empire: cf. §§ 169, 208,(4).

274. *Ly, ny*, between vowels, probably became *l′, n′* before
the end of the Empire: *fīlius, fŏlia, mĕlius, palea, tĭlia; His-*
pania, tĕneat, vĕniam.   This palatal pronunciation may be
represented by the spellings *Aureia, Corneius, fiios*, etc., S. 327.

Lly, *ll'g'*, *l'g'* were probably reduced to *l'* somewhat later: *allium*, *malleus; cŏllĭgit; ex-ēlĭgit.*

Oleum, from ἔλαιον, is an exception: cf. It., Sp. *olio*, Pg. *oleo*, Pr. *oli*, Fr. *huile;* the foreign words borrowed from Latin *oleum* indicate the same irregularity.

For *ry*, see § 296.

275. *Sy*, between vowels, doubtless became during the Vulgar Latin period *s'*, a sound similar to English *sh* in *ship: basium*, *caseus*, *mansiōnem*, etc.

Ssy, *scy*, *sty* were generally assimilated later: **bassiare, fascia, pŏstea.* Cf. *consiensia*, Pirson 72.

For the confusion of *sy* and *ty*, see § 277.

276. *Cy* and *ty*, in the second and third centuries, were very similar in sound, being respectively *k'y* and *t'y* (cf. Fr. *Riquier* and *pitié* in popular speech), and hence were often confused: Ἀρονκιανός = *Aruntianus*, 131 A.D., Eckinger 99; TERMINA-CIONES (2d century), *concupiscencia* (an acrostic in Commodian), *justicia* (in an edict of Diocletian), many examples in Gaul in the 5th century, *Lat. Spr.* 475; *defeniciones* (222–235 A.D.), *ocio* (389 A.D.), *staacio* (601 A.D.), *tercius*, S. 323; *oracionem* (601 A.D.), *tercia*, Pirson 71 ; *mendatium*, *servicium*, etc. Bon. 171 ; especially common in Gallic inscriptions of the seventh century, Stolz 51. Cf. *Vok.* I, 150 ff.; Densusianu 111.

In later school pronunciation *cy* and *ty* were sounded alike. According to Albinus (S. 321) "*benedictio* et *oratio* et talia *t* debent habere in pænultima syllaba, non *c.*" In the treatise published by Thurot (see footnote to § 259), p. 78, we are told that *ti*, unless preceded by *s*, is pronounced like *c*, as in *etiam*, *prophetia*, *quatio*, *silentium;* *ti*, furthermore, is confused with *ci*, the spelling *c* being prescribed in *amicicia*, *avaricia*, *duricia*, *justicia*, *leticia*, *malicia*, *pudicicia*, etc., also in *nuncius*, *ocium*, *spacium, tercius.*   Cf. *Gl. Reich.: audatia, speties, sotium; ambicio, inicio, spacio, tristicia,* etc.

This similarity or identity of sound led, in some cases, either locally or in the whole Empire, to the substitution of suffixes and to other permanent transfers of words from one class to the other: cf. Carnoy 151–154. Hence arose numerous double forms: *condicio conditio, solacium solatium;* later *avaritia –cia,* **cominitiare –ciare, servitium –cium,* etc.; so many proper names, *Anitius –cius,* etc., S. 324. Cf. A. Horning in *Zs.* XXIV, 545. This explains such seemingly anomalous developments as *exquartiare > It. *squarciare,* *gutteare > It. *gocciare,* etc. A number of words evidently had a popular pronunciation with *t'* and a school pronunciation with *k',* or *vice versa:* cf. It. *comenzare cominciare,* etc.[1]

277. *T'y* developed sporadically in the second century, regularly by the fourth, into *ts* (cf. § 260): crescentsian[vs], 140 a. d., S. 323; marsianesses = *Martianenses,* 3d century, Carnoy 154; zodorys = *Theodorus,* etc., S. 324, *Vok.* I, 68; *ampitζatru, Vincentζus,* Audollent 537. Servius *in Don.* (S. 320) says, " Iotacismi sunt quotiens post *ti–* vel *di–* syllabam sequitur vocalis, et plerumque supradictæ syllabæ in sibilum transeunt." Papirius, cited by Cassiodorus (S. 320): "*Justitia* cum scribitur, tertia syllaba sic sonat quasi constet ex tribus litteris, *t, z,* et *i*"; he goes on to state that it is always so when *ti* is followed by a vowel other than *i* (as in *Tatius, otia,* but not in *otii, justitii*), except in foreign proper names or after *s* (as in *justius, castius*). Pompeius says the same thing at considerable length, adding (S. 320), "si dicas *Titius,* pinguius sonat et perdit sonum suum et accipit sibilum." Consentius

---

[1] For a different explanation of the Italian and Rumanian developments, see S. Puşcariu, *Lateinisches ti und ki im Rumänischen, Italienischen und Sardischen,* 1904; reviewed in *Ltbl.* XXVII, 64.

mentions the assibilation in *etiam*, St. Isidore in *justitia*: S.
320–321. Welsh words borrowed from Latin before the fourth
century show no assibilation; but names in *–tiacum*, carried
into Brittany in the second half of the fifth century, are
assibilated (e.g., *Metiacus > Messac*).

At an intermediate stage between *ty* and *ts* — say *t's'y* — the
group, if the *t'* was rather weak, was easily confused with *sy*.
Examples are very numerous: OBSERVASIONE, 5th century,
S. 323, Pirson 71; *diposisio = depositio, hocsies, sepsies*, 6th century, S. 323; *tersio*, Pirson 71; cf. *Vok.* I, 153. Clerical usage
for a while doubtless favored *sy* for *ty*, and many words have
preserved it in various regions, especially in suffixes: *palatium*
–sium, *pretium –sium*, *ratio –sio*, *statio –sio*, *servitium –sium*,
etc.; hence Italian *palagio* beside *palazzo*, etc., and *–igia* beside
–ezza from *–itia*. Cf. *Ltblt.* XXVII, 65; *Rom.* XXXV, 480.

278. *K'y* was assibilated sporadically in the third century,
but not regularly until the fifth or sixth, after the assibilation
of *t'y* was completed: Μαρσιανός = *Marcianus*, 225 A. D., Eckinger 103; *judigsium*, 6th century, Carnoy 154; so *facio*,
glacies, *placeam*, etc. The resulting sibilant was different from
that which came from *t'y: faciam >* It. *faccia*, *vitium >* It. *vezzo*.
But the intermediate stages were similar enough to lead to
some confusion, and the ultimate products have become identical in many regions.

279. For *k', g'*, not followed by *y*, see Gutturals.

d. DENTALS.

280. The dentals were pronounced with the middle of the
tongue arched up and the tip touching the gums or teeth, as
in modern French, and not as in English: S. 301–302, 307.

281. *D* regularly remained unchanged: *dare, perdo, modus,
quid.*

Oscan and Umbrian had *nn* corresponding to Latin *nd:*
Sittl 37. There is some indication that this pronunciation was
locally adopted in Latin: AGENNÆ, VERECVNNVS, etc., S. 311–
312 ; "*grundio* non *grunnio*," *App. Pr.* If this was the case,
the central and southern Italian *nn* for *nd* (as *quannu* for
quando) may go back to ancient times: *Lat. Spr.* 476.

(1) Occasionally *d > l:* old *dacruma > lacrima; App. Pr.*, "*adipes* non
alipes." Cf. Liquids. Cf. § 289, (3).

(2) In a few words *d > r: medidies* by dissimilation > *meridies;* AR-
VORSVM = *adversum*, S. 311 ; Consentius blames "*peres* pro *pedes*," S. 311.
The cases seem to be sporadic and due to different special causes.

282. At the end of a word there was hesitation between *d*
and *t; d* may have been devocalized before a voiceless initial
consonant, and possibly at the end of a phrase : APVD APVT,
S. 365 ; *capud* in Gregory the Great ; FECIT FECED, etc., S. 365 ;
INQVID, SET, etc., S. 366–367 ; *aput, quot, set,* Carnoy 180.
Some of the confusion was doubtless due to the fall of both *d*
and *t:* see § 285.

In proclitics assimilation naturally went further, as we may
infer from the treatment of the prefix *ad–:* people probably
said not only *at te* (cf. *attendere*) but sometimes **ar Romam*
(cf. *arripere*). So the final consonant eventually often disappeared. Cf. S. 358–359. Grammarians warn against the
confusion of *ad* and *at*, etc., S. 365–366. Cf. *ad eos* and *at ea*,
etc., Carnoy 179–180; *id it, quid quit,* Carnoy 180; *a, quo* and
co, Haag 29.

Illud, through the analogy of other neuters, became *illum:*
Haag 29, *illum corpus*, etc.

283. Intervocalic *d*, perhaps at the end of the Vulgar Latin
period, became *ð* in Spain, Gaul, Rætia, northern Italy, and a
part of Sardinia: *vĭdēre > *veðere.* Similarly intervocalic *dr*,

either at the same time or later, became *ðr* in Spain and Gaul: *quadro* > **quaðro*.

In *quadraginta*, *dr* > *rr*: *quarranta*, Pirson 97.

284. *T* usually remained unchanged: *tĕneo*, *sĭtis*, *partem*, *facit*.

Tl, however, seems to have regularly become *cl*: *astŭla* > Pr. *ascla*; *stloppus* > **scloppus* > It. *schioppo*; *ustulare* > Pr. *usclar*. Cf. SCLIT· and SCLITIB· (from *stlis stlitis*), S. 312–313; Caper, "*Martulus* ... non *Marculus*," "*stlataris* sine *c* littera dicendum," Keil VII, 105, 107; *App. Pr.*, "*capitulum* non *capiclum*," "*vetulus* non *veclus*," "*vitulus* non *viclus*." For *–tulus* > *–clus*, cf. § 234.

Between *s* and *l* a *t* developed: Caper, "*pessulum* non *pestulum*" (hence Italian *pestio*, etc.), S. 315. So probably *insŭla* > ** isla* > ** istla* > ** iscla* > It. *Ischia*.

285. Final *t* fell in Volscian (*fasia* = *faciat*), often in Umbrian (*habe*), occasionally in Faliscan: Hammer 5, 7, 8. In early dialects we find such forms as CVPA, DEDE: S. 367. In Latin, final *t* disappeared early in the Empire in southern Italy, and during the Empire in most of Italy and Dacia; Rumanian, Italian (except Sardinian), and also Spanish and Portuguese show no trace of final *t* except in monosyllables. Cf. Hammer 28–32. The first sure examples of the fall in Latin are found in Pompeii; others appear later in the inscriptions in Christian Rome and northern Italy, as *ama*, *peria*, *relinque*, *valia*, *vixi*, etc.: S. 367–368, *Lat. Spr.* 472. Gaul, Rætia, and Sardinia kept the *t* late; but forms without the consonant (as *audivi*, *posui*) — possibly due to Italian stone-cutters — occur in Gallic inscriptions. Fredegarius wrote *e* for *et*: Haag 29.

Final *nt* perhaps lost its *t* before consonants: *Lat. Spr.*

473–474.   The Romance languages show forms with *nt*, with *n*, and without either consonant.   *Nt*, in general, is preserved in the same regions as *t*.   In inscriptions we find: *dedro* and *dedrot*, in Pisaurum, S. 365; *posuerun, restituerun, Lat. Spr.* 473–474.   Cf. Lindsay 124.

Final *st*, likewise, may have lost its *t* before consonants — as *post illum* but *pos' me*, *est amatus* but *es' portatus: Lat. Spr.* 473.   *Pos* is very common in inscriptions, and *es* is found: S. 368.   Cf. *pos, posquam* in R. 470.   According to Velius Longus, Cicero favored *posmeridianus;* Marius Victorinus preferred *posquam:* S. 368.   Both *st* and *s* are represented in the Romance languages.

For the confusion of final *d* and *t*, see § 282: *capud, feced, inquid* are found.   When *t* did not fall, it was doubtless often voiced, inside a phrase, before a vowel or a voiced consonant.

Caput became *capus* (Pirson 238) or **capum*.   Fredegarius uses *capo:* Haag 29.

286.   Intervocalic *t* was voiced to *d* in Spain, Gaul, Rætia, and northern Italy probably in the fifth or sixth century: cf. § 256.   Inscriptions show a few such forms as *amadus*, S. 309. Such a spelling as *retere* for *reddere* (S. 309) may indicate uncertainty in the use of *d* and *t*.

Later this *d* > *ð* in northern Gaul and Spain.   In Gaul and Spain, moreover, *tr* > *dr* > *ðr*.   Cf. § 283.

e. LIQUIDS.
(1) *L.*

287.   *L* had a convex formation, like *d* and *t* (cf. § 280): S. 306–307, 309.

288.   Priscian I, 38 (S. 324) writes: "*L* triplicem, ut Plinio videtur, sonum habet: exilem, quando geminatur secundo loco posita, ut *il-le*, *Metel-lus;* plenum, quando finit nomina vel syllabas et quando aliquam habet ante se in eadem syllaba consonantem, ut *sol*, *silva*, *flavus*, *clarus;* medium in aliis, ut *lectus*, *lectum.*" Consentius distinguishes the "sonus exilis," which he ascribes to initial and double *l* (as in *lana*, *ille*), from the "pinguis," heard *before* a consonant (as in *albo*, *alga*, etc.): S. 326. Other grammarians blame, in obscure terms, a faulty pronunciation of *l* particularly prevalent in Africa or Greece: S. 325–326. See also *Zs.* XXX, 648.

It is likely that *l* before or after another consonant had a thick sound caused by lifting the back of the tongue. *Before* consonants, this formation led in some regions, sporadically by the fourth century but regularly not until the eighth and ninth and later (*Lat. Spr.* 476), to the vocalization of *l* into *u:* καυκουλατῳ in an edict of Diocletian, 301 A.D., Eckinger 12; *cauculus* in manuscripts, *Vok.* II, 494. *After* consonants, this elevation, shifted forwards, brought about the palatalization of *l* in Spanish and Italian: *clavem* > *kl'ave* > Sp. *llave*, It. *chiave*.

According to H. Osthoff, *Dunkles und helles* l *im Lateinischen* in the *Transactions of the American Philological Association* XXIV, 50, intervocalic *l*, except before *i*, also had the thick sound — as in *famulus* (but not in *similis*): thus is explained the different fate of *a* in *calēre* > Old Fr. *chaloir* and *gallīna* > Old Fr. *geline*, etc.

289. During the Latin period *l* regularly remained unchanged: *lūna*, *altus*, *mīlle*, *sōl*. It seems to have fallen in *tribūnal*.

For *ll* > *l*, see § 161. For *ly*, see § 274. For *sl* > *stl*, *skl*, see § 284.

(1) Metathesis occurs occasionally: Consentius (S. 327) blames "*coacla* pro *cloaca*," "*displicina* pro *disciplina*"; cf. *fabŭla* > **flaba* > It. *fiaba*, etc.

(2) There are sporadic examples of the dissimilation of two *l*'s:

App. Pr., "*flagellum* non *fragellum*," "*cultellum* non *cuntellum*"; cf.
MVNTV for *multum*, *C. I. L.* IV, 1593. Cf. S. 327.

(3) Marius Victorinus (Keil VI, 8) says: "Gn. Pompejus Magnus et
scribebat et dicebat *kadamitatem* pro *calamitate*." Cf. § 281, (1).

(2) *R*.

290. *R* in Classic and Vulgar Latin was probably a gingival
or præpalatal trill: S. 307, 309, 328. It generally resisted
change: *rīdet, carrus, cŭrsus, pater.*

291. In many words, however, *rs* > *ss*. The principle seems
to have been that original *rs* remained, while old *rss*, coming
from *rtt*, was early reduced to *ss: Lat. Spr.* 471. Velius
Longus says (S. 330): "*Dossum* per duo *s* quam per *r* quidam
ut lenius enuntiaverunt, ac tota *r* littera sublata est in eo quod
est *rusum* et *retrosum.*" *Russum rusum, susum* occur in early
writers; *dextrosus, introsus, rúsus, suso, susum,* etc., in inscriptions: S. 330. *App. Pr.* has *pessica; Gl. Reich.* has *iusū =
deorsum.* The assimilation was not consistently carried out
everywhere, being probably somewhat hindered by school influence. It took place in the whole territory in *deōrsum* and
sūrsum; in most of the Empire in *dŏrsum;* in about half the
Empire in *pĕrsĭca;* locally in *aliōrsum, retrōrsum, revĕrsus,
vĕrsus.*

After long vowels the *ss* > *s* (see § 161); so *sūssum* > *sūsum,*
while *dŏssum* remained unchanged: *susum,* Waters Ch. 77;
suso susu susum, Bechtel 83: *susum* very common, R. 460–461;
diosum, R. 460. Cf. Corssen I, 243.

292. Moreover, there was a strong tendency to dissimilate
two *r*'s, although it was only sporadically carried out: in Old
Latin, *–aris* after *r* > *–alis*, as in *floralis; App. Pr.*, "*terebra
non telebra*"; in inscriptions we find repeatedly *pelegrinus*

(Sittl 74), also *ministorum, perpenna = Perperna, propietas, propio,* S. 329; *albor, coliandrum, criblare, flagrare, meletrix, plurigo* are attested likewise, *Lat. Spr.* 477. Pompeius (S. 329) says: "Barbarismus, quando dico *mamor* pro eo quod est *marmor.*" Cf. Italian *propio, dietro drieto.*

293. Velius Longus (S. 329) tells us that in elegant speech *per* before *l* was pronounced *pel,* as in *pellabor, pellicere.* Cf. PELLIGE, etc., S. 329. So Italian *per lo > pello, averlo >* (in Old It.) *avello.* This assimilation was probably not widespread in Latin; it has left very few traces in the Romance languages. Cf. Italian *Carlo, merlo, orlo, perla,* etc.

294. Metathesis is not uncommon: S. 330--331. Consentius mentions "*perlum* pro *prælum,*" S. 330. *Crocodīlus* appears as *corcodilus, cocodrilus, corcodrillus,* S. 331; cf. Italian *coccodrillo.* S. 330 notes PRANCATI. For *quatro,* **sempre,* etc., see § 245. An intrusive *r* is found in *culcitra,* Waters Ch. 38.

295. Final *r,* except in monosyllables, fell, probably before the end of the Vulgar Latin period, in most of Italy and Dacia: *sŏror >* It. *suora,* Rum. *soaru.* Sittl 11 mentions an early fall of final *r* among the Falisci and the Marsi, as in *mate, uxo;* cf. FRATE, MATE.

296. *Ry* was probably preserved through the Vulgar Latin period, although it may have been reduced to *y* in parts of Italy: *cŏrium >* *cǫryu and possibly *cǫyu (cf. It. *cuǫio*).

f. SIBILANTS.

297. *S* seems to have been dental, with the upper surface of the tongue convex (cf. § 280): S. 302, 304, 307–308.

The old voiced *s* having become *r* (S. 314–315), Classic Latin *s* was probably always voiceless and remained so in

Vulgar Latin (S. 302–304): this is indicated by the fact that intervocalic *s* is still generally surd in Spanish (*casa*, etc.) and in most popular words in Tuscan (*naso*, etc.); corroborative evidence, as far as it goes, is furnished by such spellings as *nupsi*, *plcps*, *urps*, also *maximus*, *rexi*, etc., and the development of a *p* in such words as *hiemps*, *sumpsi*. At the very end of the Vulgar Latin period, however, intervocalic *s* may have become voiced in some regions (cf. § 256): *causa*, *mīsi*, etc.[1]

Classic Latin *s* was generally preserved: *sĕx*, *ŏssum*, *cŭrsus*, *ĭste*.

298. Final *s* often fell in Umbrian (*kumate*), and occasionally in Faliscan: Hammer 5, 8. Cf. Sittl 27, who cites Umbrian PISAVRESE. In early Latin final *s* was very weak after *ŭ* and *ĭ*, and often was not written. Cicero (*Lat. Spr.* 471) says the loss of –*s* is "subrusticum, olim autem politius." Quintilian also (S. 361) notes the omission of –*s* by the ancients. Ennius and his followers down to Catullus did not count –*s* before a consonant in verse: S. 355–356. Cf. Pompeius (Keil V, 108): "*S* littera hanc habet potestatem, ut ubi opus fuerit excludatur de metro." In the older inscriptions –*s* is freely omitted, but later it is in the main correctly used until the second century of our era: *Lat. Spr.* 471. The omission is commonest in nominative –*ŏs* or –*ŭs*, but occurs also in –*ĭs* and –*ăs*, rarely in –*ās: bonu, Cornelio, nepoti, pieta, Terentio, unu*, etc., and *matrona* for *matronas*, S. 361–362. According to *Chronologie* 175–186, the nominative singular without *s* (as *Cornelio, filio*) predominated in central Italy until the time of Cæsar, when –*s* was partially restored; but by 150 to 200 A. D. the forms without *s* became common

---

[1] In the previously cited Latin treatise (see footnote to § 259), Thurot 77, *s* between vowels is described as "weak," except in compounds, such as *resolvit*. This evidently indicates a voicing in late school pronunciation.

again, and prevailed in central Italy in the third century (*eio* for *ejus*, *liberio*, etc.). Cf. *morbu = morbus*, etc., Audollent 539, 540; *filio = filios*, *C. I. L.* IX, 1938. In most of Italy, and probably in Dacia, final *s* disappeared for good from the common pronunciation in the second and third centuries, except in monosyllables (*Lat. Spr.* 471): *amātis* > It. *amate*, *sĕntīs* > It. *senti*, *tĕmpus* > It. *tempo;* but *das* > It. *dai*, *tres* > Old It. *trei* (later *tre*). Cf. Hammer 19–28, Densusianu 122–123.

In Gaul, Spain, and some other regions, –*s*, probably owing to the previous linguistic habits of the natives, was strongly pronounced and therefore preserved. Carnoy 185–206 records the omission of –*s* in many inscriptions, but notes that as this nearly always happens at the end of a line it is doubtless only a conventional abbreviation.

299. According to Velius Longus (S. 316), *trans–* became *tra–* before *d, j*, and sometimes before *m* and *p: traduxit, trajecit; tra(ns)misit, tra(ns)posuit; transtulit*. We sometimes find, however, *transduco* and *transjicio*. Both forms occur before *l* and *v: tra(ns)luceo, tra(ns)veho*.

Italy generally favored *tra–* (but *trasporre*), Gaul and Spain usually preferred *tras–* (but *traduire, traducir*).

300. In *presbȳter*, a new nominative constructed from πρεσβύτερος, the *s* fell in Italy and elsewhere through the substitution of the prefix *præ–* (as in *præbĭtor*) for the unusual initial *pres–:* hence It. *prete*, Pr. *preveire* (< *præbȳtĕrum*).

301. For prosthetic *i* or *e* before *s* + consonant, see § 230. In Old French *pasmer* (from *spasmus*) the *s* was lost probably through confusion with *es–* coming from the prefix *ex–*.

302. For *ss* > *s*, see § 161. For *sy*, see § 275. For assibilation, see Gutturals and Palatals. For *z*, see § 246 and Greek Consonants.

g. NASALS.

303. *N*, like *d* and *t* (§ 280), was dental or gingival, with an arched tongue: S. 269–270.

M and *n*, initial and intervocalic, regularly remained unchanged: *mĕus, nŏster, amat, vĕnit.* For the reduction of *mĭnus–* to *mis–,* see § 245. There was a dissimilation of two *n*'s in *Bononia* > It. *Bologna.*

304. *M* and *n*, final or followed by a consonant, were obscure and weak in Classic Latin; the preceding vowel must have been partly nasalized, and the mouth closure incomplete. According to Priscian (S. 275), "*m* obscurum in extremitate dictionum sonat, ut *templum,* apertum in principio, ut *magnus,* mediocre in mediis, ut *umbra.*" Terentianus Maurus (S. 275) says that for *n* the air comes through both nose and mouth. So Marius Victorinus (S. 275): "*N* vero sub convexo palati lingua inhærente gemino naris et oris spiritu explicabitur." The same author describes (S. 275) a sound between *m* and *n*: "Omnes fere aiunt inter *m* et *n* litteras mediam vocem quæ non abhorreat ab utraque littera sed neutram proprie exprimat." Cf. S. 276.

305. In Classic Latin the nasal naturally took before labials the form of *m;* before dentals, *n;* before *f* and *v,* probably first *m,* then *n,* as the pronunciation of these fricatives changed from bilabial to dentilabial (cf. § 320); before gutterals, *ŋ: combura, immitto, imperio; conduco, contineo, innocens; comfluo confluo, comvenio convenio; anguis, inquit, uncus* (cf. IVNCXI, NVNCQVAM, S. 278). Cf. S. 270, 279–280. The *ŋ* —or "*n* adulterinum"—is described by Nigidius (in Gellius), and also by Priscian, as between *n* and *g* (S. 275); cf. S. 269–270, 272. Before liquids the nasal was assimilated (*colligo, corrigo,* etc.), before *s* it was silent (*cosul,* etc.: cf. §§ 171, 311).

Final nasals seem to have been adapted, like medial nasals, to a following consonant: *nom paret, cun dūce, nom* or *non fēcit, iŋ carne; nol lĕgo, cur rēgibus, i senātu.* Cicero advocated *cun nobis;* Servius, *cun navibus: Lat. Spr.* 476. In inscriptions we find *cun, locun sanctum, nomem, quan floridos, quen,* S. 364; cf. *forsitam mille,* Bechtel 81 (*forsitam,* Carnoy 220).

306. In the vulgar speech of the Empire the sound before labials seems to have been indistinct, and even before dentals not always clear (S. 271–272); before *f* and *v* there was great uncertainty (cf. §§ 171, 311), and there was apparently some doubt before *gu* and *qu* (S. 272): this is indicated by such spellings as *senper, quamta, nynfis, nunquam,* S. 276–277; *conplere, decemter,* Carnoy 176; *tan mulieribus,* Carnoy 220. Cf. Carnoy 176–177. In both old and late inscriptions the nasal is often omitted altogether before a consonant: *Decebris, exeplu, occubas,* etc., *innoceti, laterna, secudo,* etc., *iferos,* etc., *defuctæ, pricipis, reliquat,* etc., S. 273, 281–285. For the change of *ŋkt* to *ŋt,* then to *nt,* see § 267: *santa,* etc., Pirson 92; *santo,* etc., frequent, S. 278.

The hesitation and inconsistency in spelling are certainly due in part to imperfect articulation, largely to mere careless-ness in cutting, but in great measure also to the mistaken efforts of later writers to restore a real or hypothetical earlier orthography: compare the treatment of prefixes, § 32.

In late Vulgar Latin *m, n, ŋ* must have been reinforced, as there is little trace of confusion in the Romance lan-guages.

307. *Mn* seems at one time to have been pronounced *m:* Quintilian (S. 286) says: "*Columnam* et *consules* exempta *n* littera legimus." Cf. Priscian (S. 275): "*N* quoque plenior in primis sonat et in ultimis partibus syllabarum, ut *nomen,* *stamen;* exilior in mediis, ut *amnis, damnum.*" Carnoy 166 has *Interamico,* for *–amn–,* from the first century.

Late inscriptions, on the other hand, show a fondness for such spellings as *calumpnia, dampnum* (cf. Bon. 189, *calumpnia, dampnare,* etc.); and *mpn* is common in the early Romance languages. It is likely that this orthography indicates a conscious and painful effort to articulate clearly. Toward the end of the Empire fashion evidently prescribed a distinct pronunciation of *mn,* counteracting a previous tendency to slur the group.

The Romance languages point to the preservation of *mn,* although it was probably assimilated into *nn* in central and southern Italy before the Empire was over (*Lat. Spr.* 476): *Interanniensis,* Carnoy 166.

308. Between *m* and *s* or *t* a *p* generally developed in Latin —that is to say, the latter part of the *m* was unvoiced and denasalized before the surd that followed; this *p* was not always written: *sum(p)si, sum(p)tus,* etc. Cf. S. 298.

309. Final *m* often fell in Umbrian (as in *puplu*), occasionally in Faliscan: Hammer 5, 8. In Old Latin it was weak: S. 356. It is often omitted in inscriptions down to 130 B. C., and again in late plebeian inscriptions; in the last century of the Republic and the first two centuries of the Empire the traditional spelling is carefully observed: early and late such forms as *dece, coru, mecu, mense, septe, unu* are very common, and conversely forms with a superfluous *m,* S. 363–364; cf. Audollent 539–540, abundant examples; *App. Pr., ide, numqua, oli, passi, pride.* The omission of *–m* and the wrong use of it are very frequent in the *Per.: que ad modum, terra,* Bechtel 79; *jacente,* etc., *accedere,* etc., Bechtel 80; *dormito* for *dormitum,* Bechtel 91; cf. Bechtel 107. So R. 462, *ardente lucernam*, etc. According to Quintilian (S. 362), Cato said *dice hanc;* he adds that there is scarcely any *m* audible in *tantum ille, quantum erat.*

Final *m* before vowels seems to have been, from early times, only a weak nasal glide: in *circueo* it disappears (S. 274), in poetry it may be disregarded (cf. *audiendu'st*, etc., S. 361). Before consonants it was assimilated (cf. TAN DVRVM, etc., S. 361): see § 305. Cf. S. 356–358, 360. Carnoy 206–221, who notes the omission of −*m* in many inscriptions under all possible conditions, reaches the conclusion that it became silent at the end of polysyllables by the first century, having disappeared very early before vowels, next before spirants and at the end of a phrase, then (by assimilation) before other consonants.

In the opinion of Schuchardt, *Vok.* I, 110–112, the preceding vowel was nasalized. The contrary view is maintained by Seelmann, 288–292. As the fall of *m* seems to have been due primarily to a failure to close the lips completely between two vowels, it is likely that the nasalization was slight.

The Romance languages point to a loss of −*m* in all words but monosyllables: *damnu(m), possu(m), tenea(m); cum, jam, quem* (*quen*, Audollent 537). Cf. Hammer 32–41.

310. Final *n* must have been indistinct (S. 358), but it seems to have been reinforced in Classic speech (S. 286). The prefix *con*− became *co*− before vowels, as in *coactum, cohaerere, cohors, coicere:* S. 274, 282. Before *gn*, too, the final *n* of prefixes fell very early, as in *cognatus, cognosco, ignotus:* S. 274. Otherwise there is no sure proof of the fall of −*n* in Latin (S. 364–365), but there is abundant evidence of its assimilation to a following labial (IM BELLO, etc., S. 361): see § 305; cf. *Lat Spr.* 473. For further assimilation, cf. Caper (Keil VII, 106), "*in Siciliam* dicendum, non *is Siciliam*": see § 311.

The Romance languages indicate the disappearance of –*n*, except in monosyllables: *nōme*(*n*), *sēme*(*n*); *ĭn*, *nōn*. It probably fell late, after the Vulgar Latin period: *Lat. Spr.* 473.

For final *nt*, see § 285.

311. Before fricatives or spirants *n* regularly fell, probably through nasalization of the preceding vowel: see § 171. This phenomenon was only partially recognized by Classic authority: –*ensĭmus* > –*ēsĭmus*, –*iens* > –*iēs*, –*onsus* > –*ōsus*, as in *vicesimus, toties, formosus* (S. 273); *ns*, however, was kept in participles, as *videns, mansus;* both forms were used in –*ē*(*n*)*sis* (according to Velius Longus, Cicero preferred *foresia, hortesia*, S. 287). Charisius (S. 286) records that "*mensam* sine *n* littera dictam Varro ait." Cf. Quintilian (S..286), "*consules* exempta *n* littera legimus."

In popular speech the fall was probably constant from early times: *cesor, cojux, cosol, coventionid, iferos, infas, libes,* etc., S. 274, 281–285; Stolz 243 ff. Plautus repeatedly uses *mostrare,* Stolz 243. Terence seems to intend a rhyme in "neque pes neque mens," *Eunuchus* 728. Such forms are frequent in inscriptions: *cofecisse, cojectis, cojugi* (very common), *covenimus, ifer* (Capua, 387 A. D.), *iferi, ifimo, ifra, iventa, resurges* (on a coin of Vespasian's reign), S. 274, 281–285. So in Greek-letter inscriptions: κλήμης, κόζους, etc., Eckinger 80, 113–115. Cf. Audollent 538, *iferi;* Carnoy 177, *cojugi*, etc., *mesis*, etc.; Pirson 94, *infas, remasit; App. Pr.*, "*ansa* non *asa*"; R. 461–462, *prægnas* repeatedly, *mesor messor = mensor.* Conversely, with a superfluous *n: fidens = fides, quiensces,* etc., S. 274, 285; *thensaurus,* Stolz 243; "*Hercules* non *Herculens,*" "*occasio* non *occansio,*" *App. Pr.; locuplens, occansio, thensaurus,* etc., R. 459.

Before *f, j, v,* the *n* was generally restored by analogy (see § 171); such words as *conjux, convenio* are really new formations: S. 274. The only sure Romance traces of the loss of *n* before these consonants in Latin are Italian *fante* and French *couvent*, although at a later date *nf* became *f* in Rætia and much of southern France.

Before *s*, the fall of *n* was permanent, and the only Romance words containing *ns* are learned terms or new formations: *mẹsa, mẹsis, pẹsat, spọsus, tọsus;* but *pensare*.

h. LABIALS.
(1) *P*.

312. *P* regularly remained unchanged: *pater, ŏpus, cŏrpus*.

(1) There was some sporadic confusion of *p* and *b*: BVBLICÆ, SCRIPIT, S. 299; *App. Pr.*, "*plasta* non *blasta*," "*ziziber* non *ziziper*"; *cannabis* and It. *canapa*.

313. In Italy and perhaps elsewhere there was a tendency to drop *p* between a consonant and an *s* or *t: redemti*, etc., Pirson 93; *scultor*, etc., S. 299.

In a part of Italy *ps* became *ss* as early as the first century: *isse* for *ipse* is found in Pompeii, and is attested by Martial and possibly by the *icse* for *ipse* mentioned by Suetonius, *Lat. Spr.* 476.

In central and southern Italy *pt* became *tt* probably early in the Empire: *scritus*, etc., S. 299; *settembres*, 7th century, Carnoy 165. In a part of Gaul *captīvus* seems to have been pronounced **caχtīvus:* it may be that in Gallic speech the *pt* of this word became *χt*, as was the case with Celtic *pt* (Dottin 100; cf. Old Irish *secht-n = septem*, Windisch 394); or perhaps *captīvus* became first **cactīvus*, under the influence of Celtic **cactos* (Welsh *caeth*) = Latin *captus* (Loth 35).

314. Intervocalic *p* probably became *b* in the fifth and sixth centuries in Spain, Gaul, Rætia, and northern Italy: see § 256. Cf. Pirson 60–61: *labidem*, etc. *Pr* likewise became *br: Abrilis*, Pirson 61; *lebræ*, Bon. 160; *stubrum*, Haag 862.

In northern Gaul intervocalic *p* and *pr*, even in clerical Latin, developed through *b* and *br* into β and β*r* by the seventh century: *rivaticus*, 629 A. D., *Vok.* I, 128; *cavanna*, *Gl. Reich.*

For *pe̦*, *pi̦*, see § 273.

(2) *B.*

315. When *b* was not intervocalic, it usually remained unchanged: *bĕne*, *blĭtum*, *oblītus.*

Mb, as in Oscan and Umbrian, became *mm* in Sicily and southern and central Italy, the *mm* being found in inscriptions as far north as Rome: *Lat. Spr.* 476. Cf. *nd*, § 281.

Before *s* or *t* it is likely that *b* regularly became *p* in Latin, although it was often written *b*: *absens apsens*, *ab– apsolvere*, *plebs pleps*, *scribsi scripsi*, *scribtum scriptum*, *trabs traps*, *urbs urps*; *App. Pr.*, "*celebs* non *celeps*," "*labsus* non *lapsus.*"

Final *b* must have been often assimilated to a following consonant: *sud die*, 601 A. D., Carnoy 165.

316. In the Empire, especially in the second century, initial *b* and *v* were much confused in inscriptions (cf. *V*): *biginti*, *bixit*, *botu*, *vene*, etc., S. 240; *Baleria*, *Balerius*, *Beneria*, *Beneti*, *Betrubius*, *Bictor*, *bos*, *valneas*, Audollent 536; African *birtus*, *bita*, *boluntas*, *Vok.* I, 98; *bivere*, very common, Carnoy 140; *baluis*, Bechtel 78; *vibit*, etc., R. 456; *bobis* in Consentius, *Vok.* III, 68.

In the Romance languages there are few, if any, traces of such an early interchange. Probably the confusion was mainly or wholly graphic, being due to the identitẏ in sound of *b* and *v* between vowels (§ 318): *Lat. Spr.* 473; cf. *Einf.*, § 120. The Spanish levelling of initial *b* and *v* does not go back to Vulgar Latin (Carnoy 139–141); the confusion is far commoner in Italian inscriptions than in Spanish or Gallic (Carnoy 142–146). We find also a change of initial *v* to *b* in north Portuguese, Gascon, south Italian, and Old Rumanian.

317. After liquids, too, there was a confusion of *b* and *v* in inscriptions, *b* being substituted for *v* much oftener than *v* for *b*: *Nerba*, *salbum*, *serbus*, *solbit*, etc., S. 240; *berbex*, Waters Ch. 57; *solbere*, repeatedly, Carnoy 140; *solbere*, etc., R. 455; *App. Pr.*, "*alveus* non *albeus*."

In all probability *v* really changed to *b* after liquids: see *V*. *B* remained unchanged.

318. Intervocalic *b* opened into *β;* the development apparently began in the first century, was well along in the second, and was completed, at least in Italy, in the third: Οὐιονία = *Vibia*, Rome, Eckinger 95; DEVERE, DEVITVM, PROVATA, etc., S. 240. As *v* also was pronounced *β*, a confusion in spelling resulted, *b* and *v* being used indiscriminately: CVRABIT, IVBENTVTIS, NOBE, etc., S. 240; IVVENTE = *jubente*, 2d century, *Einf.* 127, § 120; *cabia* = *cavea*, *Danuvium*, *Dibona*, *iubenis*, *vovis*, etc., Audollent 536–537; *devitum* (6th century), *lebis*, *redivit*, *vibi*, Carnoy 134–135; *annotavimus*, *lebat*, Bechtel 78; *devetis*, *habe* = *ave*, *rogavo*, *suabitati*, etc., R. 455–456; cf. Stolz 51, Pirson 61–62, Carnoy 134-136. Cf. *V*.

When this *β* became contiguous to a following consonant, it was vocalized into *u*: **faula*, **paraula*, **taula*, etc. Cf. *V*.

Intervocalic *br*, perhaps not until the end of our period, became *βr* in northern Gaul, Rætia, part of northern Italy, and Dacia.

(1) In the early stages of clerical Latin intervocalic *b* was pronounced *β*, as in popular speech: **faβula*, **taβula*, etc. Later, perhaps by the seventh century, it was sounded *b*.

(2) In *App. Pr.* we find "*sibilus* non *sifilus*," and Priscian (S. 300) mentions "*sifilum* pro *sibilum*"; cf. French *siffler*. Perhaps the form with *f* comes from some non-Latin Italic dialect: cf. *bubulcus* = It. *bifolco*, and a few other words.

(3) For *habēbam* > **aβęa*, see § 421.

319. *Be̦*, *bi̦* probably remained unchanged, at least in most

of the Empire: *rabies, rŭbeus*, etc.   For the analogical change
of *habeo* to *ayo, *dēbeo* to *deyo, see § 273.

(3) *F.*

320. *F* was originally bilabial (S. 294–295), but became
dentilabial by the middle of the Empire (S. 295): cf. § 305.
It is the old *f*, apparently, that is described by Quintilian
(S. 296–297); a plain description of the dentilabial *f* is given
by Terentianus Maurus and Marius Victorinus (S. 296).

(1) Grammarians speak of an alternation of *h* and *f*: *fœdus* > *hœdus*,
fasena > *harena*, *fircum* > *hircum*, *habam* > *fabam*, etc., S. 300.   The *f* and
the *h* doubtless belonged to different dialects in early Latin; according to
Varro, *Ling. Lat.* 5, § 97, the *f* for *h* was Sabine.   This phenomenon can
have no connection with the change of initial *f* to *h* in Spanish and Gascon.

321. It is probable that intervocalic *f* became *v* at the end
of the Vulgar Latin period (cf. § 256): *alevanti = elephanti*,
paceveci = pacifici, *pontevecem = pontificem*, Haag 32–33.

(4) *V.*

322. The letter *v* was doubtless originally pronounced *w;*
but, losing its velar element, the sound was reduced, probably
early in the Empire, to the bilabial fricative *β*.   During the
Empire Greek-letter inscriptions have ου or *β* for *v* (Νερουα or
Νερβα): Οὐιουία = *Vibia*, Rome, Eckinger 95; *β* for *v* is common from the first century on, Eckinger 85–91.   Velius
Longus, in the middle of the second century, says that the *u*
in *ualente* is pronounced "cum aliqua aspiratione": S. 232.

Hence arises a complete confusion of intervocalic *b* and *v*
(cf. *B.*): CVRABIT, IVBENTVTIS, etc., S. 240; *jubari* for *juvari*
in Gregory the Great.   This leads to a graphic confusion of
initial *b* and *v* in inscriptions: BIGINTI, BIXIT, BOTV, etc. (so
INBICTO), S. 240.

Later the bilabial β became dentilabial v in most of the Empire: cf. § 305.

For the substitution of w for β or v in a few words, see Germanic Consonants.

323. After liquids β seems to have closed regularly into b; this state was preserved in Rumanian (Densusianu 97, 103–105), but elsewhere the β or v was partially restored by school influence: CERBVS, CORBI, CVRBATI, FERBEO, NERBA (about 100 A. D.), SERBAT, SOLBIT, E. G. Parodi in *Rom.* XXVII, 177, cf. § 317. So *vervex* became *verbex, then *berbex*: Waters Ch. 57; BERBECES, 2d century, *Einf.* 127, § 120 (also in *Gl. Reich.*).

Hence came hesitation in spelling (*ferveo*, *ferbui*, etc.) and inconsistent results in the Romance languages: *cŏrvus* > It. *corbo corvo*, Fr. *corbeau;* *cŭrvus* > Old Fr., Pr. *corp*, Sp. *corvo;* *nĕrvus* > It. *nerbo*, Fr. *nerf;* *servare*, *servire* > It. *serbare*, *servire*.

324. Intervocalic w or β had a tendency in older Latin, as in Umbrian, to disappear between two like vowels: *divīnus* > *dīnus* (cf. Umbrian *deivina* > *deina*, Sittl 26), *obliviscor* > *oblīscor*, *si vis* > *sīs*. Cf. Lindsay 52. Also, at all times, before or after o: *bŏvis* > *bōs; devorsum* > *deōrsum; faor*, Pirson 63; *moere*, Audollent 539; Νοεμβριος, *Vok.* II, 479; NOEM[BRIS], S. 241; "*pavor* non *paor*," *App. Pr.;* cf. late *noembris*, *noicius*, Lindsay 52. "*Favilla* non *failla*" in *App. Pr.* seems to be isolated.

In the above cases the fall apparently was only sporadic. But before an accented o or u, the w or β fell regularly in most of the Empire: *aunculus*, *Vok.* II, 471 (cf. *auncli*, Pirson 63); FLAONIVS, S. 241; **paōnem;* *paōrem.

Furthermore, intervocalic w or β regularly disappeared in popular speech before any u, probably towards the end of the Republic (when *–vos* > *–vus*): FLAVS, vIvS, S. 241 (cf. *flaus* in

App. Pr., *vius* in Pirson 63); *oum*, *Vok.* II, 472 (cf. *oum* in
Probus, Keil IV, 113); *nous*, Audollent 539 (cf. *noum*, Pirson
63); *gnæus*, Lindsay 52; *datius*, Carnoy 128; *primitius*, Pirson 63; *aus*, *rius*, *App. Pr.*   Often, however, the *v* was restored, after the analogy of a feminine or a plural form: *ovum*
(beside *oum*) through *ova*, *rivus* (beside *rius*) through *rivi*, etc.
Cf. § 167.

(1) In inscriptions –vs is common in place of –vvs; in most cases this
is probably only graphic: Carnoy 128–131. The ÆVM of *C. I. L.* I, 1220,
cited by Schuchardt (*Vok.* II, 471) and others as *æum*, is evidently intended for *ævum*.

325. When intervocalic *w* or *β* became contiguous to a following consonant, it was vocalized into *u* (cf. *B*): Classic
claudo, *naufragus*, etc.; Vulgar *aucella*, *triumphaut*, etc.

(5) *U*.

326. *U* in hiatus which had not already become *w* (§§ 223–
224) probably took that sound by the end of the Vulgar Latin
period: *eccu' hīc* > *eccwịc, *eccu' ïsta* > *eccwịsta, *nŏcui* > *nọcwi*,
placuit > *placwit*.   Before this, the original Latin *w* (spelled *v*)
had become *β*: § 322.

2. GREEK CONSONANTS.

327. In Greek the surd and the sonant stops must have
been less sharply differentiated than in Latin; the sonants
were perhaps not fully voiced, and the surds doubtless had a
weak, voiced explosion: so they were not always distinguished
by the Latin ear.   The Greek liquids, nasals, and sibilants
usually remained unchanged in transmission.

328. Single consonants sometimes became double in Latin,
and Greek double consonants sometimes became single: νόμος
> *nummus;* ἐκκλησία > *ec(c)lesia*.   Cf. Claussen 847–851.

(1) Β, Γ, Δ.

329. Β, γ, δ regularly remained *b*, *g*, *d:* βλαισός > *blæsus;* γάρον > *garum;* δέλτα > *delta.* Sometimes, however, they were unvoiced into *p*, *c*, *t:* Ἰάκωβος > **Jácopus* (also **Jácomus*); γόγγρος > *conger* ^σ*onger*, σπήλυγγα > *spelunca;* κέδρος > *citrus.* Cf. Claussen 833–838.

Γμ > *um* (cf. § 268): σάγμα > *sagma sauma.*

(2) Κ, Π, Τ.

330. Κ, π, τ generally remained *c*, *p*, *t:* κόλαφος > *colaphus;* πορφύρα > *purpura;* τάλαντον > *talentum.*

Κ, however, often became *g;* π sometimes became *b;* of a change of τ to *d* there is no example, although κάνδιτος for *candidus* (Eckinger 98) seems to point in that direction: Ἀκράγας > *Acragas Agragas*, κάμμαρος > *cammarus gammarus*, κόμμι > *gummi*, κυβερνᾶν > *gubernare*, κωβιός > *gobius;* cf. EGLOGE, PROGNE, S. 346; *App. Pr.*, "*calatus* non *galatus*" (= κάλαθος); the confusion is mentioned by Terentius Scaurus and others, S. 347; — πύξος > *buxus*, πυρρός > *burrus*, cf. *bustiola* in *Gl. Reich.*

Κν > *cin* in κύκνος > *cicinus* > Old. It. *cecino.*

331. After nasals, κ, π, τ regularly came to be pronounced *g*, *b*, *d* in Greek: ἀνάγκη > *anángi*, λαμπρός > *lambrós*, ἄντρον > *ándron.* This late Greek pronunciation perhaps accounts for such cases as καμπή > Lat. *gamba*, τύμπανον > Fr. *timbre*, σάνταλον > Fr. *sandal.* Cf. Claussen 838–841.

(3) Θ, Φ, Χ.

332. The explosives θ, φ, χ became in Old Latin *t*, *p*, *c* (S. 252–253): πορφύρα > *purpura;* old inscriptions, *Pilipus*, etc., S. 259; later inscriptions, *Teodor, nimpæ, Cristo*, etc., S. 259–260. From the middle of the second century B. C. we find the spellings TH, PH, CH: Claussen 823–833. People of fashion undoubtedly tried to imitate the aspirates (Lindsay 54), but popular speech kept the old *t, p, c*, for new words as well as for old: σπαθή > *spatha = spata; κόλαφος > colaphus = colapus,* συμφωνία > It. *zampogna,* φάλαγξ > It., Sp. *palanca,* φαντασία > Pr. *pantaisar;* χορδή > *chorda = corda.*

Quintilian (S. 256) says there were no aspirate consonants in older Latin. Cicero (S. 256) speaks of using the old, unaspirated pronunciation (as *pulcros, triumpos*) in order to be better understood. The proper spelling is discussed by grammarians: S. 257–258.

The letter *h* is occasionally misused, as in PHOSIT, PACHE, etc.: S. 260. It is transposed in *Phitonis, phitonissæ,* Bonnet 141, 218; cf. *Fitonis, Fitones* in *Gl. Reich.*

333. In φάλλαινα > *ballæna,* and some other early adoptions, φ > *b;* perhaps the reason is to be sought in a Greek dialect pronunciation: Claussen 829–831. In δοχή > *doga,* etc., χ > *g:* Claussen 831. In θεῖος > It. *zio* we have a late development of θ; cf. *App. Pr.,* "*Theophilus* non *izofilus*": Claussen 833.

(1) Evidence of a late school pronunciation of θ as *ts* is to be found in Thurot 78, 79 (cf. footnote to § 259): " *T* quoque, si aspiretur, ut *c* enuntiatur, ut *æther, nothus, Parthi, cathedra, catholicus, etheus, Matheus*". . . "In principio inquam dictionis nulla prescripta causa variari compellitur, ut *thiara, Thiestes, Thestius, Thescelus, Theos.*"

334. By the first century A. D., φ had developed into *f* in some places (S. 261): DAFNE occurs in Pompeii, Claussen 828; *f* is common later in southern Italy, S. 261. Certainly as early as the fourth century (Lindsay 58) *f* came to be the standard pronunciation: *App. Pr.,* "*amfora* non *ampora*," "*strofa* non *stropa*"; Bechtel 79, *neofiti;* so ὀφήκιον for *officium,* etc., Eckinger 97. In late words φ regularly appears as *f:* φάσηλος > *phaselus faselus;* κέφαλος > It. *cefalo;* etc.

(4) Liquids, Nasals, and Sibilants.

335. The liquids regularly remained unchanged: λαμπάς >
lampas; ῥήτωρ > *rhetor.* *Rh* in common speech was doubtless
pronounced like *r.*

In σέλινον > It. *sẹdano,* and a few other words, we probably
have to do with a late Greek change of λ to δ.

336. The nasals, too, regularly remained unchanged: μαῦρος
> *maurus;* νομή > *nome.* There are, however, some indica-
tions that they were weak before consonants: βόμβος > Pr.
bobansa, etc. Cf. Claussen 845.

337. Of the sibilants, σ and ξ were regularly unchanged:
σίναπι > *sinapis;* ἔξοδος > *exodus.* In ὀσμή? > It. *orma,* σ has
probably become *r.* For πρεσβύτερος > *prebiter,* see § 300.

The unfamiliar combination ψ lent itself readily to metathesis: ψάλλειν > *psallere spallere.*

For ζ, see below.

(5) Z.

338. Z doubtless had several pronunciations in Greek. In
early Latin it was represented by *ss* or *s:* μάζα > *massa,* ζώνη
> *sona* (Plautus). From Sulla's time on it was written *z* in
Latin: Claussen 841–843. The grammarians throw no light
on the Latin pronunciation. Quintilian refers only to the
Greek letter and the lack of a corresponding Latin one; Velius
Longus discusses *z* at length, as a simple sound, but seems to
be referring only to Greek speech: S. 308. Priscian (Keil II,
36) says that ζ is sounded *sd,* but was often replaced, among
the ancients, by *s, ss,* or *d*—as in *Saguntum, massa, Medentius.*

339. Judging from inscriptions, it was pronounced in Vulgar Latin *dy,* later *y* (cf. § 272), and subsequent developments
confirm this view: *baptizare* was equivalent to *baptị(d)yare,*

zelosus to (*d*)*yelosus.* The ending –*ḭ*(*d*)*yare* became very common: see § 33.

The spelling *di* for *z* occurs repeatedly: *baptidiare* is found several times in *Per.* (90, 22, etc.; cf. Bechtel 79), and is common in inscriptions (cf. *baptidiatus,* Carnoy 163); *oridium* for ὄρυζα, *Lat. Spr.* 473. Conversely, *z* is often used for *di:* ZABVLLVS, *Vok.* I, 68; *zabulus, zacones,* Koffmane 38; *Lazis = Ladiis, zabulus, zaconus, zebus, zeta = diæta, zosum = deorsum,* R. 457–458.

In late inscriptions *z* for *j* is common: *zerax =* ἱέραξ (202 A. D.), *zanuari, Vok.* I, 69; ZESV, ZVNIOR, S. 239; Ζουλεία=*Julia,* κόζους = *conjux,* Eckinger 80. Cf. *septuazinta,* Carnoy 163.

3. GERMANIC CONSONANTS.

340. Most of the consonants offer no peculiarities, being treated as in Latin. A few, however, had no Latin equivalents: *ð, þ, h,* and *w.* Furthermore, *b* and *k* came in after the corresponding Latin sounds had undergone some modification.

341. *B* between vowels, occurring apparently only in words adopted after Latin intervocalic *b* had become β (§ 318), remained a stop: *roubôn* > It. *rubare,* *strîban > Pr. *estribar.*

G, although it can scarcely have come in time to share in the early palatalization of Latin *g* before front vowels (§§ 258 ff.), seems to have followed a similar course, and to have participated also in the later Gallic palatalization of *g* before *a* (§ 263): *gilda* > It. *geldra,* *gîga > Pr., It. *giga, geisla* > Pr. *giscle; garba* > Fr. *gerbe, garto* > Old Fr. *jart.*

K resisted front vowels: *skëna* > Sp. *esquena, skërnôn* > It. *schernire;* so *rîk-ĭtia > Pr. *riqueza,* etc. *Franko* seems to have been an early acquisition, and its derivatives palatalized their *k* before *e* and *i: frank-ĭscus* > It. *Francesco,* etc. In the

regions where Latin *c* was palatalized, in the seventh century
and later, before *a* (§ 263), Germanic *k* was modified in the
same way before all front vowels (including *a*): cf. Old Fr.
eschine, *eschernir*, *richesse;* so *blank-a* > Fr. *blanche* (but It.
bianca).

342. The spirants *ð* and *þ* were replaced in Latin by the
corresponding stops, *d* and *t:* *wiðarlon* > It. *guiderdone; hau-
niþa* > Fr. *honte*, *þahso* > It. *tasso*, *þarrjan* > Fr. *tarir*, *þrèscan*
> Pr. *trescar.* Cf. Kluge 500.

343. Germanic *h* appeared when Latin *h* had long been
silent in popular speech.

At the beginning of a word it kept its sound in northern
Gaul, but apparently was neglected in the rest of the Empire:
hanca > Fr. *hanche*, Sp. *anca; hapja* > Fr. *hache*, Pr. *apcha;
hardjan* > Fr. *hardir*, It. *ardire; hëlm* > Old Fr. *helme*, It.
elmo.   Bon. 445 notes that *ab*, rather than *a*, is used before
initial *ch: ab Chilperico*, etc.

Intervocalic *h* disappeared in most words, but in a few—
perhaps borrowed at a different date—it seems to have been
sounded *kk* in the greater part of the Empire: *fëhu* > Fr., Pr.
feu, It. *fio; skiuhan* > Fr. *esquiver*, It. *schivare; spëhôn* > Old
Fr. *espier*, Pr. *espiar;* — *jëhan* > Old Fr. *jehir*, Pr. *gequir*, It.
gecchire, Old Sp. *jaquir.*

Hs, *ht* were generally treated like Latin *ss*, *tt: þahso* > It.
tasso; — *slahta* > Old Fr. *esclate*, Pr. *esclata*, It. *schiatta; slëht*
> Pr. *esclet*, It. *schietto.*   But *wahta*, doubtless adopted at a
different time, became Old Fr. *gaite*, Pr. *gaita;* cf. It. *guatare.*

344. Germanic *w* was a strong velar and labial fricative,
at a time when original Latin *w* (spelled *v*) had become
the purely labial fricative *β* (§ 322).   It was nearer in
sound to Latin *u:* see § 326.   In the *Gl. Reich.* we find it

represented by *uu*, in *uuadius, reuuardent*, etc. Bon. 167 records *Euua, wa* (the interjection), *Waddo, walde, Wandali*,
etc. It is generally written *w* in Fredegarius, but *Wintrio* is
spelled *Quintrio:* Haag 38.

In extreme northern and eastern Gaul, in northwestern
Italy, and in Rætia this *w* apparently remained unchanged
in the Vulgar Latin period; elsewhere, through a reinforce-
ment of its velar element, it became *gw: warjan* > *warịre
guarịre, wërra > *wẹrra guẹrra, wîsa* > **wisa guịsa.*

Through association with Germanic words, the β of some
Latin words was changed to *w: vadum + watan* > *wadum,
vastare + wost– > *wastare, etc.

See E. Mackel, *Die germanischen Elemente in der französischen und
provenzalischen Sprache*, 1884; W. Waltemath, *Die fränkischen Elemente
in der französischen Sprache*, 1885; W. Bruckner, *Charakteristik der germanischen Elemente im Italienischen*, 1899.

IV. MORPHOLOGY.

A. NOUNS AND ADJECTIVES.

1. GENDER.

345. The three genders of Latin were not, in the main, dependent on sex or lack of sex. They were grammatical distinctions, whose observance was a matter of outward form. If words lost their differentiating terminations, confusion of gender ensued.

a. MASCULINE AND FEMININE.

346. Between masculine and feminine there was not much confusion, but there were some important shifts:—

(1) Feminines of the second declension nearly all became masculine: *fraxĭnus*, etc.; cf. *castaneus* for *castanea*, Bon. 194. Feminines of the fourth declension varied (*Gram.* II, 461): *dŏmus, fīcus, manus*.

(2) In Gaul, abstract nouns in *–or*, through the analogy of the great majority of abstract terms, became feminine (Bon. 503–504): *color, honor, Lat. Spr.* 483; *dolor, timor*, Bon. 504.

(3) Nouns that had a proparoxytonic accusative in *–erem, –icem, –inem, –orem*, or *–urem* were of uncertain gender (*Gram.* II, 464–467): *carcĕrem, pulĭcem, margĭnem, lepŏrem, turtŭrem.*

(4) There were some sporadic changes: *duos arbores*, Pirson 157; *cucullus* and *cuculla*, G. 293; *fons* feminine in late Latin, *Lat. Spr.* 483; *grex* became feminine.

(5) See also § 351.

b. MASCULINE AND NEUTER.

347. In Classic Latin a number of neuters became masculine: *balteum –us, caseum –us, cornu –um –us, frenum –i, nasum –us, tergum –us, vadum –us;* cf. *collus –um, lectus –um.*

In popular and late Latin this tendency was strong: ante-Classic, m. *papaver;* Plautus, m. *guttur, dorsus* (*Mil. Glor.* II, 4, 44), *lactem* (*Bacch.* V, 2, 16)); Varro, m. *murmur;* Petronius, *balneus, cælus, fatus, lactem, vasus –um, vinus,* etc., Waters Ch. 39, 41, 42, 57, Densusianu 129, 132; *collus, me[nt]us,* etc., Audollent 545; MARIS, MAREM, Densusianu 132; *castellus, fænus, lignus, signus, templus, verbus, vinus,* etc., R. 266; *sulphurem,* G. 293; *frigorem, maris* nom. sg., *marmorem, pectorem, roborem,* Bon. 348; *incipit judicius,* etc., D'Arbois 135. Beside *lūmen, nōmen, pĭper* there must have been **lūmĭnem, *nōmĭnem, *pĭpĕrem.*

Conversely we find *cĭnus,* n., for *cĭnis, cĭner,* m.; there must have been a **pŭlvus,* n., beside *pŭlvis,* m. and f. (*Lat. Spr.* 483); Petronius has *thesaurum,* Waters Ch. 46.   Cf. *gladium, laqueum, puteum, thesaurum,* etc., R. 270–272.

Cf. Bon. 345–349, 507–509. For the confusion of masculine and neuter in Africa, see *Archiv* VIII, 173.

348. The transition from masculine to neuter was facilitated by the fall of final *m* (§ 309), and also by the fall of final *s* in the regions where that phenomenon occurred (§ 298). These changes reduced considerably the distinguishing marks of the two genders:—

filiu(s)	*foliu*	*come(s)*	*corpu(s)*
filii	*folii*	*comiti(s)*	*corpori(s)*
filio	*folio*	*comiti*	*corpori*
filiu	*foliu*	*comite*	*corpu(s)*
filio	*folio*	*comite*	*corpore*
filii	*folia*	*comite(s)*	*corpora*
filioru	*folioru*	*comitu*	*corporu*
filii(s)	*folii(s)*	*comitibu(s)*	*corporibu(s)*
filio(s)	*folia*	*comite(s)*	*corpora*
filii(s)	*folii(s)*	*comitibu(s)*	*corporibu(s)*

In the second declension the only difference is in the nominative singular and the nominative and accusative plural; and
in Italy and Dacia the distinction disappears even in the
nominative singular.   In the third declension the genders are
distinguished only in the accusative singular and the nominative and accusative plural.

349. Thus the masculine and neuter inflections came to be
fused, the characteristic neuter plural –*a* being regarded as an
alternative masculine plural ending: Petronius writes *nervia*
for *nervi*, Waters Ch. 45; cf. *rivus rivora*, Zs. XXX, 635.   So
lŏcus, mūrus, for instance, give in Italian: sg. *luogo, muro;* pl.
luoghi luogora, muri mura.   Cf. § 351.

Nearly all neuters became masculine: *os locutus est*, R. 266;
donum cælestem, etc., R. 277; *hunc sæculum, hunc stagnum, hunc
verbum, hunc vulnere*, Bon. 386, 348.   *Mare*, however, perhaps
influenced by *terra*, generally became feminine: *maris*, m. and
f., Densusianu 132; *mare*, f., Haag 48.   Greek neuters in –*ma*,
if popular, generally became feminine: *cyma, sagma*.

The loss of the neuter gender for nouns was probably not
complete until early Romance times.   Cf. *Archiv* III, 161.

350. Among pronouns, the neuter forms were kept to express
an indefinite idea: *hŏc, id ĭpsum, ĭllud* or *ĭllum, quĭd, quŏd*.

Neuter adjective forms were used for a similar purpose: in
the early stages of the Romance languages we find phrases
pointing to such Vulgar Latin constructions as **mihi est grave
quod ille non veniat*, etc.

c. FEMININE AND NEUTER.

351. Classic Latin often used not only the singular for the
plural in a collective sense (as *eques, miles*, etc., in Livy: cf.
Draeger I, 4), but also the collective plural for the singular

(as *frigora, marmora, rura:* cf. Draeger I, 5–9; *Archiv* XIV,
63). So the neuter plural forms in *–a* were preserved in their
collective use after the neuter singular forms had disappeared.

This formation in *–a* was extended to many masculine
(cf. § 349) and even to some feminine nouns: *digita, fructa,
fusa, grada* occur in late Latin, *Lat. Spr.* 482. Cf. Old Fr.
crigne < ? **crīnea* = *crīnes;* It. *dita, frutta,* etc.; Sardinian,
Apulian, Rumanian *frunza* < ? **frondia* = *frondes.*

352. In late Latin and early Romance this collective plural
in *–a* came to be taken for a feminine singular: *tribula* sg.,
R. 269; *gaudia* sg., Bon. 351; *ligna ... ardet* (cf. *rama*), *Gl.
Reich.; hic est iesta,* D'Arbois 10; cf. *ne forte et mihi hæc eve-
niat,* etc., R. 435. The feminine character of such words was
doubtless reinforced by the use, for instance, of an **illæ pectora*
to match *quæ pectora: Chronologie* 199. Conversely, *palpebrum*
for *palpebra* occurs, R. 270.

Hence arose such feminine singular forms as **brachia, *folia,
gaudia, gesta, ligna,* etc., for which a new plural was created:
brachias, Audollent 548; *armentas, membras, Gl. Cassel; inge-
nias, simulachras, Gl. Reich.*

In most of the Romance territory the *–a* forms were kept
only as feminine singulars, but many were preserved as plurals
in central and southern Italy and Rumania.

353. Aside from these, few neuter nouns became feminine:
marmor, f., occurs in late Latin, *Lat. Spr.* 483. For *mare* and
Greek neuters in *–ma,* see § 349. For *cinus* = *cinis, *pulvus* =
pulvis, see § 347.

2. DECLENSION OF NOUNS.

354. For the use of cases, see §§ 85–100. By the end of
the Vulgar Latin period the cases were generally reduced,

except in Dacia, to two,—a nominative and an accusative-ablative,—the plural following the analogy of the singular. In Dacia the dative singular was to some extent preserved also: § 91. Cf. K. Sittl in *Archiv* II, 550.

355. The number of declensions was reduced to three, the fourth and fifth being absorbed by the others.

(1) The transfer from the fourth to the second began in Classic Latin and continued in vulgar and late speech: *dŏmus, fīcus,* so *frūcti, senāti; gustus* in Petronius; *manos,* Audollent 544; *jusso, passos,* Bechtel 86; *cornum, fructo fructos, gelus, genum, gradus, senatus, spiritus,* etc., R. 260–262, 270; *lacus, mercatus,* G. 282–283; *jusso, lucto,* etc., Bon. 135. All the fourth declension eventually went over. One result of the intermediate confusion was an accusative plural spelling *–us* for *–os,* which was very common in Gaul: Bon. 337–338.

(2) The transfer of nouns in *–ies* from the fifth to the first declension began also in Classic Latin: *effigies –ia, luxuries –ia, materies –ia. Acia, facia, glacia, scabia* are attested later: Densusianu 133, *Lat. Spr.* 482. All passed over in the greater part of the Empire; but *–ies* was kept in the Spanish peninsula, in southern Italy and Sardinia, and occasionally in southern Gaul, being assimilated to the third declension: cf. Sp. *haz,* Pr. *glatz,* etc. *Dies* maintained itself, as a third declension noun, beside *dia.*

Fifth declension nouns not in *–ies* went into the third: *res rem, spes spem,* etc. There was also an inflection *spes spene(m),* whence Italian *spene* (cf. SPENI): W. Heræus in *Archiv* XIII, 152.

356. The other declensions generally held their own, but there were a few shifts:—

(1) For an inflection *mama mamāne(m),* etc., see § 359.

(2) For an inflection *Bellus Bellōne(m)*, etc., see § 362. Beside *ervum ervi*, there was an *e̜rvus ervoris: Lat. Spr.* 483. *Fĭmus fĭmi*, under the influence of *stĕrcus*, apparently became *fĕmus* (*Gl. Reich.*) *fĕmŏris: cf. Old Fr. *fiens*, Pr. *femps*. *Fŭndus fŭndi* perhaps became *fŭndus* **fŭndŏris:* Old Fr. *fonz*, Pr. *fons*, Fr. *effondrer*.   Beside *termĭnus –i*, there was a *termĕn termĭnis*.

(3) On the other hand, *ŏs* > *ŏssum* (R. 259–260), *vas* > *vasum vasus* (Waters Ch. 57); so apparently *ros* > *rōsum (cf. Fr. *arroser*, It. *rugiada*, etc.); beside *coclear* there was *coclearium*. *Caput* became *capus* (Pirson 238) and **capum –i:* cf. *Ltblt.* XXVII, 367.   *Corpo* for *corpore* occurs in the *Per.*: Bechtel 86.

Greek nouns of the third declension sometimes passed into the first: *absis* > *absida*, G. 280; *lampas* > *lampada*, R. 258–259, G. 280, Dubois 258; *pyxis* > **buxida; siren* > *sirena*, G. 280.   So a few Latin nouns: *juventus* or *–tas* > *juventa*, likewise *tempesta* (*Gl. Reich.*) and probably **potesta;* but the old forms were retained also.   *Puulva* for *pŭlvis* is recorded by Audollent 416.

a. FIRST DECLENSION.

357. In countries which did not lose final *s* (§ 298), the accusative plural form came to be used as a nominative plural. This use was due in the main to the analogy of the singular, where there was only one form, and of feminine nouns of the third declension, which had only one form in the plural: *filia filia(m)*, *matres matres*, hence *filias filias*.   So *linguas*, Audollent 546.   It probably was not common until late Vulgar Latin or early Romance times.

In Italy and Dacia, where the fall of *–s* made the accusative plural identical with the singular, the nominative plural was kept instead.

(1) According to Mohl, *Chronologie* 205–209, the nominative plural in
–*as* was probably old in some parts of Italy: SCALAS, nom., 57 B.C.; LIBERTI
LIBERTASQVE, Dalmatia; HIC QVESCVNT DVS M̄RES DVAS FILIAS, Africa.
M. Bréal, *Journal des savants* 1900, Feb., p. 70, affirms that there was a
feminine in –*a* with a plural in –*as* in Oscan, and also in Latin down to
the second century B. C.; Celtic, too, had a similar plural. D'Arbois 21–24
assumes Celtic influence: *hic sunt cartas*, etc. No foreign influences are
needed to explain the practice, but they may have helped its diffusion.

358. An ablative in –*abus* is occasionally found : *Cassiabus,
feminabus, filiabus, pupillabus*, *Archiv* VIII, 171 ; *deabus, filiabus*, etc., Pirson 115–116 ; *animabus, famulabus, filiabus, vil-
labus*, Bon. 331. This form left no traces in Romance.

359. Feminine proper names and words denoting persons
often developed, rather late, an inflection in –*ánis*, etc., or
–*énis*, etc., probably under the influence of the consonantal
declension of Greek names that was in vogue in schools.
Pupils were taught to inflect *Glaucé Glaucénis, Nicé Nicénis*,
etc. (R. 264); cf. Dante's *Semelé*, etc.: hence arose *Anna
Annánis* or –*énis, mamma mammánis, amita *amitánis* (so
Juliana Julianenis in Pirson 143), cf. W. Heraeus in *Zs. fr.
Spr.* XXV, ii, 136. Some masculine person-names in –*a* had
the same declension (*Einf.* 150, § 153): *barba barbani, sa-
crista *sacristanis* (cf. It. *sacristano*), *scriba *scribanis* (cf. It.
scrivano). Both *mamani* and *tatani* are found in the third
century: W. Heraeus in *Archiv* XIII, 152–153. See G. Paris,
Les accusatifs en –ain, *Rom.* XXIII, 321 ; E. Philipon, *Les
accusatifs en* –on *et en* –ain, *Rom.* XXXI, 201 ; W. Meyer-
Lübke in *Ltblt.* XXV, 206 ; G. Salvioni in *Rom.* XXXV, 198.
In *Lat. Spr.* 483, Meyer-Lübke expresses doubt whether the
feminine –*a* –*anis* is connected with masculine *tatani*, etc.

This feminine inflection left some traces in Gaul, Raetia, and
Italy: Fr. *nonnain, putain*, etc. ; Lombard *madrane*, etc., *Rom.*
XXXV, 207.

(1) G. Salvioni, *La declinazione imparisillaba in* –a –*áne,* –o –*óne,* –e *éne* –*íne,* –i *íne* –*éne, Rom.* XXXV, 198, shows that these forms of declension were very common in the mediæval Latin documents of all parts of Italy, from 750 on: *amitane,* 218; *Andreani,* 216; *barbane,* 214–215; *domnani,* 219; *Joanneni,* 250; etc. *Attane, barbane* still exist at both ends of Italy. According to Salvioni, the starting-point of all this inflection was *bárba barbánis,* from which it was extended to other nouns of relationship and to proper names; *bárba barbánis* itself he would ascribe to the influence of the synonymous *bárbo **barbónis.* A Germanic origin is postulated by J. Jud, *Recherches sur la génèse et la diffusion des accusatifs en* –ain *et en* –on, 1907; also in *Archiv fur das Studium der neueren Sprachen* XXIV, 3–4, 405.

(2) A. Zimmermann, *Zs.* XXVIII, 343, shows that there was also an inflection in –*átis,* –*étis,* and –*ótis: Aureliati, Agneti,* etc. Cf. *Eugeneti* from *Eugenes,* R. 264, Dubois 250; *Andreate, Rom.* XXXV, 216; also *Joannentis, Rom.* XXXV, 250.

360. In general, at the beginning of the Romance period, the first declension was reduced to this pattern:—

luna	*facia*	*folia
luna	*facia*	*folia*
lune lunas	*facie facias*	*folie folias*
luna(s)	*facia(s)*	*folia(s)*

In Dacia the dative singular (*lune,* etc.) was kept also.

b. SECOND DECLENSION.

361. As neuter nouns became masculine, they assumed, partly in Vulgar Latin but mostly in Romance, the masculine inflection in those countries where the masculine and neuter differed: *vinus,* etc. Cf. §§ 347–349.

The plural in –*a,* however, was retained to a considerable extent, especially in southern and central Italy and Dacia. Some masculines took this –*a,* by the analogy of *bracchia,* etc.: **botella,* **botula, digita, fructa, rama,* etc. Cf. §§ 349, 351–352.

362. From the seventh century on,—perhaps under Germanic influence combined with the analogy of the Latin type *gúlo gulónis*, etc.,—there developed in Gaul, Rætia, Italy, and possibly Spain, a declension *–us* (or *–o*) *–ónis* for masculine proper names: *Húgo Hûgon* was Latinized into *Húgo Hugóne(m)* (cf. § 152); *avus avi* > *avo avonis*, attested in Lucca in 776 (*Rom.* XXXV, 204); hence *Pétrus* or *Pétro Petróne(m)*, *Paulus* or *Paulo Paulóne(m)*, etc.   Cf. Pirson 133: *Bellus Belloni, Firmus Firmonis*.   See E. Philipon in *Rom.* XXXI, 201; G. Salvioni in *Rom.* XXXV, 198.

Traces of this inflection are to be seen especially in French and Provençal proper names: *Foucon, Huon*, etc. So perhaps Italian *Donatoni, Giovannoni*, etc., and possibly Corsican *baboni, suceroni: Rom.* XXXV, 212–213.

363. In general, at the beginning of the Romance period, the second declension followed this pattern:—

annu(s)	*faβe(r)*	*vinu(s)*	*bracciu *–us*	*fructu(s)*
annu –o	*fabru –o*	*vinu –o*	*bracciu –o*	*fructu –o*
anni	*fabri*	*vini*	*braccia –i*	*fructi –a*
anno(s)	*fabro(s)*	*vino(s)*	*braccia –o(s)*	*fructo(s) –a*

The letters enclosed in parentheses were silent in Italy and Dacia.   In Gaul the accusative plural ending was often spelled *–us:* Bon. 337–338; cf. § 355, (1).

c. THIRD DECLENSION.

364. In the ablative there was considerable confusion of *–ī* and *–ĕ* in Classic Latin: *marī marĕ, turrī turrĕ*, etc. This was carried further in common speech: cf. *Vok.* II, 85, 87. The ablative in *–ĕ* finally triumphed, but there are some traces of *–ī:* It. *pari*, etc.

365. In the accusative plural there was still greater confusion of *–īs* and *–ēs* (*nubēs nubīs*, etc.), both in Classic and in Vulgar Latin: cf. *Vok.* I, 247–249. Apparently *–ēs* crowded out the rarer *–īs*, which left no sure traces.

Italian *pani*, etc., Rumanian *pînî*, etc., are best explained, as by Tiktin 565–566, through the analogy of the second declension: see § 368.   Cf. *folli* for *folles* in *Gl. Reich.*

366. In the nominative singular the common *–ĭs* largely displaced the less frequent *–ēs: Vok.* I, 244–247, III, 116; Caper, "*fames* non *famis*," Keil VII, 105; *App. Pr.*, "*nubes* non *nubis*"; *œdis, famis, nubis*, etc., R. 263; *famis*, etc., Sepulcri 220.

As *–ēs* and *–ĭs* came to be pronounced alike before the end of the Vulgar Latin period (cf. §§ 174, 243), it is futile to trace the Romance forms phonetically to one source rather than the other.

367. Nouns which added a syllable in the genitive, without a change of accent, tended in popular speech to use for the nominative a form in *–is, –es,* or *–e* fashioned on the model of the oblique cases: so *sæps > sæpes, stips > stipes; Jovis*, nom., in Ennius, Varro, Petronius (Waters Ch. 47); *lacte* in Ennius, Plautus, Petronius (Waters Ch. 38), Apuleius, Aulus Gellius; *bovis* in Varro, Petronius (Waters Ch. 62); *carnis* in Livy; *stirpis* in Livy, Prudentius; *suis* in Prudentius (F. D'Ovidio in *Raccolta di studii critici dedicata ad Alessandro D'Ancona* 627); *lentis* in Priscian; *calcis* in Venantius Fortunatus; *divite*, etc., Audollent 545–547; "*grus* non *gruis*," *App. Pr.; principens* (= *principis*), R. 263; *antestetis, superstitis, Vok.* III, 9; *urbis*, Haag 45; *pedis, travis* (three times), *Gl. Reich.;* cf. *Chronologie* 203, *Lat. Spr.* 481.   These forms prevailed in Romance, perhaps in late popular Latin.

In Vulgar Latin this formation was extended to words with a shift of accent: *excellente* for *excellens* in Petronius, Waters Ch. 45, 66; *audace, castore, latrone, victore, voluntate*, etc., Audollent 545–547; *heredes*, R. 263; *cardonis, papilionis* (cf. *aculionis* for *aculeus*), *Gl. Reich.; heredes*, etc., D'Arbois 85–88.

These forms, too, prevailed in Romance, except for names of
persons, which, being used mainly in the nominative and
vocative, retained and generally preferred the old nominative
form: *hŏmo*, *sŏror*, etc.; *cantātor*, *servītor*, etc.   But names of
persons in *–ans* and *–ens* usually made over the nominative:
parentis, etc. (also *presentis*, etc.), D'Arbois 85–88; so, no
doubt, *amantis, etc. (also *clamantis, etc.), but *infans* (also
prægnans).

368. In most of the Romance languages (but not Spanish),
masculine nouns made over their nominative plural on the
model of the second declension, which was regarded as the
normal masculine type: *fīlii*, hence **patri;* *lŭpi*, hence **cani;*
anni, hence **mē(n)si*.

The process may have begun in the Vulgar Latin period,
but there is virtually no evidence that it started so early: in
late Latin, however, *elifanti* is common, according to Bon. 367;
parentorum is frequent in charters; in the *Gl. Cassel*, made in
Italy in the eighth or ninth century, we find *sapienti*.

369. Neuters in *–n* and *–s* regularly kept their nominative-
accusative singular, as *nōme(n)*, *cŏrpus cŏrpu(s);* for **lūmĭ-
ne(m)*, **nōmĭne(m)*, beside the old forms, see § 347.   For the
nominative-accusative plural, however, they constructed, probably in late Vulgar Latin or early Romance, new forms on the
masculine pattern, as *nōmes **nōme(s)*, *cŏrpes **cŏrpe(s);* but
in Italy and Rumania the old ones, especially those in *–ŏra*,
were kept also (*Lat. Spr.* 482).   In these countries *–ora* was
used as a plural ending (It. *cǫrpo*, *cǫrpi cǫrpora;* Rum. *timp*,
timpurĭ), and was extended in Old Italian to the second, in
Rumanian to both the second and first declensions: cf.
Tiktin 566.

Neuters in *–r*, which apparently became masculine or

feminine earlier than the others, often developed an accusative singular in *–e(m)* as well as a nominative-accusative plural in *–es: marmorem*, Bon. 348, Zauner 30; *papaverem*, Plautus, *Pœn.* I, 2, 113; **piperem; sulphurem*, G. 293; cf. § 347. But *marmor*, etc., were kept also. *Cŏr* apparently made its plural **cŏres* instead of **cŏrdes:* according to Mohl, *Lexique* 21–38, the word shows no trace of *d* in any of the Romance languages, except Spanish *cuerdo*, and so probably goes back to an Old Latin **cŏr *cŏris = κῆρ κῆρος*; the open *o* would possibly be explained as due to a cross between this **cŏr* and the Classic *cŏr*.

Caput became **capu(m)* or *capus* (Pirson 238), and passed into the second declension: cf. § 356, (3).

370. A few feminines in *–is* apparently became neuters in *–us*, but the original forms were kept also: *cĭnis cĭnus; pŭlvis *pŭlvus*, whence Sp. *polvo*, Old Fr. *pols* (It. *polve* may come from *pŭlver*).

Incus, incūdis > incūdo, incūdĭnis: Lat. Spr. 483.

Sanguis, sanguĭne(m) also *sangue(m)*.

371. In general, at the beginning of the Romance period, the third declension must have gone about as follows (*–ĭs* and *–ēs* having coincided in the pronunciation *–es*):—

(1) No Change of Accent.

NO CHANGE OF STEM.

THINGS.			PERSONS.	
cane(s)	fine(s)	res	pate(r)	mate(r)
cane	fine	rem re	patre	matre
cane(s)	fine(s)	res	patre(s)	matre(s)
cane(s)	fine(s)	res	patre(s)	matre(s)

CHANGE OF STEM.

THINGS.			PERSONS.	
pede(s)	**arte*(s)	*corpu*(s)	*come*(s)	*vergo*
pede	*arte*	*corpu*(s)	*cómite*	*vérgine*
pede(s)	*arte*(s)	**corpe*(s) *córpora*	*cómite*(s)	*vérgine*(s)
pede(s)	*arte*(s)	*corpe*(s) *córpora*	*cómite*(s)	*vérgine*(s)

(2) Change of Accent.

THINGS.		PERSONS.		
**sermóne*(s)	**ratióne*(s)	*amáto*(r)	*soro*(r)	*parente*(s)
sermóne	*ratióne*	*amatóre*	*soróre*	*parente*
sermóne(s)	*ratióne*(s)	*amatóre*(s)	*soróre*(s)	*parente*(s)
sermóne(s)	*ratióne*(s)	*amatóre*(s)	*soróre*(s)	*parente*(s)

Letters enclosed in parentheses were silent in Italy and Dacia.

d. LOSS OF DECLENSION.

372. In Italy and Dacia, through the dropping of final *r* and *s*, declension nearly disappeared before the end of the Vulgar Latin period: cf. Audollent 545–547, nom. *alumnu*, *Glaucu*, *Romanu*, etc. It was probably lost altogether soon after, although a few double forms still remain: e. g., It. *ladro*, *ladrone*.

It disappeared early in Spain also. In most of Gaul it lasted through the twelfth century and later.

373. In Gaul and Spain the forms preserved were the accusative singular and the accusative plural. In Italy and Rumania, for phonetic reasons, the surviving cases are the accusative singular and the nominative plural.

There are, however, not a few examples of the nominative singular of names of persons.

3. DECLENSION OF ADJECTIVES.

374. Adjectives were declined after the same model as nouns. As neuter nouns assumed masculine endings (§ 347), the neuter adjective forms were less and less used; the neuter singular, however, was kept to represent a whole idea (cf. § 350), and the neuter plural (as *omnia*) was doubtless employed from time to time as an indefinite collective.

375. The principal types are:—

(1) THREE GENDERS.

–us –a –um

bonu(s)	*bona*	*bonu*
bonu –o	*bona*	*bonu –o*
boni	*bone –as*	*bona*
bono(s)	*bona(s)*	*bona*

So superlatives, as *optĭmus, –a, –um*.

–er –a –um

liβe(r)	*libra*	*libru*
libru –o	*libra*	*libru –o*
libri	*libre libras*	*libra*
libro(s)	*libra(s)*	*libra*

So *æger, ægra, ægrum*.

–er –is –e

ace(r)	*acre(s)*	*acre*
acre	*acre*	*acre*
acre(s)	*acre(s)*	*acria*
acre(s)	*acre(s)*	*acria*

(2) TWO GENDERS.

triste(s)	*triste*
triste	*triste*
triste(s)	*tristia*
triste(s)	*tristia*

(3) Originally ONE GENDER in the Nominative Singular.

*felíce(s)	félis	*prudente(s)	prude(s)
felíce	félis	prudente	prude(s)
felíce(s)	felícia	prudente(s)	prudentia
felíce(s)	felícia	prudente(s)	prudentia

(4) COMPARATIVES apparently did not reconstruct the Nominative Singular:—

mélio(r)	méliu(s)
melióre	méliu(s)
melióre(s)	melióra
melióre(s)	melióra

376. There was a good deal of confusion of types in Latin times: beside *alacer*, m. and f., there was *alacris*, m. and f., and there was probably also a feminine *alacra* and *alecra*. *Pauper* early developed a feminine *paupera* and later a neuter *pauperum: paupera, pauperum, pauperorum*, R. 275 (cf. *pauperorum*, Waters Ch. 46). *Macer, miser, sacer* passed into the –*us* –*a* –*um* class, Densusianu 142; so *tæter* > *tetrus*, App. Pr. *Declīvis, effrēnis, imbecĭllis* also assumed the –*us* –*a* –*um* inflection in the Latin period; so *trīstis* > *tristus*, App. Pr. Cf. *celerus, gracilus, præstus, sublimus*, etc., and conversely *benignis, infirmis*, etc., R. 274. *Præcox* developed a feminine *præcoca*: Neue II, 162.

In the Romance languages more adjectives went over to the –*us* –*a* –*um* type: Pr. *comuna, doussa*, etc.

4. COMPARISON.

377. For the new method of comparison, see § 56. The Romance type, not completely evolved in Vulgar Latin, was:—

carus $\begin{Bmatrix} plus \\ magis \end{Bmatrix}$ carus   ille $\begin{Bmatrix} plus \\ magis \end{Bmatrix}$ carus

However, the Classic Latin comparatives of many common adjectives remained: *altior, grandior, gravior, grevior, grossior* (G. 285), *levior, longior, major, melior, minor, pejor;* also **bellatior.* So the adverbs: *longius, magis, melius, minus, pejus, sordidius, vivacius,* etc. The old superlatives remained to a considerable extent, in the clerical language, as intensives: *altissimus, carissimus, pessimus, proximus, sanctissimus.*

5. NUMERALS.[1]

378. *Unus* was probably declined like *bonus.* It was used also as an indefinite article (§ 57) and an indefinite pronoun (cf. § 71).

Dŭo came to be replaced by *dŭi,* attested in the third century: *Archiv* IX, 558 (cf. II, 107). Its inflection at the end of the Vulgar Latin period was probably:—

dui doi (duo?)	*due doe duas doas*	*dua doa*
duo(s)	*dua(s) doa(s)*	*dua doa*

In early Romance there was doubtless much confusion of the forms.

379. The numbers between two and twenty were as follows:—

Trēs probably developed a nominative **trei,* on the model of *dui.*

Quattuor became *quattor* (*Archiv* VII, 65), also *quatro* (Carnoy 221), **quattro.*

Quĭnque, by dissimilation, became *cīnque* (*Archiv* VII, 66); so *cinquaginta* (*Archiv* VII, 70). Cf. § 254.

Sĕx, sĕpte (and **sĕtte*), *ŏcto* (and **ŏtto*), *nŏve, dĕce* offer no peculiarities. Cf. *Archiv* VII, 68.

Beside *ŭndĕce* there seems to have been **ŭndĕce.*

For *dōdĕce,* see § 225.

Trēdĕce is regular.

---

[1] See M. Ihm, *Vulgärformen lateinischer Zahlwörter auf Inschriften* in *Archiv* VII, 65.

Quattuordĕcim regularly became *quattŏrdĕce (cf. § 225), but also **quattŏrdĕce.*

Quīndĕce is regular.

Beside *sēdĕce* there was *dĕce et (or *ac*) *sĕx.*

Septendĕcim, etc., went out of use; also *unus de viginti*, etc.: G. 400. Priscian (Keil III, 412) mentions *decem et septem*. Beside this *dĕce et sĕpte* there was **dĕce ac sĕpte;* so *dĕce et (or *ac*) *ŏcto*, *dĕce et (or *ac*) *nŏve.*

380. The tens, beginning with 20, are irregular: cf. § 142.

Vīgĭntī, *trīgĭnta* regularly became *viįnti*, *triįnta* (§ 259): βειεντι occurs in a sixth century document of Ravenna, *Vok.* II, 461; *trienta*, *Archiv* VII, 69. These forms easily contracted into *vinti*, *trĭnta* (*vinti*, *trinta: Archiv* VII, 69), which account in general for the Italian, Provençal, and French words; Rumanian has new formations. But beside these we must assume for Spanish something like *vįinti, *trįinta, with an opening of the first *i* and an early shift of accent, probably anterior to the fall of the *g; trígínta* is, in fact, mentioned as a faulty pronunciation by Consentius, Keil V, 392. Cf. G. Rydberg in *Mélanges Wahlund* 337.

This change of accent apparently occurred everywhere for the subsequent tens: *quadráinta, *cinquáinta, *sexáinta, *septáinta *settáinta, *octáinta *ottáinta, *nonáinta **nováinta;* the *septua–* and the *octo–* of 70 and 80 were made to conform to the type of the others. Outside of the Spanish peninsula *–áinta* apparently became *–ánta*. Furthermore the *dr* of *quadráinta became *rr: quarranta* is found in an inscription, perhaps of the fifth century (Pirson 97; *Zs. fr. Spr.* XXV, ii, 136; *Archiv* VII, 69).

381. *Cĕntu* was regular. For *ducĕnti*, *trecĕnti*, etc., there were probably new formations, such as *dŭi cĕntu, etc.

Mīlle was regular. For its plural it had *dŭi mīlle or **dŭi mīl(l)ia*, etc.

382. The ordinal numerals, after 5th, were probably not very commonly used: the Romance languages show many new formations; in northern Italian, Provençal, and Catalan the distributive ending *–ēnus* was employed (*septēnus* for *sĕptĭmus*, etc.).

Prīmus, *secŭndus*, *tĕrtius*, *quartus*, *quīntus* were generally kept, inflected like *bŏnus;* but some languages have new formations even for these.

The ordinals were best preserved in Italy.

B. PRONOUNS AND PRONOMINAL ADJECTIVES.

383. The nominative and accusative remained; and the dative was preserved in personal, demonstrative, relative, and interrogative pronouns. The ablative gave way to the dative and accusative. The genitive was usually lost; but *cūjus* was kept, and so was the genitive singular and plural of *ĭlle*, *ĭpse*, and *ĭste*.

1. PERSONAL PRONOUNS.

N. B. — For the *use* of personal pronouns, see § 60.

384. As the pronouns came to be expressed more and more, *ĭlle* and also *hīc*, *ĭpse*, and *ĭs* were used to supply the lacking pronoun of the third person: cf. §§ 60, 67. Examples occur as early as the second century: *Franz. ?* II, 262. *Hŏc* served as an indefinite neuter. *Inde* assumed the function of an indefinite genitive: *nemo inde dubitat*, Regnier 110.

385. *Ego* lost its *g* in all the territory, but probably not until the end of the Vulgar Latin period. According to Meyer-Lübke, *Lat. Spr.* 484, *eo* occurs in manuscripts of the sixth century.[1] See § 263.

---

[1] But his reference to *Vok*. I, 242 is incorrect.

In the last syllable of *tĭbĭ*, *sĭbĭ* the short *i* prevailed, and
was carried into *nōbīs*, *vōbīs*. On the pattern of *mī < mihi*,
there were formed *tī*, *sī* beside *tĭbĭ*, *sĭbĭ;* these are found, according to *Lat. Spr.* 484, from the sixth century on; cf.
Franz. ⸗ II, 243–244.

386. The inflection was probably reduced to: —

ẹo	nọs	tu̯	vọs		
mị	nọβe(s)	tị teβe	vọβe(s)	sị seβe	sị seβe
me̦	nọs	te̦	vọs	se̦	se̦

2. POSSESSIVES.

387. *Mĕus, tŭus, sŭus* were declined like *bŏnus; nŏster, vŏster*, like *līber*. But *mī* was used, beside *mĕus, mĕa*, as a masculine and feminine vocative (G. 281–282); *mi domina* is
common, G. 282, Dubois 261–262. For the plural of the third
person, *illōru* came, in the Romance languages except Spanish,
to replace *sŭus*, etc.

By the analogy of *mĕus*, there was a *seus:* C. I. L. XII,
5692, 9; cf. *siæ*, IX, 3472.

Sous is found in Gaul, *Zs. fr. Spr.* XXV, ii, 135: perhaps it
is only a phonetic spelling of *sọus < su̯us*, but it may represent
a pronunciation *sọus* with an *o* opened by dissimilation (cf.
§ 167). There doubtless was a **tọus* also.

Vester disappeared. Vulgar Latin *vŏster* may be a survival
of the Old Latin *vŏster*, or a reconstruction on the model of
nŏster: cf. § 199, (1).

388. In archaic and popular Latin there was a short *sus sa
sum*, probably used originally in the unaccented position: *sas,
sīs* occur in Ennius, *sam* in Festus; *so* is found in C. I. L. V,
2007. There must have been similar short forms for the first
and second persons singular: *mīs*, indeed, is used by Ennius.

The full inflection is found in the sixth century: *Franz.* ∂
II, 244.

These forms survived in Romance: Old It. *fratelmo, madre-
ma,* etc.

3. DEMONSTRATIVES.

N. B.— For the *use* of demonstratives, see §§ 61–68. For their function as definite
articles and personal pronouns, see §§ 60, 67–68, also § 392.

389. When *ille* and *iste* had a really demonstrative force,
they came to be compounded usually with the prefix *ecc'* or
eccu': see § 65. Cf. *Franz.* ∂ II, 283–304.

390. The inflection of *ille* developed considerably in popular speech. *Ipse* and *iste* followed a similar course; we find,
however, the special forms *ipsus* for *ipse* and *ipsud* for *ipsum,*
R. 276; *Franz.* ∂ II, 274.

Ille, nom. sg. m., was partially replaced, probably in the second half of the sixth century, by *illi,* framed on the model of
quī: Bon. 114, *illi = ille, ipsi = ipse;* cf. *Franz.* ∂ II, 246–260.

Through the analogy of *cūjus, cūi,* the m. *illīus* gave way to
illūjus, and the dat. sg. m. *illī* was replaced in part by *illūi.*
The former, however, subsequently went out of use, and the
latter is not found in Calabria, Sicily, Sardinia, and the Spanish
peninsula. *Illius (ipsius, istius),* having become archaic in
popular speech, sometimes occurred as a dative: *Franz.* ∂ II,
277–279. There was another dative form, *illo,* used by Apuleius and others (Neue II, 427; R. 275; Quillacq 83); but it
disappeared from late Latin, being confused with the ablative
and the accusative. The Old Latin genitive *illi (ipsi, isti),*
was abandoned: cf. *Franz.* ∂ II, 273, 275.

In the dat. sg. f., beside *illī,* there was *illæ* (or *ille*), used by
Cato and others (Neue II, 427; R. 275; Audollent 302); and
from that, on the model of *illūi* (and perhaps of *quei*), was

made *illæi* (*illei*), which was used beside *íllī* and *íllæ*. In the genitive, on the same pattern (influenced perhaps by *quejus*), was constructed *illæjus* (*illejus*), which crowded out *illīus*.

Illujus, illui, illejus, illei are found from the sixth century on: Zs. XXVI, 600, 619. Cf. *Lat. Spr.* 484: *illujus, illui, illejus, illæ, ille; ipsujus, ipseus*.

Illōrum displaced the f. *illārum*. It came, furthermore, to be used, in Romance, for the dat. m. and f. *íllīs*, which, however, did not entirely disappear. In parts of northern Spain and southwestern France *illōrum* seems to have become **illūrum*, through the analogy of *illūjus, illūi*.

The neuter *íllud* was replaced by *íllum:* Neue II, 426; R. 276.

391. The popular inflection, at the end of the Vulgar Latin period, was something like this (brackets indicating forms not kept in Romance): —

ęlle ęlli	ęlla	ęllu
[ellujus]	ellejus	
ęlli [ęllo] ellúi	ęlli ęlle ellęi	ęlli
ęllu ęllo	ęlla	ęllu ęllo
ęlli	ęlle	ęlla
ellǫru ellǫru?	[ellaru] ellǫru ellúru?	
ęlli(s) ellǫru	ęlli(s)	
ęllo(s)	ęlla(s)	ęlla

392. When unaccented, these words tended to lose their first syllable (see § 157): *tū íllam vídēs > *tu 'la' vede(s); vídēs tū ípsam clavem > *vede(s) tu 'sa' clave'?* *Lui* and *lei* are found after the seventh century: *Franz. ə II, 281–283.*

Ille and *ipse* were used freely as definite articles from the fourth century on: Densusianu 177. *Ille* prevailed, except in Sardinia, Majorca, a part of Catalonia and Gascony, and some dialects on the south shore of France. Cf. *Franz. ə II, 271–272.*

4. INTERROGATIVE AND RELATIVE PRONOUNS.

N. B. — For the *use* of these pronouns, and the substitution of *qui* for feminine *quæ*,
see §§ 69–70.

393. In Christian inscriptions from the fifth century on,
quī takes the place of *quĭs*, and also of the feminine *quæ*. Beside *cūjus*, *cūi* is found a corresponding feminine *quejus*, *quei*:
see Mohl in *Zs.* XXVI, 619.

The combined inflection of *quī* and *quĭs*, by the end of the
Vulgar Latin period, was probably reduced, in common speech,
to something like this: —

quị	*que*	*quị*	*cǫd quẹd*
cuju(s)	*quẹju(s)*	*cuju(s)*	*cuju(s)*
cuị	*quẹị*	*cuị*	*cuị*
que	*qua*	*que*	*cǫd quẹd*
cǫ?	*qua*	*cǫ?*	*cǫ?*
quị	*que*	*quị*	*que*
cǫs?	*quas?*	*cǫs?*	*que*

The genitive was probably not used everywhere; perhaps it
was kept only in Spain. *Unde* and *d'ŭnde,* 'whence,' took the
meaning 'of which': Bon. 580.

394. *Qualis,* inflected like *trĭstis,* was used as an interrogative pronoun and adjective. In the Romance languages
(*ĭl*)*le* + *qualis* came to be employed as a relative pronoun.

5. INDEFINITE PRONOUNS AND ADJECTIVES.

395. For these, see § 71. *Alter, nūllus, sōlus, tōtus, ūnus*
doubtless developed an inflection like *bŏnus:* gen. *nulli,* etc.,
R. 276; dat. *solo, toto, uno,* etc., R. 276–277. *Alter,* however,
assumed a dative **altrūi,* on the model of *illūi,* etc.

C. VERBS.

1. THE FOUR CONJUGATIONS.

396. There was some confusion of conjugations; the first and fourth were least affected. In the *Peregrinatio* the second decidedly preponderates over the third (Bechtel 87); in other texts the third gains at the expense of the second.

The second gained most in Spain, the third in Italy, the fourth in Gaul. Eventually Spanish and Portuguese discarded the third, Sicilian and Sardinian the second.

New formations went into the first and fourth.

a. FIRST CONJUGATION.

397. The first conjugation generally held its own, defections being few and partial.

Beside *do, dant* and *sto, stant* there came into use **dao, *daunt* and **stao, *staunt:* Rum. *daŭ, staŭ;* Old It. *dao;* Pr. *dau, daun, estau, estaun;* Pg. *dou, estou.* Mohl, *Lexique* 47, would connect these forms with Umbrian *stahu,* but it seems more likely that they were late Latin formations due to an effort to keep the root vowel distinct from the ending. Cf. Probus, "*adno* non *adnao,*" *Lexique* 47.

In northern Gaul there may have developed with **stao* a **stais* and a **stait,* on the analogy of (**vao*), **vais, *vait* (see § 405): cf. *Lexique* 47–54.

The Italian present subjunctive *dia* from *dare* is associated by Mohl, *Lexique* 47 and *Pr. Pers. Pl.* 30, with Umbrian *dīa.* It is entirely possible, however, that the form is a later, Italian development due to the analogy of *sia:* see § 419, (2).

398. For new formations, — such as *abbreviare, follicare, werrizare,* etc., — see §§ 33–35. Germanic verbs in *–on* and in

–an (but not *–jan*) regularly went in the first conjugation: *roubôn* > It. *rubare, wîtan* > It. *guidare.*   Cf. § 36.

b. SECOND CONJUGATION.

399. Even in Classic Latin there was some confusion between the second conjugation and the third: *fervĕre, tergĕre.* In Vulgar Latin the second lost some verbs to the third in most of the territory: **ardĕre, *lucĕre, lugĕre* (R. 283), *miscĕre* (R. 284), **mordĕre, *nocĕre, *ridĕre, respondĕre* (Bechtel 88: *responduntur*), *tondĕre, *torcĕre* (for *torquēre*).   Other verbs passed over locally or occasionally: *seditur,* Bechtel 88.

400. Some verbs went into the fourth, probably through the pronunciation of *–e̦o* as *–io* (see § 224): **complīre, florīre* (R. 284), **implīre, *lucīre, lugīre* (R. 284), **putrīre.*   The inchoative *–ēscĕre* then became *–īscĕre: *florīsco, lucīsco, *putrīsco.*

Habēre, at least in Italy, sometimes became *habīre:* ·Vok. I, 266 ff.; *havite, C. I. L.* V, 1636; *habibat, Itala,* Luke VI, 8; *avire* in many Italian dialects in which *e* does not phonetically become *i,* and even in early Tuscan (cf. E. Monaci, *Crestomazia italiana dei primi secoli* I, p. 20, l. 10, etc).   According to Mohl, *Lexique* 108–109, this is a peculiarity of ancient Umbrian.

401. While retaining *habeo, habes, habet, habent,* the verb *habēre,* under the influence of *dare* and *stare,* adopted the forms **ho* or **hao, *has, *hat, *hant* or **haunt.*

c. THIRD CONJUGATION.

402. The third conjugation gave a few verbs to the second, perhaps beginning with those that had a perfect in *–ui,* such as *cadere *cadui, capere *capui, sapere sapui: sapere* was influenced, especially in Italy, by *habēre; capere* may easily have imitated *sapere,* and *cadere* may have followed *capere.*

In Spain all the third conjugation verbs eventually passed into the second. This transition was probably helped by a partial fusion of *ĕsse* and *sedēre*.

403. The anomalous *pŏsse pŏtui, vĕlle vŏlui* naturally went over to the second conjugation, assumed the infinitive forms *potēre, *volēre,* and conformed their inflection more or less to the regular type. *Vĕlle,* however, was discarded in Spain and Sardinia.

(1) *Potere, potebam* occur repeatedly in the sixth century (*Pr. Pers. Pl.* 24), *potebo* is found in the *Gl. Reich.*, *potebas* in Fredegarius (Haag 60). *Posso* for *pŏssum* is used by Gregory and Fredegarius (*Pr. Pers. Pl.* 24), *poteo* is attested in 745 A.D. (*Pr. Pers. Pl.* 25). The present indicative must have been inflected something like this:—

pǫssu pǫsso pǫtęo *pǫssęo	*potęmu(s)
pǫte(s)	potęste(s) *potęte(s)
*pǫte(t)	pǫssun(t) *pǫten(t)

The present subjunctive must have had corresponding forms.

(2) *Volimus* is found in the sixth century (*Lat. Spr.* 478), *volemus* in the seventh (*Pr. Pers. Pl.* 21); *voles* is found in the *Gl. Reich. Volestis,* framed on the pattern of *potestis,* is twice used by Fredegarius (*Pr. Pers. Pl.* 21). The present indicative forms must have been something like this:—

*volęo	volimu(s) volęmu(s)
vǫle(s)	volęste(s) *volęte(s)
*vǫle(t)	*vǫlen(t)

The present subjunctive must have been similarly inflected.

404. Beside *facĕre* there doubtless existed **fare* (*Facere* 48), strongly influenced by *dare* and *stare. Dare* and *facere* were associated in old formulas: *Lexique* 53. Furthermore, a suggestion of shortening existed in the monosyllabic imperative *fac* (also *fa: Zs.* XXV, 735), which must have led to *fate beside *facĭte*. The present indicative certainly had several sets of forms, one series being on the pattern of the first conjugation, but the present subjunctive retained its old inflection (see *Facere* 72, 121; *Zs.* XVIII, 434): —

facịo	*fao	*fo	*fácimu(s)*	*fáimus	**famu(s)*
face(s)	*fais	*fas	*fácite(s)*	*fáitis	**fate(s)*
face(t)	*fait	*fat	*facịun(t)*	*faunt	*fant

There was also a rare infinitive *facire*, which occurs several times in the sixth and seventh centuries: *Facere* 13.

405. *Vadĕre* supplied its missing past tenses from *īre* and other verbs. These other substitutes, whose origin constitutes one of the most discussed problems in Romance philology, resulted — to cite only the principal types — in the verbs *allare or *alare* (used in northern Gaul), *annare (used in southern Gaul), *andare (used in Spain and Italy). It is now generally thought that *allare and *annare developed in some peculiar way (perhaps through distortion in military commands) from *ambŭlare*, which is very common in late Latin in the sense of 'march' or 'walk.' *Andare is commonly traced to *ambĭtare, coming either from *ambĭtus* or, more probably, from *ambŭlare* with a change of suffix. C. C. Rice, in the *Publications of the Modern Language Association of America* XIX, 217, argues that the three verbs sprang from Latin *annare* (= *adnare*) and its derivatives *annŭlare, *annĭtare. For a bibliography of the subject, see Körting. Cf. also A. Horning in *Zs.* XXIX, 542; H. Schuchardt in *Zs.* XXX, 83; *Lexique* 56–78. Both *ambulare* and *alare* occur in the *Gl. Reich.* *Amnavit* is found on a sixth century African vase: see F. Novati in *Studi Medievali* I, 616–617.

Ire and the other substitutes were introduced also into the

present. The present indicative, moreover, was influenced by
facere fare: —

vado	**vao*	**vo*	*vádimu(s)*	*imu(s)* etc.	
vade(s)	**vais*	**vas*	*vádite(s)*	*ite(s)* etc.	
vade(t)	**vait*	**vat*	*vadun(t)*	**vaunt*	**vant*

406. Verbs in *–io* tended to pass into the fourth conju-
gation (see, however, § 416): **capīre*, beside **capēre; cupīre*,
Lucretius (*Lat. Spr.* 477), Densusianu 148, Bon. 426; *fodīri*,
Cato; *fugīre*, St. Augustine (*Lat. Spr.* 477), common in the
Vulgate (R. 285), Sepulcri 229, Bon. 427, Haag 60, *Gl. Reich.;*
morīri, Plautus, and **morīre.*

Some others went over, at least locally: **fallīre; gemire*,
Pirson 148; *occurire*, Pirson 148; **offerīre, *sofferīre*, by the
analogy of *aperīre* (*sufferit*, R. 286; cf. *deferet, offeret*, Bechtel
90; *offeret*, first half of the 7th century, Carnoy 112); **sequīre*,
beside **sĕquĕre.*

Dīcĕre, probably in the Vulgar Latin period (cf. *Lexique* 62),
developed a form **dīre*, doubtless suggested by *dīc* (cf. *fac* and
*fare, § 404) and helped by the analogy of *audīre.*

d. FOURTH CONJUGATION.

407. The fourth conjugation usually held its own, and
gained some verbs from the others.

For new formations, — such as **abbellīre, ignīre*, — see § 34.
Germanic verbs in *–jan* regularly went into the fourth conjugation in Latin (Kluge 500): *furbjan* > It. *forbire; marrjan* > Fr.
marrir; parrjan > Fr. *tarir; warnjan* > It. *guarnire.* Cf. § 36.

For the intrusion of the inchoative *–sc–* into this conjugation, see § 415.

2. FUNDAMENTAL CHANGES IN INFLECTION.

408. Of the personal forms of the verb there remained in
general use in Romance only the following tenses of the active
voice, the entire passive inflection having been discarded: the

indicative present, imperfect, perfect, pluperfect, and in some regions the future perfect; the subjunctive present, pluperfect, and in some regions the perfect; the imperative present. For instance: *amo, amabam, amavi, amaram, (amaro); amem, amassem, (amarim); ama.* See Syntax.

Of the impersonal forms of the verb there remained: the present active infinitive, the present participle, the perfect participle, the gerund (especially the ablative case), and probably in some standing phrases the gerundive. For instance: *amare, amans, amatus, amando, (amandus?).* The supine fell into disuse from the first century on. See Syntax.

409. The entire passive inflection came to be replaced, towards the end ·of the Vulgar Latin period, partly by active and reflexive constructions but mainly by a compound of the perfect participle with *ĕsse·* (in northern Italy *fĭĕri*): *lĭttĕra scrībĭtur* > *lĭttera scrĭpta ĕst* (or *fĭt*).

Deponent verbs became active: *mentire, operare,* etc., R. 298; cf. R. 297–302, 388–389. Conversely, some writers substituted the deponent for the active inflection of a few verbs: Petronius, *rideri,* etc., R. 304; cf. R. 302–304.

Cf. §§ 112–114.

410. The Latin perfect was kept in its preterit sense. In its perfect sense it was replaced, in the Vulgar Latin period, by a compound of *habēre* and the perfect participle — in the case of neuter verbs, *ĕsse* and the perfect participle: *fēci* > *habeo factum; reverti* > *reversus sum,* R. 289. Similar compounds replaced the pluperfect and the future perfect. See §§ 121–124.

The old pluperfect indicative (*amāram, audīram*) was kept, as a preterit or a conditional, in various regions: see § 124. In the subjunctive the pluperfect was used instead of the imperfect, which disappeared everywhere but in Sardinia (*fa-cheret*, etc.): *amārem*>*amāssem, audīrem*>*audīssem;* cf. § 118.

The old future perfect — *amā(vĕ)ro* — fused with the perfect subjunctive — *amā(vĕ)rim* — and apparently remained more or less in use, as a future indicative or subjunctive, in all regions except Gaul and Rætia. It is best preserved in Spanish and Portuguese, but is found also in Old Rumanian and Macedonian. There are traces of it in Old Italian, sometimes confused with the pluperfect indicative and later sometimes with the infinitive (*ápriro, póteri, crédere*, etc.): see C. De Lollis in *Bausteine* 1; V. Crescini in *Zs.* XXIX, 619.

411. The old future, with the exception of *ĕro*, was crowded out by the present and by new formations, especially by the infinitive combined with the present indicative of *habēre* (*amābo*>*amar' habeo*): see §§ 125–129. In this compound all the various forms of the present indicative of *habēre* were used (see §§ 273, 401): **amar' –ábeo, –áyo, –áo, –ó;* **amar' –ábe(s), –ás;* **amar' –ábe(t), –át;* **amar' ában(t), –áunt, –ánt.* In the first and second persons plural, *habēmus* and *habētis* eventually, as they came to be regarded as mere endings, were reduced to *–ẹmu(s), –ẹte(s),* to correspond to the dissyllabic or monosyllabic *–áyo, –ábe(s), –ábe(t),–ában(t)* and *–ó, –ás, –át, –ánt:* **amar' –ẹmu(s),* **amar' –ẹte(s).*

On the model of this new future, an imperfect of the future, or conditional, came to be made, in late Vulgar Latin and Romance, from the infinitive combined with the imperfect or the perfect of *habēre* (see § 130): **amar' –abe(b)a(m)* or **amar' –abui.* In these formations the unaccented (*h*)*ab–* disappeared, as in the first and second persons plural of the future: **amar' –ẹ(b)a,* **amar' –ẹsti,* etc.; but **amar' ábui,* etc. In Italian we find, beside *–ía* from *habēbam* and *–ábbi –ébbi* from *habŭi,* a form in *–éi* (*ameréi*), which has prevailed in the

modern language, while in Old Italian the *ei* was sometimes
detached and used as a preterit of *avere:* it is probably due to
the analogy of the first person singular of the weak preterit
(*credéi*, hence *crederéi*), cf. § 426.

412. The imperative disappeared, except the present, second
person singular and plural: *ămā, amāte; tĕnē, tenēte; crēdĕ,
crēdĭte; audī, audīte.* The first and third persons were supplied
from the present subjunctive. In some verbs the present subjunctive was used instead of all imperative forms. See § 115.

Instead of the plural form, the second person plural of the
present indicative came to be used: *adferte > adferitis,* R. 294.
For the monosyllabic *dic, duc, fac,* writers sometimes employed
dice, duce, face: R. 294.

3. INCHOATIVE VERBS.

413. The Latin inchoative ending *–sco* was preceded by *ā–,
ē–, ī–,* or *ō–.* The types *–āsco* and *–ōsco* were sparingly represented and were not extended in late and popular Latin; they
have bequeathed but few verbs — such as Pr. *irāisser < irāscĕre,
conóisser < co(g)nōscĕre* — to the Romance languages. The
types *–ēsco* and *–īsco* — as *parēsco, dormīsco* — were extended
in the third century and later, and lost their inchoative sense.

414. There is some evidence of a confusion of *–ēsco* and
–īsco in Latin. Virgilius Grammaticus (Sepulcri 194) mentions
double forms of inchoative verbs, such as *calesco calisco,* etc.
Clarisco, erubisco, etc., are common in Gregory the Great:
Sepulcri 193. Cf. *criscere,* etc., in *Vok.* I, 359 ff.

In Veglia, the Abruzzi, Sardinia, and a part of Lorraine
neither of these two endings left any trace. Only *–ēsco* survived in the Tyrol, the Grisons, French Switzerland, Savoy,
Dauphiné, Lyons, the Landes, Béarn, and Spain — Sp. *parecer,*

florecer; –*esco* was preferred also in Rumanian.   Elsewhere, although there are traces of –*ēsco*, –*īsco* prevailed — Fr. *il fleurit*, It. *fiorisce*.   For Pr. *despereissir*, etc., see E. Herzog in *Bausteine* 481.

415. The ending –*īsco* eventually entered into the formation of the present stem of fourth conjugation verbs.   There is no direct evidence of this in Latin, nor are there any traces of it in Spanish, Portuguese, Sardinian, or southern Italian; but in the earliest texts of France, northern and central Italy, Rætia, and Rumania we find a type

*finisco	*finimu(s)*
*finisce(s)	*finite(s)*
*finisce(t)	**finiscun(t)*

The –*sc*– then generally disappeared from the infinitive — It. *fiorire*.   Later, in some regions, the –*sc*– was carried throughout the present indicative (Fr. *finissons*, *finissez*); it also penetrated the present subjunctive (Fr. *finisse*), and in some districts eventually the present participle and the imperfect indicative (Fr. *finissant*, *finissais*).

See *Archiv* I, 465; *Zs.* XXIV, 81; *Rom.* XXX, 291–294; *Lat. Spr.* 478.

4. PRESENT STEMS.

416. Many verbs in –*io* dropped the *i* whenever it was followed by another vowel.   In the present participle this was a regular phonetic development (see § 225): *audientem* > **audente*, *facientem* > **facente*, *partientem* > **partente*, *sentientem* > **sentente*.   Hence forms without the *i* were introduced more or less into the indicative and subjunctive: *audio *audo*, **dŏrmo*, *partiunt *partunt*, *sĕntiam *sĕntam*, etc.

By the analogy of these, the *e* was occasionally lost in the second conjugation: *vĭdeo *vĭdo*.   On the other hand, by the

analogy of *capiunt, faciunt,* etc., the second conjugation ad-
mitted such forms as **habeunt, *vĭdeunt,* etc., beside the regular *habent, vĭdent,* etc.

417. The verbs *struĕre, trahĕre, vehĕre* developed infinitive
forms **strúgere, trágere, végere* (*tragere* and *vegere* are used by
Fredegarius, Haag 34) and a whole present and imperfect
inflection with –*g*–, as **trago, *tragam, *tragēbam.* The guttural
was derived from the perfect indicative and the perfect participle — *struxi structus, traxi tractus, vexi vectus* — on the
analogy of *ago actus, figo fixi, lego lectus, rego rexi rectus, tego
tectus,* and also *fingo finxi fictus, tango tactus,* and probably
*cingo cinxi cinctus, jungo junxi junctus, pango panxi panctus,
plango planxi planctus, ungo unxi unctus,* etc.

There may have been also **strúcere, *trácere, *vécere,* based
on the analogy of *dico dixi dictus, duco duxi ductus.*

Cf. *Substrate* VI, 131.

418. The verbs *dare, debēre, dīcĕre, facĕre, habēre, pŏsse,
stare, vadēre, vĕlle* underwent considerable changes in the
present: see §§ 273, 397, 401, 403–406, 412, 416.

419. *Esse* was made into **ĕssĕre,* to bring it into conformity
with the usual third conjugation type. Considerable alterations
were made in the present indicative and subjunctive. For the
use of *fĭĕri* for *ĕsse,* see § 409. The Spanish use of *sedēre* for
ĕsse is probably later than our period.

(1) The present indicative shows some signs of a tendency
to normalize its erratic inflection by making all the forms begin with *s*. The old *esum* cited by Varro (*Pr. Pers. Pl.* 128)
went out of use. Italian *sei* and Rætian *šeš* point to a **sĕs*
beside *ĕs;* Italian *siete* and Rætian *siede,* etc., indicate a **sĕtis*
for *ĕstis,* while there is some evidence of an alternative **sŭtis*
on the model of *sŭmus;* Old Italian *se* for *è,* Provençal *ses* for

es, usually understood as reflexive forms, may go back to *sĕt and *sĕst for *ĕst*. In the first person plural *sŭmus* became *sŭmus* and *sĭmus* (see § 220); *sŭmus*, the usual Classic form, was preferred in Spain, Portugal, northern Gaul, and the Tyrol (Sp. *somos*, Old Fr. *sons*, etc.); *sĭmus*, which was used, according to Suetonius, by Augustus, and by various purists of the Augustan age (Stolz 58), prevailed in southern Gaul, Italy, Dalmatia, and Dacia (Pr. *sem*, Old It. *semo*, etc.): cf. *Lat. Spr.* 479; *Pr. Pers. Pl.* 130; *Rom.* XXI, 347. Provençal *esmes* < *ĕsmus seems to be a new formation on the analogy of *ĕstis;* Mohl, *Pr. Pers. Pl.* 135, would derive it from old *esĭmus*, which existed with *esum*. The present indicative inflection was doubtless something like this : —

sǫm		sǫmu(s)	sęmu(s)	*ęsmu(s)
ęs *sęs		ęste(s)	*sęte(s)| *sǫte(s)?
ęst *sęt? *sęst?		sǫnt		

(2) In the present subjunctive the analogy of other third conjugation verbs tended to introduce the characteristic vowel *a*. It is likely, too, that from early times there was a reciprocal influence of *fiam*, etc., and the Old Latin optative *siem*, etc. (cf. *Lexique* 51): *fiet* is common for *fit*, Pirson 150; *fiam* replaces *sim* in northern Italy and Dacia. Hence comes an alternative inflection *sĭam, etc., which ultimately prevailed : —

sęm *sęa		sĭmu(s)	siámu(s)
sĭs *sęa(s)		sĭte(s)	*siáte(s)
sęt sęa(t)		sęnt	*sęan(t)

For *sĭat*, see *sead* in *Vok.* II, 42. *Siamus*, according to *Lat. Spr.* 478, occurs in Italian documents of the eighth century.

5. IMPERFECT.

N. B. — For the loss of the imperfect subjunctive, see § 118.

420. The endings were *–ābam*, *–ēbam*, *–iēbam*, *–ībam*. In the third conjugation *–iēbam* regularly developed into *–ēbam*,

just as *–ientem* > *–entem* (see §§ 225, 416): *faciēbam* > *facēbam.
In the fourth conjugation *–iēbam* and *–ībam* existed side by
side from early times (Neue II, 445), *–ībam* — as in *munībam*
— being common in early Latin and recurring at later periods
(Lindsay 491); *–ībam*, which stressed the characteristic vowel
of the fourth conjugation, prevailed in popular speech, and
–iēbam disappeared: *vestibat*, etc., Dubois 277–278.

421. *Habēbam*, pronounced *αβεβα* (cf. § 318), developed
another form, *αβεα, probably through dissimilation. Hence
came an alternative ending *–ea* for *–εβα*, which in Romance
was widely extended, affecting all the conjugations but the
first: It. *vedéa*, *credéa*, *sentía*. It is common to nearly all the
Romance territory except Rumania: *Lat. Spr.* 479.

6. PERFECT.

422. We must distinguish two types, the weak and the
strong: the weak comprises the *v–* perfects in which the *v* is
added to a verb-stem (*–āvi*, *–ēvi*, *–īvi*), the strong includes all
others. Verbs of the first and fourth conjugations generally
had weak perfects, those of the second and third had mostly
strong. Only six verbs — all of the second conjugation and
most of them rare — regularly had a perfect in *–ēvi*: *deleo*, *fleo*,
neo, *–oleo*, *–pleo*, *vieo*; *silevit* for *siluit* occurs also, R. 287.

All first and fourth conjugation verbs with strong perfects
probably developed a weak one in Vulgar Latin: *præstiti* >
præstavi, R. 289; *salui* > *salivi*. For further encroachment of
the weak type on the strong, see § 426.

a. WEAK PERFECTS.

423. A tendency to keep the stress on the characteristic
vowel, and also a general inclination to omit *v* between two *i*'s
(see § 324), led early, in the fourth conjugation, to a reduction

of *-ĭvĭstī* to *-īstī* and *-ĭvĭstis* to *-īstis*, which brought about, still early, the further reduction of *-ĭvī* to *-īī* and **-īī*, *-īvit* to *-ĭit* and **-īit*, *-īvĕrunt* to *-ierunt*, and, later, the reduction of *-ĭvĭmus* to *-īmus* and probably **-immus* (the lengthening of the *m* being due to compensation and also, perhaps, to a desire to distinguish the perfect from the present). For *-ĭit*, as in *lenĭit*, see Servius *ad Aen.* I, 451; for *-ierunt*, see Neue III, 452–454; for *-īmus*, as in *repetīmus*, etc., see Neue III, 449.

Then a contraction of the two vowels gave, in the first and third persons singular and the third person plural, *-ī*, *-ĭt*, **-īrunt*: *audī*, Neue III, 434 (cf. S. 241: 65–121 A.D.); *petĭt*, etc., Neue III, 446–448; "*cupĭt* pro *cupivit*," Priscian XII, 17 (Keil II, 587); *perĭt, petĭt, redĭt*, Bayard 60; *perĭt*, etc., Bon. 440.

A contraction without the fall of *v*, in the third person singular, gave rise, locally, to an alternative form, **-īut:* It. *servío*, etc.

424. The loss of *v*, carried into the first conjugation, gave rise early to a reduction of *-āvĭstī*, *-āvĭstis*, *-āvĕrunt* to *-āstī*, *-āstis*, *-ārunt*. Much later *-āvī > -āi*, *-āvit > āit* and *-āt*, *-āvĭmus > -āmus* and probably **-āmmus: calcai* (Probus), *edificai*, *probai* (Probus), *Vok.* II, 476; σεγναι, Densusianu I, 152; — *laborait*, *C. I. L.* X, 216; *speclarait*, *Vok.* II, 476; *dedicait*, *Lexique* 46; "*fumât* pro *fumavit*," Priscian XII, 17 (Keil II, 587); *denumerat*, *judicat*, Fredegarius (Haag 55); — *cælebramus*, *memoramus*, *vocitamus*, Gregory of Tours (Bon. 440); *speramus*, Fredegarius (Haag 55). The third person singular in *-ait* is found in Old Sardinian: *Lat. Spr.* 479.

A contraction without the fall of *v* gave rise, in the third person singular, to *-aut;* and, in the first person plural, probably to **-aumus: triumphaut* in Pompeii, Densusianu I, 152. This *-aut* prevailed in Romance: It. *amò* and *amáo*, etc.   The

*–*aumus* is preserved in some Old French dialects near Douai: *Rom.* XXX, 607.

425. The forms in the first and fourth conjugations, therefore, were: —

–ávi	–ái			–ívi	*–íi	–ii	–í
–ásti				–ísti			
–áve(t)	–áut	–áit	–át	–íve(t)	*–íut	*–íit –iit –ít
–ávimu(s)	–ámu(s)	*–ámmu(s)	*–áumus	–ívimu(s)	–ímu(s)	*–ímmu(s)
–áste(s)				–íste(s)			
–árun(t)				*–írun(t)			

With the exception of –*ivi* in Old Italian, the forms with *v* were not preserved in Romance.

Verbs in –*ēvī* doubtless had a similar inflection: *delēi, *delēsti*, etc. Some other second conjugation verbs apparently adopted this perfect: *silevit*, R. 287.

426. Compounds of *dare* had a perfect in –*dĭdī* (*crēdĭdī*, *perdĭdī*, *vēndĭdī*, etc.), which in Vulgar Latin became –*dédi* (see § 139): *perdedit*, etc., Audollent 544. This –*dedi* was extended to many other verbs in –*d*–: *prandidi*, Keil IV, 184; *descendidi*, *respondidi*, *Lat. Spr.* 479, 480; *ascendiderat*, *descendidit*, *incendederit*, *odedere*, *pandiderunt*, *prendiderunt*, *videderunt* (cf. *edediderit* with an extra –*de*–), R. 288.

Through the analogy of –*āi*, *–*ēi*, *–*īi*, helped by dissimilation, this –*dédi* became *–*déi*. Hence arose eventually an inflection *–*déi*, *–*désti*, *–*dét*, *–*dém(m)u(s)*, *–*déste(s)*, –*dérun(t)*, from which there came a set of endings *–*éi*, *–*ésti*, etc., corresponding to the –*ai* –*asti*, etc., and the –*ii*, –*isti*, etc., of the first and fourth conjugations: so *caderunt*, *Gl. Reich.* In some of the Romance languages these endings were carried into other verbs of the third and even the second conjugation (It. *battéi*, Pr. *cazét*); in Provençal they invaded the first also (*améi*). In Dacia, on the other hand, they apparently did

not develop at all. In Italy, under the influence of *stetti* <
*stětui, dare had (beside *diẹdi* < *dĕdi*) a perfect *dẹtti*, whence
arose an inflection –*dẹtti*, etc., and a set of endings –*ẹtti*, etc.,
beside –*dẹi* and –*ẹi*.

Through these endings the weak type encroached somewhat on the strong. In Italy all strong verbs except *esse*
introduced weak endings in the second person singular and
the first and second persons plural: It. *presi, prendesti*, etc.;
cf. *plaudisti* for *plausisti*, R. 286, also *vincisti, Gl. Reich.* In
Rumania, where there was no –*dẹi*, the –*ui* and –*si* types were
extended.

A few weak verbs adopted strong inflections: *quæsīvi* >
**quæsi, sapīvi* > *sapui*.

b. STRONG PERFECTS.

427. There are three types — those that add *u* to the root,
those that add *s*, and those that have nothing between the
root and the personal endings: *plac-u-i, dīc-s-i = dīxi, bĭb-i.*
In the first class the *u* lost its syllabic value and became *w*
(cf. § 326): *placwi̥*, etc.

428. The –*ui* type, according to Meyer-Lübke, *Gram.* II,
357, included from the start not only perfects of the *placui*
sort, but also all perfects in –*vi* not made from the verb-stem
(cf. § 422), — such as *cognōvi, crēvi, mōvi, pāvi*, — this ending
being pronounced *wui*, but written *vi* to avoid the doubling of
the *v*. At any rate, the development of the *vi* indicates that
it was sounded *wui̥, wwi̥*, or *βwi̥* in Vulgar Latin: cf. It.
conọbbi, crẹbbi, etc.; Pr. *mọc*, etc.

This perfect disappeared from the first and fourth conjugations: *crepui* > **crepavi, necui* > *necavi*, etc.; *aperui* > *aperii
**apersi, salui* > *salivi salii* *salsi, etc   In the second and
third conjugations it maintained itself very well: *cognovi, crevi,*

gemui(?), *messui*(?), *molui, movi, pavi, tenui, texui.* It lost *posui* (>*pŏsi*), *silui* (>*silevi*), and possibly a few others.   On the other hand it received many additions: *bĭbi* > * *bĭbui; cĕcĭdi* > * *cadui* * *cadedi; cēpi* > *capui,* Haag 56, *Lat. Spr.* 479 (so * *recĭpui*); *expavi* > *expabui, Lat. Spr.* 479; *lēgi* > * *lēgui* * *lĕxi: natus sum* > * *nacui; pepĕrci* > *parcui,* R. 288; *sapivi* > *sapui; sēdi* > * *sēdui; stĕti* > also * *stĕtui; sustŭli* >* *tolui* * *tolsi; texi* > *texui, Lat. Spr.* 479; *vēni* > also * *vēnui; vīci* > also * *vĭncui* * *vĭnsi; vīdi* > also * *vīdui* * *vĭdui; vīxi* > also * *vĭscui;* etc. Cf. A. Zimmermann in *Archiv* XIII, 130; *Zs.* XXVIII, 97.

429. Of the –*si* class, — which comprised perfects in –*si,* –*ssi,* and –*xi,* — some thirty-five were preserved: *arsi, cinxi, clausi, coxi, divisi, dixi, duxi, excussi, finxi, fixi, frixi, junxi, luxi, mansi, mīsi* (also * *mĭssi,* perhaps on the model of *mĭssus,* cf. § 163), *mulsi, pinxi, planxi, pressi, rasi, rexi, risi, rosi, scripsi, sparsi, –stinxi, strinxi, struxi, tersi, tinxi, torsi, traxi, unxi, vixi. Sensi,* however, became * *sentii.*

In Vulgar Latin there were perhaps some thirty or more new formations: *abscō*(*n*)*si,* Keil VII, 94; * *accē*(*n*)*si;* * *apĕrsi;* * *attĭnxi;* * *copĕrsi;* * *cŭrsi;* * *defe*(*n*)*si;* * *ērsi* from *ērĭgo;* * *franxi;* * *fūsi;* * *impĭnxi;* * *lĕxi;* * *mŏrsi;* * *occīsi;* * *offĕrsi;* * *pē*(*n*)*si; pĕrsi, Lat. Spr.* 480; *pŏsi,* R. 288; * *prē*(*n*)*si;* * *pŭnxi;* * *quæsi;* * *redĕmpsi;* * *respō*(*n*)*si;* * *rōsi;* * *salsi;* * *sŏlsi;* * *sŭrsi;* * *taxi,* * *tanxi;* * *tē*(*n*)*si;* * *tŏlsi;* * *vĭnsi;* * *vŏlsi.* Some of these—* *defensi,* * *fusi,* * *morsi,* * *occisi,* * *pensi,* * *prensi,* * *responsi,* * *rosi,* * *tensi* — assumed the *s*– perfect through having an *s* in the perfect participle.

Cf. *Einf.* § 165.

430. Among the –*i* perfects, the reduplicative formations were discarded in Vulgar Latin, with the exception of *dĕdi* and *stĕti* (also * *stĕtui*), whose reduplicative character was no longer

apparent; compounds of *dare* usually formed their perfect like
the simple verb (cf. § 426; but *circumdavit* in *Gl. Reich.*),
while compounds of *stare* tended to follow the regular first
conjugation model (*præstĭti* > *præstavi*, R. 289). *Cĕcĭdi* became **cadui* or **cadedi; fefelli* > **falii; peperci* > *parcui*,
R. 288. The other reduplicative perfects either disappeared
or passed into the *–si* class: *cucurri* > **cŭrsi; momordi* >
*mŏrsi; pependi > **pē(n)si; pupŭgi* > **pŭnxi; tetendi* >
*tē(n)si; tetĕgi > **taxi *tanxi.*

The other *–i* perfects were greatly reduced in number in
Vulgar Latin. Some simply disappeared, some became weak,
some went over to the *–ui* or the *–si* type: *ēgi, vĕrti; fūgi* >
*fugii; bĭbi > **bĭbui, cēpi* > *capui, lēgi* > **lēgui, sēdi* > **sēdui;
accendi* > **accē(n)si, defendi* > **defē(n)si, frēgi* > **franxi, fūdi*
> **fūsi, lēgi* > **lĕxi, prendi* > **prē(n)si, solvi* > **sŏlsi, vīci* >
*vīnsi, volvi > **vŏlsi.* There were no additions. Two of
the old perfects maintained themselves intact, and two more
were kept beside new formations: *fēci, fui; vēni *vēnui, vīdi
vĭdui.

431. In *fui* the *u* was originally long, but it was shortened
in Classic Latin; Vulgar Latin seems to show both *ū* and *ŭ*.
In an effort to keep the accent on the same syllable throughout
(cf. §§ 423–424), *fuĭsti* > **fusti, fuĭstis* > **fustis;* then *fuĭmus*
generally became **fum(m)us, fuit* was often shortened to
*fut, and *fuĕrunt* became **furunt.* There may have been also,
through dissimilation, a form **fŏrunt.*

The prevailing inflection, with some variations, was probably
something like this: —

fui̯ foi̯		*fǫm(m)u(s)
*fǫsti̯		*fǫste(s)
fǫe(t) fue(t) *fǫt *fut		*fǫrun(t) *furun(t) *fǫrun(t)? fǫerun(t)?

7. PLUPERFECT AND FUTURE PERFECT.

432. When preserved at all, these tenses followed the old types: *plácuĕram* (cf. § 137), *placuĭssem, plácuĕro; díxĕram, dixĭssem, díxĕro; fécĕram, fecĭssem, fécĕro.* In formations from weak perfects only the contracted forms were used: *amāram, amāssem, amāro; delēram, delēssem, delēro; audī(e)ram, audīssem, audī(e)ro;* cf. *alaret, ortaret* in *Gl. Reich.* Bayard 60–61 notes that St. Cyprien employed only the shortened forms — *petisset,* etc. — before *ss.*

433. In some regions a tendency to keep the accent on the same syllable throughout the pluperfect subjunctive led to a change of *–assēmus, –assētis,* etc., to **–ássĭmus, *–ássĭtis,* etc.: It. *amássimo amáste,* Sp. *hablásemos habláseis;* but Pr. *amessém amessétz,* Fr. *aimassións aimassiéz.*

8. PERFECT PARTICIPLE.

434. Verbs which had no perfect participle were obliged to form one in order to make their passive and their perfect tenses: *fĕrio, *ferītus.*

435. In the first conjugation *–ātus* was preserved and was extended to all verbs: *frictus > fricatus; nectus > necatus; sectus > secatus;* so the new *alatus, Gl. Reich.* The ending *–ĭtus,* in the first conjugation, generally fell into disuse: *crepitus > *crepatus; domitus > domatus,* R. 295; *plicitus > plicatus; sonitus > *sonatus; tonitus > *tonatus; vetitus > vetatus,* R. 296. Nevertheless there were some new formations in *–ĭtus: *lĕvĭtus, prŏvĭtus, rŏgĭtus, vŏcĭtus;* cf. *Lat. Spr.* 480.

In the third conjugation *–ātus* disappeared: *oblatus > offertus* (*Gl. Reich.*), *sublatus > *suffertus,* by the analogy of *apertus, copertus; sublatus* (from *tollo*) > *tŏllĭtus* (*Gl. Reich.*).

436. In the fourth conjugation *–ītus* was preserved and was extended to nearly all verbs: *saltus*>*salītus; sensus*>*sentītus; sepultus*>*sepelītus,* old and found in all periods, Pirson 152, *Gl. Reich. Apertus* and *copertus,* however, were kept; and *ventus* generally became **venūtus.*

In the third conjugation *quæsītus*>**quæstus.*

437. In the second conjugation the rare *–ētus* disappeared as a participial ending: *complētus,* etc., were kept only as adjectives.

438. The ending *–ūtus,* belonging to verbs in *–uere* and *–vere.* (*argutus, consutus, minutus, secutus, solutus, statutus, tributus, volutus*), offered a convenient accented form, corresponding to *–ātus* and *–ītus.* It was extended to nearly all the verbs that had an *–ui* perfect: **bibutus, *habutus, *parutus, *tenutus, *venutus, *vidutus,* etc.; but *status.* It did not always, however, entirely displace the old perfect participle: *natus* was kept beside **nascūtus.*

Eventually *–ūtus* was carried further, — as **credutus, *perdutus, *vendutus,* — and in Sicily encroached largely on *–ītus.*

On the other hand, **mŏvĭtus* and **mŏssus* were formed beside **movutus, *sŏlvĭtus* (or **sŏltus*) beside *solutus, *vŏlvĭtus* (or **vŏltus*) beside *volutus.*

439. The ending *–ĭtus* tended to disappear (cf. § 435): *absconditus*>*absco(n)sus; bibitus*>**bibutus; creditus*>**credutus; fugitus*>**fugītus; molitus*>**molutus; paritus*>**parutus *parsus; perditus*>**perdutus *persus; submonitus*>**submo(n)sus; venditus*>**vendutus.* A few of these participles, however, remained, and there were some new formations in *–ĭtus: gĕmitus?, pŏs(i)tus, sŏlitus; *lĕvitus, *mŏvitus, prŏvitus, rŏgitus, *sŏlvitus* (or **sŏltus*), *tŏllitus, vŏcitus, *vŏlvitus* (or **vŏltus*).

440. The ending *–tus* was kept for some twenty verbs, occasionally with a change of stem: *cinctus; dictus; ductus; exstinctus; factus; fictus finctus,* R. 295; *fractus *franctus; frīctus; lectus; mistus; pictus *pinctus; punctus; rectus; scriptus; strictus *strinctus; structus; *surtus* for *surrectus; tactus? *tanctus?; tinctus; tortus; tractus.* There were a few new formations in *–tus: offertus, *quæstus, *suffertus, *vīsĭus;* and perhaps **sŏltus, *vŏltus* (cf. § 439).

About fifteen verbs probably replaced *–tus* by *–ātus, –ītus,* or *–ūtus: captus *capītus; cognōtus > *conovūtus?; crētus > *crevūtus?; fartus > *farcītus* and *farsus, Lat. Spr.* 480; *frīctus > fricātus; mōtus > *movūtus?* and **mŏssus; nectus > necātus; pastus > *pavūtus?; saltus > *salītus* and **salsus; sectus > secātus; sepultus > sepelītus; tentus > *tenūtus; texus > *texūtus; ventus > *venūtus* and *venītus,* Bechtel 91; *vĭctus > *vincūtus* and **vinctus; vīctus > *vixūtus.*

441. The ending *–sus* was generally kept: *acce(n)sus; arsus; clausus; defe(n)sus; divīsus; excussus; fixus; fusus; ma(n)sus; mĭssus,* also perhaps **mīsus* by the analogy of *mīsi; morsus; pe(n)sus; pre(n)sus; pressus; risus; rosus; sparsus; te(n)sus; tersus; to(n)sus; visus,* also probably **vistus.* Several of these developed also a participle in *–ūtus: *pendutus, *vidutus,* etc. *Salsus,* 'salted,' maintained itself beside *saīītus.*

A few verbs replaced the old form by one in *–ītus* or *–ūtus: expansus > *expandutus; falsus > *fallītus; fusus > fundutus, Gl. Reich.; gavīsus > *gaudutus; messus > metītus,* Dubois 282; *sensus > *sentītus; sessus > *sedutus.*

On the other hand, there were some new formations in *–sus: absco(n)sus,* Keil VII, 94, *Lat. Spr.* 480, R. 295 (very common); *farsus, Lat. Spr.* 480; **mossus; *parsus; *persus; *salsus; *submo(n)sus.*

9. PERSONAL ENDINGS.

442. For the reduction of –*io* to –*o*, see §416.

443. Meyer-Lübke, *Grundriss* I², 670, assumes that in Italy –*ās* and –*ēs* became –*i*. The evidence, historically considered, does not support this view. Italian *lodi* and Rumanian *lauzi*, from *laudas*, are correctly explained by Tiktin 565–566 as analogical formations.

444. As unaccented *ē*, *ĕ*, and *ĭ* came to be pronounced alike (§243), great confusion ensued between –*ēs* and –*ĭs*, –*ĕt* and –*ĭt*. This confusion is very frequent in the *Peregrinatio:* Bechtel 88–89, *colliget*, etc.

445. In southern and to some extent in northern Gaul the first person plural lost its final *s*, perhaps in the Vulgar Latin period: *vidēmus* > Pr. *vezém*. This is not a phonetic phenomenon, as –*s* did not fall in this region. It may be that –*s* was dropped because it was regarded as a characteristic of the second person, as *t* was of the third (cf. *Pr. Pers. Pl.* 73–80):—

ámo	*amámu
ámas	amátes
ámat	ámant

446. According to Mohl, *Pr. Pers. Pl.*, forms like **cánomus*, due to Celtic influence, were used in northern Gaul instead of *canĭmus*, etc.; then the accent was shifted to the penult — **canómus*, whence came the French –*ons*. This theory has not found acceptance.

447. In strong perfects the first person plural, –*ĭmus*, — through the analogy of –*ĭstis* and –*ĭsti*, and doubtless of weak perfects as well, — tended, perhaps after our period, to stress its penult: *fēcĭmus* > Pr. *fezém*. There are traces of this in inscriptions and elsewhere: S. 47, 53. The shift, however, was not universal, as there are in Italian and French remains of the original accentuation.

448. In the present indicative and imperative, *–ĭmus, –ĭtis, –ĭte* generally became, in the sixth or seventh century, *–ẹ́mu(s), –ẹ́te(s), –ẹ́te,* — the penult assuming the accent, to match *–ámu(s), –áte(s), –áte* and *–ẹ́mu(s), –ẹ́te(s), –ẹ́te* and *–ímu(s), íte(s), íte* in the other conjugations. The shift was perhaps helped by the analogy of the future — *mīttĭmus,* for instance, being attracted by *mittēmus: Pr. Pers. Pl.* 30, 64. Rumanian, however, kept the old accent (Tiktin 596): *úngem, úngeţĭ; vĭndem, víndeţĭ;* etc. There are some traces of its preservation in southeastern French dialects also. Furthermore, *facĭmus, facĭtis* and *dīcĭmus, dīcĭtis* kept their old forms in many regions.

449. For the reduction of *–iunt* to *–unt,* see § 416. Beside *–ent,* in the second conjugation, there was an ending **–eunt* (**habeunt,* etc.), — due to the analogy of *–iunt,* — which was particularly common in Italy: cf. § 416.

The endings *–ent* and *–unt* came to be very much confused (**crēdent, *vĭdunt,* etc.); their interchange is frequent in the *Peregrinatio:* Bechtel 88–90, *absolvent, accipient, exient, responduntur,* etc. According to Mohl, *Pr. Pers. Pl.* 112, the confusion goes back to early Italic. The Classic distinction was best kept in Gaul and northern Italy; in Spain and Portugal, Sardinia, and a part of southern Italy, *–ent* prevailed; in central and the rest of southern Italy, Rætia, Dalmatia, and Dacia, *–unt* was preferred.

450. In the perfect, the third person plural ending *–ēre* was discarded. The ending *–erunt,* in Classic Latin, sometimes had a short *e* (*ĕ* is common in the comic poets, Virgil wrote *tulĕrunt,* etc.); in Vulgar Latin this vowel was apparently always short: *débuerunt, díxerunt, víderunt.* Cf. § 137.

INDEX.

N. B.—Arabic numerals refer to Paragraphs. Words printed in Roman type belong to ancient, words in *italics* to modern languages.

adpretiare 25
adpropiare 25
ad semel 47
ad sero 47
adsteti 139
ad subito 47
adtonitus 32
ad tunc 47
ad ubi 47
aduc 250
adulescentulus 37
adunare 25
Adverbs 73–5
æ 174, 178, 209–10, 228,
  243, 244
  accented 174, 178, 209–10
  unaccented 174, 178, 243,
  244
  -æ = -e 174, 244
æcclesia 228
ædis 366
ægis 188
æliens = eligens 259
æques = e- 175
æquus = e- 175, 210
æteneris = itineris 201
Æthiopia 188
æum = ævum 324 (1)
a foras 47.
a foris 47
agennæ = -nd- 281
agere = ajere 259
aggio 273
aggravatio 37
Agneti 359 (2)
agnetus = -na- 194
-ago 37
Agragas 330
Agrientum 259
agurium 228
agustas 228
Agustus 228
ahenum 250
ai > æ > e 209
αι 188
Aiax 188, 222
aiglon 37 (-o)
Aiiax 222

aiio 222
-*aio* 39 (-arius)
aios = ἅγιος 272
Aix 86
ajutit = adjutet 272
-al 37
alacer 195 (1)
alare 405, 435
alauda 19
alaudula 37
alba spina 43
alberca 19
albeus 317
albor = arbor 292
-ale 37
alecer 195 (1)
Alesander 255
alevanti = eleph- 321
Alexander 38, 255
alguem 71
alguien 71
-alia 37
alicer 195 (1)
alicunus 71
alid = aliud 71
alio(r)sum 291
alipes = ad- 281 (1)
aliquanti 71
aliqui 71
aliquis 13, 71
aliquot 71
-alis 39
alium 224
alius 71
allare 405, 435
allegorizare 19
alleviare 34
allium 274
a longe 47
alques 71
alter 71, 233, 395
altiare 34
altior 377
altissimus 377
altitia 37
alto (**adv.**) 40
altra 233
altrui 395

alumnu (**nom.**) 372
am 78
amadus = -t- 286
amantis (**nom.**) 367
amào 424
amaricare 34
ama(t) 285
ambitare 405
ambolare 232
ambulare 10, 232, 405
amei 424
amenus 215
amfora 334
amicicia 276
amido 187
amistat 154
amita 239, 359, 359 (1)
amitane 359 (1)
amitanis 359
amma 16
amnavit 405
amð 424
a modo 47
amourette 37 (-ittus)
ampitzatru 277
ampora 334
amurca 186
amure 203
amygdalum 19
an 11, 14, 83
-an 36
-âν 36
anangi 331
anathema 19
anathematizare 19
anc 40
anc = hanc 251
anca 343
ancilia 187
ancora 150, 187
-ancus 37 (-incus)
-anda 37
andare 405
andata 37 (-ta)
Andreani 359 (1)
Andreate 359 (2)
andron 331
anellus 37, 42

anemis 232
–aneus 39, 42
angelice 40
angelus 19
Angers 86
angliscus 39
angostia 208 (1)
anguil(l)a 163
ang(u)lus 233
angustiare 34
Anicius 276
animabus 358
animalico 37 (–icca)
Anitius 276
Annanis 359
annare 405
annata 37 (–ta)
Annenis 359
annitare 405
annotavimus = –bi~ 318
annulare 405
anos = annos 247
–ans 39
anser 13
anta 239
ante 96
antemittere 46
antestetis (nom.) 367
–antia 37
anticus 226
antiefne 184
antiphona 184
anus = annos 244
–anus 39, 42
Aorist 124
apcha 343
aperii 428
apersi 428, 429
apertus 436
apotheca 182
apothecarius 39
apparescere 35
appo 78
apprendere 12
ápriro 410
apsens 315
apsolvere 315
apte = –æ 244

apud 14, 78, 282
aput 282
aqua 164, 223
aquilotto 37 (–ottus)
–ar 37
Arbonenca 37 (–incus)
arbor (masc.) 346 (4)
arb(o)rem 235
arboricellus 153
ardente(m) 309
ardere 399
ardire 343
–are (infin.) 33, 34, 36, 397–8
–are (nouns) 37
ares = aries 225
aretem 225
argentum 259
–aria 37
–aricius 39
arida (noun) 13
ar(i)dorem 219
ar(i)dus 237
aries 225, 255
ariex = –s 255
–aris 39
–aris > –alis 292
–arius 39
armeise 184
armentas 352
–aro 39 (–arius)
Aroncianos 276
arrespex = haruspex 251
Arrius 251
arroser 356 (3)
arsi 429
arsus 441
artemisia 184
artetico 184
arthriticus 184
Article 57, 68, 392
artic(u)lus 234
arvorsum = adversum 281 (2)
arvum > arum 226
–as 38
–as > –i 443
ascella = axilla 42, 255

ascendiderat 426
ascetes 182
ascla 284
asculta 228
a semel 47
aspargo 31
aspectare 25
Aspirates 249–52, 265
aspra 233
–asse 161
–assem 161
–ássemus 433
–ássetis 433
Assibilation 277–8, 260–1
Assimilation 229 (3), 255, 264, 265, 267, 269, 282, 293, 307, 310, 315
Asti 86
astula 284
at 11
at = ad 282
–ata 37 (–ta)
–aticum 37
atque– 24, 65
atque ille 24
atque ipse 65
atque is 65
atrium 12
atta 16, 359 (1)
Attane 359 (1)
atticissare 33
attinxi 429
Attitta 37 (–ittus)
–attus 37
at ubi 48
–atus 37 (–ta), 39, 42
    participle 435, 440
au 178, 211–3, 228, 229 (7)
    accented 178, 211–3
    unaccented 228, 229 (7)
        au > o 229 (7)
av 189
auca 13, 236
aucellus 13, 325
aucidere 212
audace (nom.) 367
audi = audivi 227, 423
audiendu'st 309

fervere 399
fervura 37
fesit 260
feu 343
fezem 44
fiaba 289 (1)
fiam 419 (2)
fib(u)la 235
ficatum 16, 141
ficit 197
fictus 440
ficus (**masc. and fem.**) 346 (1)
ficus (**2d decl.**) 355 (1)
fidens 311
fiele 160
fiens 356 (2)
fieri 112, 409, 419 (2)
fiero 160
fiet 419 (2)
figel 242
fiios = filios 274
filiabus 358
filias (**nom.**) 357 (1)
filiaster 13
filio(s) 298
filius 155, 274; = filios 244
filix 197
fillio 247
Fimes 86
Final Syllable 240–5
finctus 440
finis (**adj.**) 17
finiscere 35
finxi 429
fio 343
fiorentino 154
fioretto 37 (–ittus)
fiorisce 414
fir– 29
fircum 320 (1)
Firenze 86
Firmus –onis 362
fiscla 234
fistula 234
fistus 197
fixi 429
fixus 441

flaba 289 (1)
flagrare 292
flaonis 324
flator 37
flaus 240, 324
flavor 37
fletus 11
fleuma 268
fleurit 414
fleuve 208 (2)
floralis 292
florecer 414
Florentinus 37
florire 400
florisco 400
flovium 208 (2), 217
fluviorum 224
foces 213
focus 8, 12
fodiri 406
folia 352
follia (**noun**) 18
follicare 33
fons (**fem.**) 346 (4)
fons 356 (2)
fonte 205
fonz 356 (2)
foras 81, 96
forbatre 29
forbire 407
Foreign Words 19; **see Germanic Words and Greek Words**
foresia 311
foris 81
foris– 29
forisfacere 29
forismittere 46
formaceus 39
formosus 161
formunsus 208
forsitan 305
forte 40
fortescere 34
fortia 37
fortis 10
   fortis fortis 55
fossato 37 (–ta)

fractus 440
fragellum 289 (**2**)
fragilis 233
fragrantia 37
fra(g)rare 270
Francesco 341
franctus 440
Frankensis 39
Frankiscus 39, 341
Franko 341
franxi 429
frate 295
fratelmo 388
frat(t)re 164
frax(i)nus 239; (**mc.**) 346 (1)
fraumenta 268
frecare 201; cf. 256
frenum –us 347
fricatus 435, 440
fricda = frigida 238, 259
frictus 440
frigare 256; cf. 201
frigdaria 219, 231
frigdura 37
Frigia 187
frig(i)dus 166, 200 (1), 233, 238, 259
frigora 351
frigorem 347
frixi 429
frondifer 11
frualitas 263
fructa 351, 361
fructus (**2d decl.**) 355 (1)
frundes 205
frunza 351
frutta 351
fugii 430
fugire 406
fugitus 439
fŭi 431
ful(i)ca 237
fumát 424
fundus (**3d decl.**) 356 (2)
fundutus 441
funtes 205
funus 11
fuore 160